CHOSEN CHILDREN

CHOSEN CHILDREN

New Patterns of Adoptive Relationships

William Feigelman and Arnold R. Silverman

foreword by
H. David Kirk

PRAEGER SPECIAL STUDIES • PRAEGER SCIENTIFIC

New York   •   Westport, Connecticut   •   London

Library of Congress Cataloging in Publication Data

Feigelman, William.
  Chosen children.

  Bibliography: p.
  Includes index.
    1. Adoption—United States. 2. Foster parents—United
States—Family relationships. 3. Children, Adopted—
United States—Family relationships. 4. Social case work
with children—United States. 5. Family social work—
United States. I. Silverman, Arnold R., 1940-   . II. Title.
LHV875.64.F44   1983   362.7'34'0973   83-13972
  ISBN 0-275-90974-3 (alk. paper)

Library of Congress Catalog Card Number: 83-13972
ISBN: 0-275-90974-3

First published in 1983

Praeger Publishers, 521 Fifth Avenue, New York, NY 10175
A division of Greenwood Press, Inc.

Printed in the United States of America

The paper used in this book complies with the Permanent
Paper Standard issued by the National Information Standards
Organization (Z39.48-1984).

10 9 8 7 6 5 4

We dedicate this book to our children,
Jesse, Ana, Elana, and Ari, from whom we
learned the richness of parenthood, and
to our parents, whose sacrifices taught
us the value of childhood.

Acknowledgments

Our work has been in progress since the fall of 1973, and we would like to take this opportunity to thank many of those who have contributed their time and talent to our research. Without them *Chosen Children* would not have been possible. First, and most important of all, we are deeply appreciative of the time and efforts given by the hundreds of adoptive parents who completed our questionnaires in 1975 and 1981. Our instruments were long and detailed, but the responses of parents were overwhelmingly cooperative. In addition, many offered further aid and information with extremely useful comments and letters. We also wish to thank the officers of the many adoptive parents' organizations who gave us their utmost cooperation. Without them we never would have had a sample. There were a number of parent group leaders who extended themselves beyond all measure in cooperating with our research. We would have liked to mention them specifically in these acknowledgments, yet in the interests of preserving the anonymity of our respondents, they must remain unnamed.

H. David Kirk of the University of Waterloo (Ontario) and Eugene Weinstein of the State University of New York at Stony Brook were particularly helpful to us in the development of the 1975 questionnaire. Through her careful typing, Charlotte Hanzman of the department of sociology at Nassau Community College enabled us to turn our early questionnaire drafts into readable documents.

We would never have been able to complete the research for *Chosen Children* without the generous support of the National Institute of Mental Health, the Research Foundation of the State University of New York, and the Sabbaticals Committee of Nassau Community College. Their support provided the released time and assistance that greatly facilitated our work.

We are indebted to members of the mathematics, computer science, and academic computing departments of Nassau Community College for their generous assistance in managing and analyzing our data base. James Partridge, Mauro Cassano, and Tom Taylor all provided help beyond what anyone could reasonably expect from colleagues. We also wish to acknowledge the advice and help of Irene

Carley and Tony Pisacano of Nassau's academic computing department. Ellen Liebman of the University Computing Center of the University of California, Berkeley, was most helpful in the analysis of our data during Professor Silverman's tenure as a visiting scholar at that institution. A number of our undergraduate students at Nassau Community College made substantial contributions to the coding and analysis of our data. In particular we wish to thank Mildred Alder, Peggy Bertrand, Andrew Ceraulo, Pat Murphy, Bette Russell, Nancy Sica, and Tracey Stock.

Russell Middleton of the University of Wisconsin was a thoughtful and responsive mentor to Professor Silverman in the completion of his dissertation, portions of which served as a basis for analysis presented here. Nan Maglin of the Borough of Manhattan Community College read the manuscript carefully and helped us to excise the worst of our offenses against the English language.

Last, and very important, we wish to thank our wives for the long hours of child care and household responsibilities that they had to assume to make this work possible. We also wish to thank Beverly and Ruth for their careful comments on our work, which reflect both their professional training in social work and sociology and their experience as parents. We extend our appreciation to our spouses in the knowledge that we stand ready to do the same for them in the future.

Foreword

It is both an honor and a pleasure for me to be writing some preliminaries for the reader of this book. It is an honor because the authors have done thoughtful and meticulous research in one of the most difficult areas of social life. And it is a pleasure because, far from producing a mere technical treatise, they have managed to speak to all of us in terms of human experience and sentiment. But while it bears the stamp of genuine sentiment, this book is devoid of a sentimentalism that has been the curse of so much writing about adoption.

What should be the task of a foreword? Should it be an introduction to the work? Should it be a critique? Should it be an apology? I have chosen none of these routes. The authors have provided a very satisfactory introduction to their book; constructive criticism will undoubtedly flow from the pens of reviewers; as for apology, none is needed. On the contrary, one might ask why it has taken so long for a truly incisive assessment of the most revolutionary of family arrangements, the family constituted by the adoption of children across racial and national lines. What I have chosen to do here is to add a few pertinent notes of my own. I shall try to write some comments between the lines, as it were, as an "old hand" in this venture of studying adoptive kinship.

First of all, some very general impressions. I have been excited by the authors' reporting style: they have taken me, as they will take you, into each chapter by way of a family portrait. In their introductory chapter we meet the Thorntons, whose family arrangement gives us a first glimpse into the subject of the book. In chapter 2 it is the Nelsons' history that leads us into the circumstances of people who take children with physical or developmental problems. Again and again we meet real people, real families, albeit under the guise of pseudonyms, whose thoughts and actions illuminate the path to understanding the authors' sociological inquiries. Although the first seven chapters are all introduced in a similar mode of the case study, I was always equally intrigued. Each case is not so much a "study" as it is a window through which to look into the more impersonal characteristics of a changing family scene.

Now I have come to the words that must be emphasized: the changing family scene. In 1951, when I was wrestling with the problems of designing research for a doctoral dissertation, it dawned on me that the adoptive family can be understood as a special and particularly poignant example of social change in human affairs. It is now common for people outside of academic sociology to recognize that our world is characterized by change; changes in technology, changes in styles of life, changes in populations coming together, changes in health patterns, changes in life expectancy; changes in what is meant by "family." One-parent families have existed for years, but they were created by death of a parent rather than by divorce. Adoptive families have been legalized for decades, but only recently have there been substantial numbers of people with children born to them and children adopted in addition, or with children whose bodies or minds do not conform to the accepted standards of desirable offspring, or children whose appearances at once betray that their ancestry is different from that of the adoptive parents.

These changes are the most obvious, the most visible. But all adoption involves less obvious and less visible changes in the lives of the family members. When the involuntarily childless become parents by adoption, they move into a new status, the status of parenthood. When the illegitimate child becomes legitimated by the act of adoption, that child has likewise moved, into the status of legitimacy. When the child who has been an only child receives a sibling by birth or by adoption, that child has gained a new status, that of "elder" brother or sister. Adoption is, then, a constant reminder of change within the family. But it is also a reminder of change between families and in the society at large. No longer is it necessary for adopters and adoptees to hide or play down the fact of adoption. It has become more and more an accepted part of social life in modern societies.

In one area of social change adoption has in fact become so common that it has made for new and relatively unrecognized difficulties. With the rise of the divorce rate, and the consequent rate of remarriage, there has come a tendency for the new husband-wife unions to use adoption as a way of affirming the new stepparent relationships. That this is not always a desirable answer to a changing family arrangement has been recognized by recent legislation in Great Britain, a reform that is overdue in Canada and the United States. Even though Professors Feigelman and Silverman have not made reference in this book to the issue of stepparent adoptions, their work is otherwise centrally informed by the realities of social change. In that sense it might very well have been given the subtitle "A Sociological Study of Social Change in Family Life."

There is among the chapters one that may at first glance seem not to belong in this book. It is the chapter dealing with the controversy over the rights of adult adoptees searching for information about their ancestral roots. How are we to understand this chapter about adult adopted persons and the current limitation of their access to birth information, except in the larger context of social change? Let me put it this way: in more traditional times, with more traditional rules of family life, the loyalty of children to parents was assumed, if not always acted upon. More and more of life in the world of families has become voluntary, including the marital bond itself — and, thus, the cohesion of the family. In adoption the parent-initiators have the choice of the social mobility into parenthood. In everyday family life adult children have the right to move away from the place where parents live, and even the right to remove themselves from the social and psychological sphere of the parental family. Only in adoption is the loyalty of children to parents enforced by a law that forbids the adult "child" to move beyond the closed circle of the adoptive family. In my book *Adoptive Kinship: A Modern Institution in Need of Reform* (Toronto: Butterworths, 1981) I have argued that only when the adoptive family becomes as open as the family whose children are born into it, can adoptive kinship truly come into its own. What the authors of the present book have done by incorporating the subject of the adult adoptee's violated rights is this: they have correctly understood that adoption is first and foremost an indicator of social change in the family and in the society in which that family exists.

Earlier in this foreword I spoke of the human and humane manner in which the more technical aspects of the several chapters are introduced. I want now to make at least a brief incursion into the technical sociological parts. One of the more troublesome aspects of contemporary social science has been the tendency of its practitioners to report research findings primarily in terms of successes — that is, in terms of data that support the assumptions or hypotheses of the investigators. Readers who are acquainted with the history of science know that this is not how scientific knowledge has grown. A dependable body of scientific knowledge has come about at least as much by disproving hypotheses and theories.

What I have appreciated about the work of these authors has been, in this regard, their candidness: they have let me and their other readers see with what assumptions they have approached their inquiry, and on more than one occasion they have shown us that these assumptions were mistaken. For instance, in Chapter 2 they say, ". . . contrary to the hypothesis, persons with religious affiliations — with the exception of Jews — seemed more accepting of handicapped and retarded children." In Chapter 6 the authors discuss the adjustment of transracially adopted adolescents, and remark:

> . . . We . . . hypothesized that adolescent Korean adoptees would be better adjusted in racially and ethnically diverse communities than elsewhere. Consequently we expected that residence in urban settings would facilitate the personal adaptation of the nonwhite adoptees in our sample. . . .
>
> Our data did not confirm these expectations. The adolescent Korean adoptees who were reportedly well adjusted tended to live in rural communities. Over 90 percent of the older Korean adoptees living in rural communities were described as having problem-free adjustments, compared with 75 percent among urbanites, and 65 percent among those living in suburbs. The successful adjustment of Korean adolescents in rural communities is especially striking.

After this kind of declaration of discrepancy between hypothesis and findings, the authors further explore the actual conditions discovered, helping us understand, or at least helping us in trying to make sense of, a complex and often seemingly contradictory set of circumstances in the lives of these adoptive families.

While their starting point is the concerns of the social scientist, the authors are attuned to the interests of both child care professionals and adoptive families. One of the most interesting and useful aspects of this book is its constant attention to the implications of the findings for social policy and social casework practice. Feigelman and Silverman have brought fresh and impressive data to bear on the issues of transracial adoption, single parent adoption, and a number of other issues, which now confront policy makers and caseworkers. Often, the writers demonstrate that previously held ideas about adoptive families cannot be sustained under close empirical examination. They show that single adoptive parents can provide secure and lasting placements even for children with unusually troubled pasts. Their data reveal that transracially adopted black children do not develop the serious adjustment and identity problems that some have predicted and that living in close proximity to Afro-Americans is not essential for being well adjusted. Many adoptive parents questioned say they are prepared to accept the unsealing of adoption records. All of these findings are contrary to widely held beliefs in the field of child care and social work.

Although they are not the first to advance some of these notions, they have taken the lead in giving these ideas solid empirical grounding. More important, perhaps, than any single conclusion is their more general implication that adoptive families and, indeed, all family relationships, are in a process of dramatic change. It must be understood that these social changes are transforming both the content and the meaning of professional social work with individuals and families.

Thomas Kuhn has suggested that major changes in thinking are often initiated by those outside a discipline, but working with its problems. I believe that the present writers, with their distinctive sociological vantage point, provide a useful stimulus to rethinking older ideas, models, and policies in social work.

Let me now return to my writing-between-the-lines. While the present work is avowedly concerned with very practical applications of social knowledge, the authors have again and again addressed questions and problems of sociological theory of the family. Whether or not it is readily acknowledged by family sociologists, it is this part of the sociological discipline that has been particularly poor in systematic theoretical development, and most lush with idiosyncratic outgrowths purporting to be theoretically sound. Readers of Chapter 2 in particular will recognize the care that has been taken in this work to hold the questions and findings up against theoretically sound insights that have been proffered by sociologists in recent years. It is thus not only a work of careful research inquiry, but also one in which the research has been anchored in sociological theory and in which sociological theory stands to gain from the exploration and its findings.

In the rest of this foreword, I must speak more personally than I have done up to now. Why have the authors singled me out as the contributor of a foreword? I need not be reticent to admit it: I have been the first sociological investigator to carry out systematic researches into the inner and outer worlds of the adoptive family. Furthermore, my studies have been cross-cultural, so that by the mid-1960s it was possible to speak with some degree of assurance about the life conditions of parents and children in adoption. The theory that sought to explain the special conditions and the contradictions of adoptive parent-child relationships was reported in a book of mine that has influenced much contemporary thinking about adoption, *Shared Fate, a Theory of Adoption and Mental Health* (New York: The Free Press, 1964). That theory was based on empirical studies spanning the years between 1951 and 1962, and involved more than 2,000 families in Canada and the United States. This empirically based theory suggested that the differences that are clearly built into adoption by nature and by social and legal contrivances must not be denied. In fact, it showed that if such differences are denied by the adoptive parents, such denials tend to reduce the capacity of the parents to create adoptive families of strength and vitality. If adoptive parents could acknowledge that their parenthood is different from the parenthood of fertile couples, who create their own offspring, they could more readily identify themselves with the special conditions of the adoptee.

Let it here be remembered that every adoptee, as child and as adult, has to come to grips with having once been given up by biological parents. That is a hard thing to do; and it becomes harder, the "shared fate" theory suggests, if the parents cannot accept the reality of their atypical position as adoptive parents. So the "shared fate" theory has also become a program for more satisfactory adoptive parent-child relations: it has said that if adoptive parents want to maximize the chances that theirs will be a family of strength and solidarity, they must first of all acknowledge the inherent difference in their own parental status. Thereby they will more likely learn to empathize with the special circumstances that have brought the child into their family. Such empathy will make it easier for the parents to hear their child's questions and problems concerning the meaning of adoption as having been given up by others. Clearly, this theory and its program for parenthood have very powerful implications, especially for those who adopt across racial, ethnic, national, and physical normalcy lines. As the reader will see shortly in the book itself, the authors have built on the work that was reported in *Shared Fate* and on related studies by others. But I am especially pleased that in the context of the present work, my own has been both tested and refined.

Having spoken personally as an author and sociologist who has been concerned with matters involving adoptive kinship, I must go one step further and speak as adoptive father. In previous publications I have felt free to discuss this dual role, but up to now I have not had reason to speak about the fact that several of my four children were adopted across racial and ethnic lines. When they were adopted, in the early and mid-1950s, such adoptions were relatively rare; at that time our family was seen as an oddity. But perhaps because of our marginality as a family, I was able to observe some matters that I might not as readily have seen had we been more sheltered within a larger group of similarly constructed and like-minded families. In the past I had not seen fit to discuss my insights and experiences of the early years as a father of transracially adopted children. Now, in the context of the work by these authors, it becomes justifiable. In Chapter 4 we are told:

> Paul Dinitz was described by his parents as having only occasional emotional problems. Matthew Dinitz [the adoptive father] described his son's adoption as working out well in all aspects. Neither of Paul's parents felt that he had any physical or growth problems. His father had only one reservation:
>
>> I sometimes worry that Paul isn't aggressive enough in dealing with his problems. He'd rather run away from things than face them. If he'd just stand up to some of the kids at [the parish school] who tease him, they'd stop. Carol — our Korean daughter — wouldn't let anyone get away with calling her names behind her back. She's spent some time in the principal's office because of it, but there's no more teasing. Paul [who is black] has to learn to do some of that.

I have quoted this entire section from the present work because it reminded me of some relevant events in the life of my family. The first, chronologically, has to do with a clearly white sibling standing up both for herself and for her brother when she was in third grade and he in first in the same school. One day the teacher called us in to complain about our daughter's aggressive behavior. She apparently had hit another child over the head with her lunch box. When confronted, our daughter said at once that she had indeed done so. What had set her off, we asked. Well, the other child had called her brother a "nigger." "You have a nigger brother," the other girl had said, and wham, she had been clobbered. My response was quite direct also; I let my daughter know that I appreciated her immediate action, and cautioned her not to do harm. And we so informed the teacher, whose response I don't recall.

But Matthew Dinitz wanted his son to stand up for himself. Mine did, but I did not know about it until many years later. Our oldest son had chosen to go to a boarding school when he was 16, a rather special school where, in addition to doing academic work, the young people learned to live a hardy life, doing chores in forest and house, cutting wood and baking bread. When it came the younger boy's turn, he resisted; he preferred to stay in the big urban high school where he had started two years before. I asked why, but I did not get a very satisfactory reply. Some years after this young man had left the high school and was holding down a responsible job, he confided to me why he had wanted to stay at the high school in the city. "You see," he said, "I had fought for my place in that school. For a term I had to defend my gym locker against all kinds of mischief, and more than once I had to fight some kid physically when I was called names." What my son had told me was that he had become attached to the place that had become very much his as a result of his having stood up for himself and having become one of the boys, irrespective of color. For me this was a revelation. When I asked why he had not told me, he laughed. "You know well enough what would have happened, Dad; you would have blustered into the school and made a fuss. It wouldn't have been good for me. I had to do it myself."

As I read over the chapters on the adjustment of transracially adopted children in this work, I remembered another episode in the life of my family. I tell it here because it sheds light, it seems to me, on a matter that has not been raised in the present book but that ought to be part of the awareness of all people interested in transracial adoption and all professionals who assist in such adoptions in any way. I refer to the issue of the parents' readiness to stand up for the family, for the child, and ultimately for the dignity of transracial adoptive parenthood. Here is what happened:

A year earlier we had moved into a neighborhood in the Montreal area where we believed a new community would soon be flourishing. It had been planned by a famous city planner; the homes were comfortable, the streets were wide, there was ample parkland where the children could play; a new school was being built, and there was talk of a shopping center nearby. We had every reason to assume that the neighborhood would soon be not only a mix of English and

French-Canadian families, but also of other people who, by the late 1950s, were coming from the Caribbean and from Asia. One day I heard that a black family had bought a house a street or two away; it seemed to confirm my hunch that this would turn out to be a good place for raising our family. Not long thereafter I was told by a neighbor that the people across from the black family had held a neighborhood meeting to see what could be done to get the black family to move out. Gossip travels fast; even our older children, then in first grade, had heard the rumor.

I decided to make some inquiries about the people who had hosted the antiblack meeting. I learned that they had just adopted an infant girl. At supper I mentioned to our children that I would do something about those people and their interference in the life of the community. To my surprise, the children tried to have me be quiet, not rock the boat. I decided that something would have to be done and, furthermore, that my children should be clearly aware of what I was about to do. While we were still at supper, I got up, went to the telephone, and called the neighbors who had held the meeting. I identified myself, and told them I felt bad that I had been excluded from so important a meeting. Might I come over and talk with them? They tried to put me off; there would be a second meeting soon. But I pressed — no, I couldn't wait. There was something important I had to tell them immediately. I managed to get them either curious or anxious. I was invited to come over that evening. My children pressed me to tell them what I thought I would do, but I said: "Wait; I'll soon be back with the news." I went away as uncertain and anxious as I suspect these neighbors were.

When I entered the house, I spoke to them immediately about their newly adopted infant, and congratulated them. They offered to take me to the baby's room. "No," I said, "that can wait to another time that's more appropriate. First things first." What did I want, then? I told them about the community study we had initiated at McGill two years earlier, a study in which we had asked adoptive parents to speak about their experiences with the attitudes of other people. It was a study that included adopters in New York, Ohio, California, Ontario, and Quebec. We had received more than 1,500 replies. And there was a common theme in the experience of these parents, I told the neighbors. That theme was that the adoptive family was regarded by others as different from the family constituted by birth and blood.

And what did this have to do with them? I said something about my own adoptive family. Yes, they knew about us, but they felt it was different with us; we were not a "Negro family." So I told them how angry this made me, how it meant that I would have to deny the reality of my children's ancestors, which neither my wife nor I was ready to do. Furthermore, although they had adopted a Caucasian child, as we had in our first move into adoption, this in no way shielded them from being regarded as "different" by outsiders. So they had a choice, I said: to emphasize a false homogeneity in our community, or to accept the reality, and perhaps even the desirability, of a heterogeneous neighborhood. After all, whether they had realized it or not, by adopting they had become a "heterogeneous family."

I cannot remember more about this interview with these neighbors, except my own discomfort and theirs. They led me to the door, where I said something about wishing them a good life with their new daughter, a life that would be better if they could act like people who can let difference into their lives with comfort. When I came home, the children asked what happened, and I told them as best I could. What I hoped would come through for them was that their parents could stand up for their family as it was. That it came through in part, at least, seems supported by this evidence: the assault on the "nigger spouting" child occurred two years later, when we were temporarily living in another community in a distant part of the continent. But there was another, and for me equally gratifying, result of my having stood up to this community outrage: the neighbors I had visited completely dropped the matter, and the black family became a very firmly embedded part of our neighborhood.

I see that I have taken longer to write personally than I had intended. A prologue should not take more space than is strictly necessary for welcoming the real actors of the play. Let the curtain, therefore, rise on this important book.

H. David Kirk

Victoria, B.C., Canada

Contents

List of Tables

1
Introduction

Jim and Betty Thorton live in the Chicago suburb of Oak Park, Illinois. Jim, age 42, is the director of a social agency serving visually handicapped adolescents; Betty, 39, a former elementary school teacher, is now a housewife. She spends her spare hours writing childrens' textbooks. Three of her books have been published.

During the early years of their marriage, Jim and Betty never talked much about how large a family they would ultimately have. Both came from relatively prosperous homes — he is the son of an attorney; she is the daughter of a dentist. They always assumed they would have as many children as they could afford. After they started raising their family, they heard about several families in their church who had adopted Asian orphans. They admired what these people had done, and began to discuss whether they might also adopt an Asian orphan. The more they discussed it, the more attractive the idea became; the couple felt they should do something tangible to support the principle of international Christian brotherhood. They are politically liberal, and they are concerned about controlling the world's population explosion.

The Thornton family now consists of Betty and Jim; Brian, to whom Betty gave birth 13 years ago; Keith, also a biological child, who is now 11; and Sally, the Thorntons' biological daughter, who is 8 years old. Six-year-old Tommy, also known as Thon, is a Korean-born baby Betty and Jim adopted five years ago. The most recent member of the Thornton family is Jenny, born of black parents in Chicago, who was adopted two years ago, when she was six.

Jenny has very limited sight. Jim learned about her and her availability for adoption through his social service agency.

The Thorntons don't regard themselves as a very unusual family; they feel great affection for each other and a sense of being inseparably linked to each other. Yet, to the outside world their family group may seem odd, perhaps freakish. The Thorntons spend most of their spare time together. While no one in their extended family has openly disapproved of their family's composition, Betty and Jim have gotten hints of restrained acceptance of their adoptions by some relatives, particularly on the part of Betty's parents. They anticipate that eventually their parents will fully accept Tommy and Jenny. In the meantime, they keep to themselves.

We might wonder about the Thorntons — how widespread families as theirs are today. Why may such families as theirs be increasingly common? What prompts people like Betty and Jim Thornton to adopt children like Thon and Jenny? We may also wonder what the future will be for Tommy Thornton — he is no longer living in the Korean culture and has a family who obviously are not Korean. How will Tom's appearance, different from his parents' and his community's, create a barrier for him in meeting his needs and in realizing the hopes for him of both his birth and his adoptive parents? The same questions might be raised about Jenny Thornton. How can she, a black growing up in a white American family — in a racist society — develop positive feelings toward herself and her blackness? Does she have a better or poorer chance to realize her potential growing up in a transracial adoptive family? How does her development compare with that of her Asian brother Tommy (and of other Asian transracial adoptees), her other brothers and sisters, Brian, Keith, and Sally? How does her future compare with theirs, and with what it would have been if she had been raised in a black adoptive or biological family? These are questions about the Thorntons that need examination.

Another family we might mention and have questions about are the Olsens. Nancy Olsen, its head, is a nurse who lives in Los Angeles. She is 38 years old. She was married for four years and then divorced. One morning, on her way home from work, she heard a broadcast — sponsored by the Department of Social Services of Los Angeles — that told of the availability of seven-year-old Maria, a Mexican-American girl believed to be borderline retarded, who needed a loving home. The announcement mentioned that applications from single adults would be considered.

The possibility of becoming a parent was exciting to Nancy Olsen. After a lengthy period involving two home studies and considerable discussion of her plans with her parents and friends, Maria finally came to live with Nancy as her adopted daughter. At first Maria wet her bed frequently and was given to fits of sullen rage; she was convinced that Nancy would ultimately return her to the state agency. Nancy took much time off from work to help Maria adjust to her new home. Now, five years later, Maria is twelve, has many friends, and is a good student. Her main worry is her appearance. She feels very uneasy and displeased about her shortness and her very dark skin. She and Nancy have established mutually meaningful and fulfilling family feelings. Nancy has an application pending with the Department of Social Services to adopt another child.

In the early 1960s it would have been almost unthinkable — and certainly almost impossible — to arrange a single-parent adoption like Maria's by Nancy Olsen. What accounts for the new possibilities permitting such single-parent adoptions? What prompts people like Nancy Olsen to seek adoptive parenthood? How common is her experience with single-parent adoption? Was it exceptional, or common and typical? Would Maria's chances have been more favorable if she had been placed in a two-parent home?

Another family we will be interested in studying is the Ragusas. Nicholas Ragusa is 41 years old. He is a foreman for a large electrical contractor and lives in the lower-middle-class community of Massapequa Park, Long Island. His wife, Mary Ann, is 37 years old and is a full-time housewife. Both Nicholas and Mary Ann come from families of four children. From the earliest days of their marriage they had expected to raise their own large family. They were very surprised and disappointed when they encountered difficulties in conceiving children. At first each thought the other was to blame. They found themselves arguing frequently and even considering divorce. After much agonizing they reluctantly sought medical counsel. They learned, after two years of seeing every fertility specialist affiliated with the best New York city hospitals and trying all the recommended measures, that they were only remotely likely to be able to have biological offspring. It seemed like the end of the world. As they accepted the idea of their infertility, the possibility of adopting children began to crystallize.

In 1969 the Ragusas finally overcame their reluctance to pursue adoption. They approached the Nassau County Department of

Social Services. They had little trouble adopting. From the date of their application until Jamie was placed in their custody was a period of eight months. Now Jamie is almost 13 years old, a good student in school, well liked by his classmates, and the star player on his junior high school soccer team. When the Ragusas started to think about adopting a second child, in 1974, the Department of Social Services had no infants available. They were told their names would be put on a waiting list, and they would be likely to wait no less than five years before they would even be considered. The fact that they already had a child put them in a lower priority category than couples who had no children. After that they pursued adoption with all the private agencies in their area, with much the same result.

Just when they were beginning to give up hope, the Ragusas read of an organization in their community that was helping couples to complete Colombian and other Latin American adoptions. The article showed pictures of some of the beautiful children that were being adopted by American families, some of whom lived in their vicinity. A little over a year later the Ragusas were aboard a plane en route to Bogotá, Colombia, where they were to pick up their daughter Joanna. That was in 1976. Now Joanna is eight years old and about to enter third grade. Again, we might wonder about Joanna — how will she grow up in an alien culture, where she is identifiably different from her parents with her jet black straight hair, her almond-shaped eyes, and her dark skin? We may also wonder about her parents, a conservative and diffident couple — whether they are up to enduring the many stares and irritating questions outsiders often ask about why Joanna looks so different from the other members of their family. Are people like the Ragusas likely to be as able adoptive parents as others, such as the Thorntons, who pursue adoption for social and humanitarian reasons? Or perhaps the Ragusas, with their strong personal motivation and commitment to succeeding as adoptive parents, may be more effective parents than the "bleeding heart" liberal types like the Thorntons.

Our examination of adoption wouldn't be complete without considering people like Sheila Shapiro. Sheila is now 28 years old and works as an editorial aide for a Boston publishing company. She was adopted when she was only 14 months old. Harold and Vivian Shapiro are the only parents she has even known. She was their only adopted child. As a child Sheila's parents never got around to telling her that she was adopted. People always remarked on how closely she resembled Vivian. Sheila therefore assumed that she was their natural offspring. Yet, as she grew older, every now and then things were said around the house that led her to wonder whether there was some unacceptable difference between her and other children. The sometimes strange behavior of her parents confused and disturbed her — she never connected it with adoption. Then, when she was 12, an aunt she rarely saw let slip a bit of information that was supposed to be a family secret. Later she confronted her mother about it, and Vivian confirmed her suspicions that she was adopted. Sheila was greatly angered by her family's deceit, but eventually forgave her mother and father. She was sure of their love for her; it must have been their feelings about infertility that led them to suppress this important piece of information about her.

Yet, it continued to puzzle her: what were her "real" parents like? Did she have any brothers and sisters? Was she in any way like them? Her adoptive parents didn't receive a great deal of information from the lawyer who arranged the independent adoption. They were far too anxious to ask many questions, fearful they might cause some last-minute hitch that would prevent them from getting their daughter. The lawyer who had arranged the adoption had since retired from his practice and had moved to another state.

Sheila's interest in her genealogical origins peaked when she was a college sophomore. In the many conversations she had with her roommates at the dormitory about career goals and personal values, the idea of finding out more about herself and her origins took on especially significant meaning. Eventually, with her mother's help, the lawyer was found, and agreed to act as an intermediary to facilitate a reunion if Sheila's birth mother could be found, and if she wanted the reunion. Some months later Sheila met her birth mother; she also learned that she had a half brother and a half sister, whom she met several times. They have written to each other, although the correspondence has begun to diminish.

Sheila feels much better about herself for having made this inquiry. She is convinced that the information she has acquired will be even more valuable to her when she starts to raise her own family. She is dating a fellow now whom she expects to marry. She is grateful for her adoptive parents' aid in expediting her reunion and feels this has strengthened her relationship with them. We may wonder about other adult adoptees and whether most carry out the search such as Sheila did. We may also wonder whether the search is most likely to be made when a child finds out later in life about his or her adoptive origins, as contrasted with those who may obtain this information about being adopted when they are much younger.

What role do adoptive parents usually play in facilitating or discouraging search efforts? Is the pattern of adoptive parents' suppressing, then supporting, search efforts — Sheila's experience — the most common one? What kinds of adoptive parents are more likely to have children searching for their birth parents? We may also ask whether the interest in searching is linked with personality problems. Or is it associated with optimal psychological adjustment? And what, if any, social and psychological attributes among adoptees can be linked with the interest in making contact with one's birth parents?

The families who have been mentioned — the Thorntons, Olsens, Ragusas, and Shapiros — are composites of real families who participated in our study. The names and certain attributes have been changed to preserve the privacy and anonymity of our respondents. However, although fictitious here, these families are very real analytically and empirically. Their cases suggest a great deal about what is happening in the realm of adoptions today, and some of the most significant transformations that are taking place. These are the central issues in our study; these issues and questions will be further explored and developed within the context of our research.

BACKGROUND OF THE RESEARCH

Our work will be aimed at examining the transformations occurring in the realm of American adoptions. Our emphasis will be on evaluating the more fundamental social changes and changes within the American family's behavior that have spawned such innovations in adoptions. We intend to describe and delineate these novel and emergent patterns, to investigate their sociocultural and social structural bases, and to probe their consequences for the families and individuals involved. Our study will also evaluate the role of social service professionals in serving adoptees and adoptive parents.

It will focus on the kinds of experiences that adoptive parents and children have with social service professionals, how their needs may be served and thwarted in that association, and what may be needed to enable social service agencies to better serve their adoption clientele.

Thus, the work is envisioned to have academic and practical implications. It is seen as scholastically significant to academic professionals in the fields of psychology, sociology, and social work because it delineates the patterning of social forces surrounding current and changing adoption relationships. We also anticipate that our efforts should be of value to the many social work practitioners active in the area of adoptions — those who formulate and revise adoption policies, as well as the many who carry out such programs. Attorneys, judges, psychologists, and all others who serve adoptive families in some way should have an interest in the issues taken up in this volume. Last, and by no means least, our work is intended to have particular significance for those with a personal involvement in adoption: adoptive parents, adoptees, and birth parents who have considered surrendering or have surrendered children for adoption.

If we accomplish our objective of placing adoption in a systematic social science perspective, then we should have a great deal of useful information to offer the groups mentioned above. It is our hope here to illuminate some of the perplexing questions associated with adoption in the 1980s, to account for some of the more novel and noteworthy aspects of adoption, and to dispel some of the prevalent myths about it.

Our study, which began in 1973, is based upon an extensive examination of existing research and publications on adoption. In addition to summarizing and critically evaluating earlier adoption studies, we conducted a mailed questionnaire survey based on a nationwide sample of adoptive families. Most of these data were collected between November 1974 and March 1976. Our sample was drawn from three groups: the membership lists of adoptive parent groups in different regions of the country; a list of adopting families given by a large adoption agency; and the names of adopting families not affiliated with adoptive parent organizations who were known to the heads of the parent groups that participated in the research.

Members of adoptive parent groups were overrepresented in the sample — approximately 80 percent of sample members belonged to such groups. Some 1,100 copies of the questionnaire were sent out, and one follow-up letter was sent to tardy respondents. Ultimately some 60 percent of the sample population returned usable questionnaires, yielding a total sample of 737 adoptive families.

Respondents received their children from a variety of sources: domestic and foreign, private agencies, regional social service departments, and independent adoptions. Seventy-six percent of responding families had adopted overseas, and 24 percent had adopted domestically. Eighty-nine percent had adopted through private agencies and regional social service departments; 11 percent had adopted independently. The sample, one of the largest taken in any adoption study, included all major types of adoptions. It intentionally included an overrepresentation of families typifying newer and emerging adopting patterns: transracial adoptions, fertile adoptive parents, and single-parent adoptions. We felt this inclusion of large numbers of the particular groups we were interested in studying was entirely appropriate, given our largely exploratory aims.

All but 20 of our responding parents were white. Given the small number of nonwhite parents we decided to defer the analysis of nonwhite adopting families until a larger and more representative sample could be obtained.

In 1975 adopting parents were asked to respond to a detailed list of questions about their most recently adopted child. Parents described the racial and national origins of their most recently adopted child in the following terms:

White children born in the United States	13 percent (96)
Afro-American children	8 percent (58)
Korean children	40 percent (298)
Vietnamese children	20 percent (144)
Colombian children	6 percent (46)
Other children	13 percent (95)

In 1980 and 1981 we sought to contact the respondents to our earlier survey. Despite our efforts to resurvey our sample population directly or through their adoptive parent organization, we were unable to administer our follow-up survey to 26 percent of respondents because they had moved and their postal forwarding requests had expired. Of the remaining 545 possible respondents, 68 percent cooperated with our follow-up study, yielding a total of 372 responding families. The two surveys comprise the data base for the present study.

CHANGING ADOPTION PATTERNS: CAUSES, ISSUES, AND QUESTIONS

No one knows for certain how many children are adopted in America. There is no central government agency that regularly tabulates adoptions. Nor is this being done by state social service agencies. Adoption is usually a very private matter, often treated with extreme guardedness and even great secrecy. Once adoptions are made, the information about them is usually sealed and not available to anyone, particularly to those directly involved in the adoption process: the adopting parents, the adoptees, and/or the birth parents. The secrecy surrounding adoption is felt by many to be necessary to assure the well-being of all parties. Such attitudes and actions, however, tend to obscure adoption from social analysis.

Our society has not always been as ignorant of adoption as it now may be. Until as recently as 1971 the National Center for Social Statistics, a branch of the former Department of Health, Education and Welfare (now Department of Health and Human Services), reported adoption statistically annually. The total number of adoptions in the country was never more completely tabulated than during 1957-71. Yet, since the early 1970s some of the more populous states — New York, California, Pennsylvania, Michigan — have failed to furnish adoption figures. This has undermined the accuracy of any national tabulations. The last year for which state-wide enumerations of adoptions were collected by the National Center of Social Statistics was 1976. This declining effort at tabulating adoption statistics says a great deal about the priorities of our society and the level of national interest in children's services. Americans are able to learn far more readily the number of cans of dog food sold, or the number of people buying electric hair dryers, than they can acquire information about children requiring certain kinds of social services.

The best available tabulations of adoptions showed 169,000 in 1971, a considerable increase from the 91,000 reported in 1957 (Bonham 1977). Evidence suggests that after 1971 there may have been a decline in adoptions, to 149,000 in 1974. Gordon Scott Bonham estimated the number of adoptions nationwide for 1972-74 from the figures reported for 1969-71. If the ratio of reporting to nonreporting states remained the same for both periods, then there is an indication of a downward spiral from the peak of 175,000 adoptions in 1970.

One should bear in mind the important distinction between relative and nonrelative adoptions. A relative adoption would most typically be one in which a divorced woman remarries and her child is adopted by his or her stepfather. It would also include the rarer adoption of a child into the family of another relative after the death of one or both parents. Such relative adoptions have been increasing. In 1951 they comprised 49 percent of all adoptions. By 1974 they amounted to 64 percent of all adoptions (Bonham 1977). Thus, the largest part of the decline in adoptions in the 1970s appears to be among nonrelative adoptions. Also, some of the increase in adoptions during the 1960s can be accounted for by the rise in relative adoptions.

Although relative adoptions predominate in the totality of adoptions, we will focus our attention on children adopted by nonrelatives. These children are the ones who attract the attention and require the assistance of social service agencies. Children adopted by nonrelatives are usually adopted in infancy. The National Center for Social Statistics reported that 84 percent of such children were less than a year of age at adoption in 1971. Most adoptions by nonrelatives were of children born out of wedlock; in 1971 the National Center for Social Statistics reported that 87 percent of nonrelative adoptions involved such children.

Adoptions may be done through social agencies, such as state social service departments, or through private adoption and/or child welfare agencies. Adoptions can also be arranged independently — that is, between the adoptive parents and the biological parent(s), usually with a facilitator, such as an attorney, physician, or clergyman. During the early 1960s independent adoptions accounted for a greater percentage of all adoptions than they did in the early 1970s. The proportion of adoptions by nonrelatives arranged independently of agencies dropped from 43 percent in 1960 to 22 percent in 1970 (Meezan 1978). In the early 1970s available statistics suggest that independent adoptions stabilized at approximately 20 percent (Meezan 1978). Adoption specialists anticipate that as those seeking to adopt through agencies encounter greater difficulties in getting children, they are likely to be driven to adopt independently. Thus, independent adoptions are likely to form an ever greater portion of all adoptions in the future. Such a trend, if it has begun to occur, has yet to be noticed in the increasingly meager array of adoption statistics.

Most American adoptees are born in the United States, although growing numbers of adopted children are coming from abroad. Before 1970 the Immigration and Naturalization Service reported variations in international adoptions of up to 2,000 during any given year in the 1960s. Since 1970 there have been approximately 5,000 international adoptions annually, peaking at over 6,500 in 1976 and 5,139 in 1980, the last year for which statistics are available. In 1974 international adoptions accounted for approximately 9 percent of all nonrelative adoptions.

The emerging trend of international adoptions is primarily transracial. This was not always true. At first international adoptions were predominantly same-race. White parents, often families of American servicemen, adopted homeless white children from the war-ravaged countries of Western Europe. As a result of war relief, in later years the adoptions of European-born children virtually terminated. More recently white American parents have adopted children of Asian ancestry. Adams and Kim (1971) reported that 73 percent of international adoptions were of European-born children in 1948-57 and only 27 percent were of Asian-born children. Since 1958 Asian adoptions have predominated. For example, in 1970 Asian adoptions comprised 56 percent of all foreign adoptions (Adams and Kim 1971). By 1980, the last year for which statistics are available, Asian adoptions had steadily advanced, coming to represent more than 75 percent of all foreign adoptions (U.S. Immigration and Naturalization Service 1983). Today Asian-born children come principally from the Philippines, India, the Republic of China, Japan, Thailand, and, most of all, Korea.

There has been a remarkable increase in the number of Latin American children adopted. In 1970 South and Central American children adopted by American families comprised less than 5 percent of all foreign-born adopted children (Adams and Kim 1971). By 1980 such children comprised 29 percent of all foreign adoptions, numbering 1,499 children (U.S. Immigration and Naturalization Service 1983). The greatest number of these children are from

Colombia. American adoptions of black children from Africa have been, and remain, extremely isolated occurrences. Thus, the predominant tendency of foreign adoptions nowadays is for white American parents to adopt children of Asian or Latin American ancestry.

Adoptions of white and black children born in the United States show differing patterns. White adoptions increased during the 1960s, then fell during the early 1970s. For blacks the trend has been one of modest expansion until 1974 — the last year for which national statistics are available (Bonham 1977). Yet, despite the great and expanding expression of concern for the needs of black children, their share of nonrelative adoptions did not rise greatly between 1957 and 1974. In 1957 they constituted 9 percent of all nonrelative adoptions; in 1971, 12 percent, a figure that merely reflects the proportion of blacks in the total population (Kadushin 1977).

Transracial black/white adoptions have increased significantly over the years. Before the 1950s and early 1960s, such adoptions were virtually unheard-of and nonexistent. During the late 1960s they increased, and peaked at 2,574 in 1971 (Opportunity 1975). After that they began to fall, reaching 1,056 in 1976, the last year for which data are available (Opportunity 1976). In 1969-76 they comprised from 20 to 35 percent of the nonrelative adoptive placements of black children (Opportunity 1969-76).

Although data remain fragmentary and incomplete, evidence is beginning to emerge that points to dramatic increases in the numbers of older and handicapped children being adopted. In Massachusetts it was reported that in 1969-72 the number of older children (those over a year of age) adopted showed a 200 percent increase, from 44 to 124 per year (Massachusetts Adoption Resource Exchange 1969-72). In 1975 the Child Welfare League of America reported that 14 percent of the children placed by the reporting public agencies were mentally and/or physically handicapped (Haring 1976). In earlier years adoptions of these children would have been unacceptable and very difficult to arrange. They were especially rare — if they could be found at all. Now such adoptions appear to comprise a growing minority in current placement practice.

Do Americans approve of and accept adoption? Poll results suggest that they do. One public opinion poll conducted among a representative sample of adult Americans found that over half of the respondents would consider adopting a child if they already had two children and wanted a larger family (Commission on Population Growth and the Future, 1972). Nearly half the women in another study said that they would adopt a child if they found they were unable to have the number of children they expected to have (National Center for Health Statistics 1974). Studies also indicate that the acceptance of adoption is greater among the more highly educated and affluent and among those bearing fewer children (Bonham 1977). Thus, adoption appears to be widely accepted as Americans have become more highly educated and have fewer biological children.

What are the common features of today's adoptive parents? They are not greatly distinguishable from most other American parents. One study found adoptive parents to be between the ages of 25 and 35, and to be more highly educated and more successful economically than their nonadopting counterparts (Braden 1970). Although earlier studies suggest that most adopting parents are childless, more recent evidence indicates that as many as half of all adoptive parents have biological offspring (Bonham 1977). Some have had their biological offspring prior to adoption; others have biological children after they adopt. Research evidence suggests that the former pattern is nearly twice as common as the latter (Bonham 1977).

Recent evidence suggests an unmistakable trend to adoption among fertile parents. Bonham's study noted that the percentage of childless wives who adopted decreased from 6 to 4 percent between 1955 and 1973, and that the number of fertile and subfertile women who adopted increased during this same period from 3 to 7 percent. Fertile parents still represent a distinct minority, but their numbers appear to be growing appreciably.

In the past, couples who adopted were likely to be in their late twenties and early thirties. Many child welfare agencies used to require couples to present proof of infertility in order to qualify for adoptive parenthood. It was usually after years of attempting to conceive children and seeking medical help that couples – in these age groups – would be likely to apply to agencies for children. Growing numbers of older couples are beginning to appear among the ranks of adoptive parents – husbands and wives may be in their late thirties, forties, and even fifties. In our adoption survey sample, including a preponderance of less traditional adoptive parents, it was noted that nearly half of the husbands and 37 percent of the wives

were over 35 when they last adopted. These older couples still
represent a decided minority among the ranks of adoptive parents,
but their numbers are increasing.

Before the early 1960s very few single adults considered the
possibility of becoming adoptive parents. Child welfare agencies
were at that time – and many still are – extremely dubious about
the capabilities of single individuals to provide adequate care for
adopted children. The few single individuals who in the past pursued
adoptions were suspected of being mentally ill, homosexual, or
otherwise unsuitable as parents. Today, however, we are beginning
to see growing numbers of single-parent adoptions and widening
acceptance of them among social work practitioners. There has even
been a small but increasing number of cases where placements have
been made with openly homosexual parents (*The New York Times*,
1983). Most often women are single adoptive parents, representing
anywhere from 80 to 95 percent of that population (Branham
1970; Feigelman and Silverman 1977).

Another issue that has come to the fore concerns the unsealing
of adoption records and the rights of adoptees to use the information
in them to seek their birth parents. Available evidence remains
unclear on how widespread the inclination to search for one's birth
parents is among adult adoptees (Sorosky, Baran, and Pannor 1978).
One study found that nearly two-thirds of adult adoptees of today
desired much more information than they had obtained about their
genealogical origins (Children's Home Society 1977). There is much
controversy over the unsealing of adoption records and the effects
this would produce upon adoptees, adoptive parents, and biological
parents.

In earlier times the sealing of adoption records was taken for
granted as necessary to ensure an adoption's success. It was seen
as necessary to protect the interests of all those involved – adoptee,
adoptive parents, birth parents – from invasions of privacy by
would-be blackmailers and scandalmongers. Those advocating the
opening of adoption records contend that adoptees who are denied
full information about their origins may suffer permanent psychological damage, and are being deprived of a fundamental civil right
– full knowledge about themselves. Those favoring the continued
sealing of adoption records see this as necessary to enable those who
adopt to be effective parents. Many contend that adoptees are likely
to suffer confusion about their own personality and about parental

allegiance with the opening of adoption records. Some maintain that if adoption records were not sealed, many birth parents would be unwilling to surrender children for adoption because of their fears of subsequent embarrassing disclosures.

Here, then, are the issues of concern in this volume: the new and growing patterns of transracial and international adoptions and of adoptions of older and handicapped children; the adoptions of children by older, fertile, and single parents; and the growing interest among adult adoptees in finding their birth parents and the controversy concerning the unsealing of adoption records. We are interested in what social changes have given rise to these trends and what their social ramifications have been among these particular families and individuals.

American adoption practices and their transformations cannot be fully understood without taking account of the family and other groups. Many of the changes that we are witnessing in adoptions are outgrowths of changing family life. There are five particular areas of overall family change that appear to have had an especially strong influence on current adoption practices: diminishing fertility and family size; the postponement of marriages; the pattern of increasing divorce and the growing social acceptability of single-parent families; expanded availability of family welfare programs and greater tolerance of nontraditional family life-styles; and the extension of greater legal rights to children.

Jessie Bernard cogently sums up the trend toward diminishing fertility since the 1960s:

> Among currently married women, the average number of expected children in 1967 was 3.1; in 1978, 2.3; among women 18-34, 2.1. The Roper poll of 1980 found that the two children women said they wanted was half the number they said they wanted in 1970. The number of children under 5 dropped 9 percent between 1970 and 1979. (Bernard 1981, p. 53)

The drop in fertility has reduced the demand for adoptions. Couples who would have wanted to adopt one or more children have curtailed their demands. This is consistent with the apparent downward trend of adoptions during the early 1970s. Declining fertility has also had an impact on the supply side of adoptions. It has reduced the number of children who might otherwise be available for adoption. Declining fertility has been especially critical in diminishing the number of babies available. It has given rise to numerous cases of baby selling, the "black" or "gray" market in adoptions, where babies have not uncommonly been sold for $20,000 or more (McTaggert 1980). The declining availability of infants has led people like the Ragusas to seek a Colombian-born child, and others to select a hard-to-place child – an older child, a minority child, a child in less than good health.

Another factor affecting the supply of adoptable children is the changing pattern of illegitimate births. Since the overwhelming majority of nonrelative adoptions involve children born out of wedlock, we need to establish whether illegitimate births have declined during recent times. Available evidence suggests they have not. During the period from 1957 to 1974 there was a doubling of illegitimate births, from 201,700 to 418,100 (Bonham 1977). For whites, as the rate of illegitimacy has risen, there has been a concomitant decline in the tendency to surrender such children for adoptive placement (Bonham 1977). Factors other than changing illegitimacy rates will be needed to explain the diminishing supply of adoptable infants.

The postponement of marriage also appears to have relevance for adoptions. During the first six decades of the twentieth century, the average age at marriage dropped for both men and women. In 1900 men averaged about 26 years of age when they first married; women averaged about 22. By 1960 the respective figures were 23 and 20. Since 1960 the trend has been upward. In 1976 the figures were 23.8 for men and 21.3 for women (Leslie 1982). Paul Glick and Arthur Norton (1977) report that the proportion of women still single at ages 20-24 had increased by 50 percent since 1960, from 28 to 43 percent.

The impact of postponing marriage on adoptions is complex. On the one hand, as it contributes to the overall diminution of fertility, it tends to reduce the demand for adoptions. On the other hand, as it leads people into attempting to conceive children at later ages, it contributes to increasing infertility and subfertility, thus leading more people to seek adoptions than would have otherwise done so. Although problems of infertility have been eased somewhat by advances in medical technology – by such innovations as in vitro fertilization, pioneered by the British doctors Edwards and Steptoe, and other sophisticated techniques – on the other side of the coin there has probably been an increase in infertility because of changing life-styles, modern birth control methods, and the tendency to postpone marriage.

Some medical experts estimate that in the 1950s one couple in ten had infertility problems; now, with people starting to raise families later in life and having complications from birth control techniques, it is estimated that the figure has risen to one out of six (Kleiman 1979). Thus, on balance it is highly probable that the tendency to postpone marriage may have contributed to maintaining, if not expanding, the demand for adoption.

One of the most important factors affecting the declining availability of infants for adoption has been the growing trend among unwed mothers to retain custody of their children. Leslie Aldridge Westoff cogently sums up recent trends in this area:

> In the past most black teenagers kept their babies and most white girls aborted or gave them up to a hungry adoption market. In recent years the trend has been reversed. Many black girls with more options open to them are either having legal abortions or considering adoption. And more white teenagers who have children out of wedlock have begun to keep them. Thus in 1966 an estimated 65 percent of white illegitimate babies were given away for adoption; in 1971 Dr. John Kantner and Dr. Melvin Zelnick of Johns Hopkins put the estimate at 18 percent. Ten years ago only one out of three decided to keep and raise their illegitimate babies; five years later four out of five chose that alternative. Today the proportion is doubtless even higher. (Westoff 1976, p. 14)

Analysts such as Westoff see a variety of factors as important in the emerging trend among younger white women to keep their out-of-wedlock children: changing social and sexual mores, the withering away of many of the traditional moral prohibitions of earlier times, and the greater financial and other support that is presently available from parents and society. Now parents and society — with expanded social services and welfare benefits — will more often help young mothers financially rather than disown them. The growing presence and acceptance of single-parent families also has reduced the need for relinquishment.

Another aspect of family life that has had a decisive impact on adoption patterns is the rising rate of divorce. Gary Lee writes:

According to the Vital Statistics Reports provided by the Department of Health and Human Services, the 1979 divorce rate in the United States was 5.3 divorces per 1,000 population. This compares with a rate of 3.2 only ten years earlier and a rate of 2.2 as recently as 1962. The trend, as everyone knows, has been sharply upward since the mid-sixties. (Lee 1981, p. 68)

The continuing rise of divorce has created a significant expansion in the number of single-parent families. Seventeen percent of all childen are now living in single-parent families; as many as four children out of ten born in the 1970s will spend at least part of their childhood in a single-parent family (Newsweek 1978). The rising incidence and social acceptance of divorce and single-parent families have affected adoptions in two ways: they have encouraged young, white, unwed mothers to retain custody of their children; and they have led child welfare agencies to think more positively about single adults as potential adoptive parents.

As family changes have brought about reductions in the numbers of healthy white infants available for adoption, at the same time there has evolved a surfeit of prospective adoptive parents; this has led child welfare agencies to reevaluate their adoption policies and practices. Adoption agencies have always tried to balance the needs of all parties involved in adoptions: birth parents, adoptees, and adoptive parents. Until the late 1950s they put primary emphasis on serving the interests of adoptive parents. Agencies often did what they could to "match" parent and child, selecting a child for a particular couple as nearly like them as possible in coloring, body build, temperament, and ethnic and religious background. This emphasis was clearly directed at accommodating the needs of the adoptive parents, offering them a child as much as possible like the one they might have had if they were fertile. Since the 1960s the pendulum has begun to swing toward emphasizing the needs of the adopted child. In 1959 the Child Welfare League of America put forth new standards for adoptive practice:

The primary purpose of an adoption agency is to help children who would not otherwise have a home of their own and who can benefit from family life, to become members of a family. . . . An adoption service should not have as its main purpose to find children for families. (p. 6)

Since the early 1960s child welfare agencies have put forth much more effort to serve children needing placement. This has led to vastly increased placements of special-needs children — minority, older, and handicapped children — who had not been considered adoptable.

The proliferation of single-parent families has led to a reevaluation of the capabilities of unmarried adults to become adoptive parents. As family patterns have changed, agency workers have increasingly concluded that children are better off in a single-parent family or some other nontraditional family arrangement than in an institution or a series of foster placements. Thus, the parental capacities of single adults, older couples, fertile parents, and others have achieved greater recognition and acceptability in current adoptive placement practice. Family changes have removed many of the traditional barriers that excluded certain groups and individuals from being adopted or adopting. With these changes the range of adoption possibilities has been vastly extended.

It would seem that the connection between the civil rights movement and the efforts of Sheila Shapiro to find her birth parents is very tenuous. Yet, we feel these happenings have a striking affinity. When we consider the civil rights movement initiated by blacks during the 1950s and 1960s, the emerging feminist movement it helped engender, the youth rebellion of the 1960s that helped to end the war in Vietnam and the draft, and extended the right to vote to 18-year-olds, we see a long and continuous line of civil rights-oriented activities. Such increasing concern for civil rights has also impacted upon how children are regarded, awakening a new interests in children's rights (Margolin 1978). In recent years legal trends have moved significantly toward abandoning the view of children as the property of their parents. We can see these trends manifested in the growing concern about and "discovery" of the problem of child abuse (Pfohl 1977). Certainly child abuse existed in the past. It may even have been more virulent. Yet, it has achieved social recognition only as the inviolable rights of children have attained wider acceptance and appreciation.

Numerous other changes have taken place in state laws pertaining to children's rights. For example, in New York State child offenders accused of serious crimes must be given all the legal protections and judicial safeguards that are available in adult courts.

In Connecticut children are now able to sue their parents for malfeasance of their custodial responsibilities. In the area of adoptions, the issue of expanded children's rights has most frequently been concerned with the child's right to a permanent home (Goldstein, Freud, and Solnit 1973). One of the most controversial questions to be raised here concerns the issue of at what point the parent who places a child in foster care relinquishes parental rights.

These and other recent questions have exerted an important impact on adult adoptees, fostering greater rights-seeking behavior on their part. It has helped spawn a new mood of questioning among them, challenging the sanctity of adoption records. Today's adoptees are increasingly insisting upon their right to full disclosure of information about themselves and their genealogical origins.

A secondary element in current efforts among adult adoptees to know more fully about themselves has its basis in movements fostering expanded ethnic pride and self-knowledge. In recent years numerous ethnic and religious minorities have expressed interest in their origins. This has been true among blacks, Hispanics, Native Americans, Jews, and many others. The emerging fascination with "roots" has awakened widely felt genealogical interests. When a television dramatization such as Alex Haley's *Roots* is able to attract the largest audience ever, our society may be peaking in its preoccupation with genealogical matters. It would appear that this increased interest in genealogy has some bearing on adoptees' efforts to search for their birth parents.

In our analysis we intend further exploration of the linkages between changes in society and those in the realm of adoptions. We intend to go as far as we possibly can to identify more fully the patterning of social forces associated with emerging trends in adoption. We will examine in greater detail most of the issues mentioned here: adopting hard-to-place children, adoption by fertile couples, single-parent adoptions, transracial and international adoptions, the search for birth parents by adult adoptees. We are hopeful and confident that such a sociological emphasis will enlarge our understanding of the developments going on in adoption, and of the social realities and problems of today's adoptive families. Moreover, we anticipate such sociological knowledge will be enormously useful for offering guidance in the kinds of treatment and services needed by today's adoptive families and for helping to identify and locate families for the many thousands of needy children presently lacking them. Such considerations have prompted our present efforts.

2
Social Factors Linked with
Adopting Hard-To-Place Children

Bob and Betty Nelson have a large family by today's standards — six children. Rob Jr., Patrick, and Nancy were born to Betty 16, 14, and 12 years ago, respectively. Four years after Nancy's birth the Nelsons adopted Thomas from Korea. He was an infant when he joined the family, and now is approaching nine. Around the time of the Vietnamese "babylift," in 1976, the Nelsons learned of the availability of Kathy — then three — who was in an orphanage in Saigon; she became the fifth member of their family. The last child to become a Nelson was Matthew, whom the Nelsons learned about from their adoptive parent group. Matthew is a black child, now ten. He's been living with them for the last three years. At first they were concerned that Matthew was mildly retarded; he functioned slowly and was unusually quiet and reserved. These doubts appear to have vanished as Matthew has become a better-than-average student in his fifth grade class. He's not noticeably shy, although he tends to be on the quiet side with his other brothers and sisters and his few school friends. The Nelsons belong to a Congregational church, although they attend services rather infrequently. Bob writes science textbooks; Betty is a part-time interior decorator. Together they make over $60,000 annually. They live in the affluent community of Ladue, a suburb of St. Louis.

When asked about their willingness to adopt various types of hard-to-place children, Bob and Betty both indicated that they could easily adopt an Asian, black, or older child — as they had done. They indicated some reservations about adopting a slightly retarded child. They also said they would not consider a child with a serious physical handicap that was not correctable. As far as they are concerned, their family is complete.

Another family in our sample is the Steins. David Stein is a junior high school teacher. Linda, his wife, was an elementary school teacher before and shortly after she and David married. Now she is a housewife. After five years of unsuccessfully attempting to conceive a child, the Steins adopted Jane, a fair-haired, blue-eyed white infant, seemingly in excellent health. They adopted her through a lawyer in their hometown of White Plains, New York. Four years later the Steins learned of a woman who was about to give birth to an out-of-wedlock child that she intended to surrender for adoption. They heard about this case from another member of their adoptive parent group who had previously been a client of the lawyer who was representing the birth mother. That was how the Steins got Paulette, who was born in Florida to white parents. Three years later, after the Steins thought they had completed their family, they were surprised to find out that Linda was pregnant. At present the Steins have three girls: Jane, twelve; Paulette, eight; and Rebecca, four. Both born in Jewish families, David and Linda attend religious services infrequently, usually going to synagogue only on the high holy days.

When we asked David and Linda about their willingness to consider different kinds of hard-to-place children, they indicated that they could not consider a child with physical or emotional handicaps, a black child, or an older child. They also indicated some reservations about adopting an Asian child.

Another couple, Sally and Jim Bradshaw, had a family that sounded like the United Nations. Their family was one of the largest of those in our sample, consisting of eight children, six of whom were adopted. Jennifer, their first child, was born to them eleven years ago. Two years later they adopted Paula from Korea through the Holt Agency. She was four when she was adopted; she came to their family with some serious emotional problems. Christopher came next, a five-year-old black boy with a deformed leg. They learned about him from the Minneapolis Department of Social Services. Gregory was next, a six-year-old Vietnamese boy they adopted through Lutheran Social Services in 1975. Phillip was born to them in 1977. In the following year the Bradshaws added seven-year-old Jessica to their family. She was born to black and Hispanic parents and came from metropolitan Chicago. In 1979, when the Bradshaws thought their family was complete, they learned that homes were needed for some Vietnamese boat children. They opened their doors to Kim and Li, an orphaned brother and sister, now aged 15 and 18, who have been living with them off and on. The Bradshaws are active in their Lutheran church, which they attend regularly. They live in Red Wing, a small town in Minnesota, from which Jim commutes to his job as director of a private social service agency. When Sally finds the time, she writes children's stories. Their income is about $30,000 annually. Both are very active adoption advocates in their home state.

When they were asked about their willingness to adopt all the various hard-to-place children — black, Asian, older, and seriously handicapped — they indicated that they would adopt them all easily. They did, however, express some reservations about adopting a slightly retarded child.

The Maffetones were another family in our sample. Joseph and Susan have been married for 15 years, are both of Italian-American ancestry, and are active in their local Roman Catholic parish. They have two biological children: Amy, fourteen, and Robert, eleven. In 1974 they decided to adopt additional children if and when they expanded their family. The following year, with the help of their priest and International Social Services, they learned of the availability of Paul, a one-and-a-half-year-old Vietnamese foundling who was being cared for in a church orphanage in Saigon. He became their third child. They have since adopted Sarah, who joined them at age three. When she was eight months old, she was diagnosed as having cerebral palsy. Now Sarah feeds herself, but she is not yet toilet-trained. Her vocabulary is growing. There is a possibility Sarah may be able to walk with braces, but it is still too early to tell. Spaulding for Children helped the Maffetones obtain Sarah.

Joseph, aged 36, is a lineman for the Long Island Lighting Company. He and Susan live in a modest home in Ronkonkoma, New York. Susan is a full-time housewife with few career aspirations, although she used to work as a secretary. Both Joe and Susan completed high school. In addition, Joe finished a year of college, going nights to the community college near his home. The annual income of the Maffetone family is between $20,000 and $25,000. When asked about being willing to adopt different kinds of hard-to-place children, the Maffetones indicated that they could easily adopt an Asian, older, handicapped, or retarded child. They did, however, indicate some reservations about adopting a black child.

The above four cases suggest considerable variability in each family's willingness to adopt different hard-to-place children. Some families, like the Nelsons, Bradshaws, and Maffetones, seemed very willing and eager to adopt almost all of the available kinds of special-needs children. Others, like the Steins, were clearly reluctant to become adoptive parents for hard-to-place kids. Some families, like the Maffetones, were willing to adopt handicapped and retarded children but were unwilling to adopt blacks. Others, like the Nelsons, had no reservations about adopting blacks, but were hesitant to adopt retarded children.

We wondered whether couples' being willing to adopt special-needs children was in any way linked with other social characteristics. Did people of any particular religious affiliations, belonging to any common occupational groups or social classes — or any other categories — have any greater inclination than others to adopt special-needs children? We also wondered whether this inclination to adopt the hard-to-place is associated with any particular family patterns. Is it associated with being fertile or infertile? In short, we were interested in finding out why some families, rather than others, were more inclined to parent hard-to-place children. These questions — and others — will be explored in the present chapter.

First, we were concerned whether there were any discernible trends in families toward parenting the many different kinds of special-needs children available for adoption. Were there any kinds of children who were more likely or unlikely to be acceptable to adoptive parents? Or do the interests in and aversions to different kinds of special-needs children merely reflect the idiosyncrasies of different families?

We asked our respondents whether they would be willing to adopt various kinds of hard-to-place children. The following groups were included: Asian children; blacks; older children (over eight); those slightly retarded; those with serious, noncorrectable physical handicaps. Respondents were asked whether they could adopt these children easily, could adopt with some reservations, or could not consider such children for adoption. Our results indicated that Asian children were clearly the preferred group, with 83 percent able to adopt these children easily. The next most desired groups were older children and black children, with approximately 25 percent willing to adopt these group members. The least wanted groups were the retarded and handicapped children. Table 2.1 shows these data.

The trends offer few surprises. The hardest-to-place group is those children whose care imposes the most demanding obligations on parents. Black children are the next most difficult group, reflecting the deep-seated prejudice in America against blacks. Perhaps the most interesting part of these findings will be noted in comparing our results with an earlier study of these questions undertaken by David Fanshel (1972). In 1960 Fanshel asked these questions of a sample composed of 97 white parents who adopted at least one Native American child. He noted considerably less receptivity to adopting black children; in fact, he observed less willingness to adopt blacks than to adopt the developmentally disabled. Fifty-eight percent could not consider black children, compared with 42 percent who could not consider adopting retarded and physically handicapped children. We think the remarkable change in increasing willingness to adopt black children reflects growing tolerance in American society. A number of poll results, including those of the Gallup organization (Harris 1978), indicate substantially diminished antiblack attitudes among white Americans today as compared with those expressed during the late 1950s and 1960s. Such changing

TABLE 2.1
Willingness to Adopt Hard-to-Place Children
(percent)

	Adopt Easily	Some Reservations	Could Not Consider
A slightly retarded child	4	29	67 (702)
A seriously handicapped child, not correctable	5	30	65 (699)
A black child	26	32	42 (700)
A normal older child (over 8)	27	35	38 (706)
An Asian child	83	11	6 (706)

sentiments have apparently affected adoption attitudes. It is an interesting question — one that remains to be investigated — whether the hierarchy indicated by our adoptive parent respondents would be found among members of the adult population without adopted children.

Our interest in public attitudes and behavior toward hard-to-place or special-needs children is by no means simply an academic and theoretical matter — it is a question of enormous practical implications. While estimates vary at any given time, in recent years there have been anywhere from 250,000 to 750,000 children without the benefits of family membership. According to a report of the U.S. Children's Bureau, dated April 1981, the latest available data showed 502,000 children in foster care in 1977 (U.S. Dept. of Health and Human Services 1981). Minority children — blacks, Hispanics, and other racial and ethnic minority groups — are over-represented among these children. In 1977 they comprised 37 percent of all children in foster care (U.S. Dept. of Health and Human Services 1981). Many of these children are older, with the greatest number in elementary and junior high school. Disproportionally larger numbers of these children have physical and psychological disabilities. In 1977 over 101,000 of these children were legally free for adoption (U.S. Dept. of Health and Human Services 1981).

Juanito Rodriguez is typical of today's waiting children. At age 11 he has known more families than most people do in a lifetime. Juanito's father is a 37-year-old black man names Miles Jones. Jones hasn't been able to manage his life effectively since his army days. A Vietnam veteran who has had long spells of unemployment and sporadically works in various semiskilled blue-collar positions, he has had chronic problems from heavy drinking. His common-law wife, Esmeralda Rodriguez — Juanito's mother — is a Hispanic woman of 32; she is a part-time seamstress. She has repeatedly tried to make a go of it with Jones during his brief intervals of relative sobriety. They have had two children: Juanito and Melinda, now nine. Esmeralda has put both children in foster care at various times during her years with Jones. Most recently she resolved to care for Maria, her third and last-born child, herself. Maria, now five years old, is the product of her union with her second husband, Felix Martinez. Esmeralda began to live with Martinez shortly after she gave up on Jones. Martinez insisted that she surrender Juanito and Melinda for adoption when they began living together. Although she still had some feelings for the children, she recognized that she had had little contact with them over the years, and that this was probably the best thing for both of them. Most recently Esmeralda has separated from Martinez. She intends to make a go of things on her own, living with Maria.

Juanito has had very limited contact with his birth parents. He is now in his third foster placement. His school records show frequent disciplinary problems. He reads on a third grade level. He was left back in school once and now is in the fifth grade. He liked the family he lived with for two years in his second foster placement. At that time his mother reclaimed him in a last-ditch effort to restore her family with Miles Jones. Juanito doesn't have many positive feelings for his present foster parents, even though he's been living with this family the longest. They frequently talk about moving out west, starting a new life for themselves, and returning the two foster children presently in their care to the agency. Juanito has frequent disagreements and conflicts with the three birth children of his foster parents. At various points during his childhood he has seen a child psychiatrist. He has been given medication for his occasional hyperactive behavior. Juanito likes sports but doesn't belong to any teams. He rarely plays with the other children in the neighborhood. He is an especially distrusting and wary boy with no close friends. His social worker — the sixth social service professional to manage his life — is extremely dubious about finding an adoptive placement for him.

Most of the children living apart from their birth families are in foster homes. Smaller numbers are in a variety of nonfamilial settings, such as shelters, group homes, and other institutional facilities. The general plan for children in these kinds of care facilities is that such arrangements are temporary. The ultimate goal is that they will eventually be returned to their birth parents, once the parents regain their capabilities or acquire sufficient resources to resume parental functioning. Yet, all too often, this does not happen, and childhood is spent moving through a series of foster homes and institutions. A Massachusetts study revealed that of all children in foster care in that state, 67 percent had been in the system two or more years; it also found that 83 percent of the children under care were never returned to their parents (Gruber 1973). A New York City study found that of all children under two years of age who were placed in foster care, half were in foster care five years later; approximately half were never returned to their birth parents (Fanshel 1978; 1979). Studies in other states show that over 40 percent of the children in foster care remain in placement from one to five years (National Commission on Children in Need of Parents 1979).

A heavy burden is sustained by our society to support this enormous variety of child care arrangements. As we indicated before, there is no accurate and up-to-date census of the numbers of children presently receiving such aid. Nor is there any overall tabulation of the costs these differing child care arrangements entail. Yet, it is estimated — even acknowledging the very meager and inadequate amounts given to foster parents — that foster care expenses alone cost taxpayers in excess of $2 billion annually (National Commission on Children in Need of Parents 1979). Foster care is the largest single item in the child welfare budget; it is generally acknowledged to be one of the least expensive alternatives of all the many welfare services offered to children living apart from their families. By promoting the adoptions of many of these children — even where some adoptions would be subsidized — costs could be greatly reduced, especially in the longer term.

We may ask what happens to the children who are nurtured in these "temporary" settings. Many studies testify to the disadvantages children sustain when they grow up apart from families (Fraiberg 1977; Bowlby 1952; Spitz 1945; Provence and Lipton 1962). Diminished ability to survive infancy, heightened feelings of insecurity and aggressiveness, and depressed educational attainments are a few of the manifold adverse developmental problems that are likely to occur. Often irreversible social and psychological damage results, ultimately causing such persons as adults to be disproportionally represented among the ranks of the unemployed, the mentally ill, drug abusers, and criminals. The costs that society sustains in caring for such persons drastically escalates. The importance of permanence for normal socialization is regarded as so great that numerous analysts presently conceptualize it as something to which children are entitled. It is not simply that children need families, but that they have an inalienable right to belong to them, to reap the benefits that such membership confers, and to avoid the anguish and damage that denial of such opportunities would inflict upon them (Goldstein, Freud, and Solnit 1973; Fraiberg 1977).

Children denied the full benefits of family life receive various forms of aid from public and private programs. From help in restoring family functioning — such as job training, mental and physical health care, family counseling, drug rehabilitation, homemaker aid, direct financial support — to foster care, adoption services, protective aid, temporary shelters, and more, an almost unending array of services is provided. Yet, despite the plethora of programs and the well-intentioned efforts of many, the problems often persist barely diminished. Children often spend the greatest portion of their childhoods moving through the child welfare system, avoiding the more obvious perils of abuse and neglect but lacking the advantages of care and constancy available in enduring family relationships.

Fanshel's study (1979) of children receiving foster care in New York City turned up some interesting and important findings. He found that half of the children in the foster care system were eventually returned to their birth parents; actually, close to 60 percent were returned to their families when one considers an additional 7 to 8 percent who eventually went to live with other relatives. Only about 10 percent were adopted by their foster families or by other adoptive parents. The approximately 30 percent remaining were discharged to their own responsibility, institutionalized, dead, or their whereabouts unknown. The last-mentioned group represents significant numbers of children whose needs are apparently unmet by prevailing child welfare programs. Although adoption is by no means the only solution for problems of child neglect, clearly its expansion could contribute a great deal to alleviating these difficulties.

A large number of the many children now in foster care are free for adoption, and many more children could be freed if opportunities for their adoptions were available. Yet in the past, and even now to some extent, it has been thought that such children are unadoptable. Many agency workers would be very pessimistic about the prospects of finding adoptive homes for many waiting children. Many would think it would be utterly hopeless to find a home for a sibling group of two school-age black children, one of whom is suffering from a mild-to-moderate emotional adjustment difficulty — typical instances of today's waiting children. Of course there is an increasing recognition of improving placement prospects for special-needs kids. Many more agency workers are coming to realize that there may be homes somewhere in the community for these children. The trouble is, however, that locating these homes takes a commitment and resources that go way beyond the capabilities of most agencies.

In most public and private child welfare agencies, very little time and effort are devoted to pursuing adoption possibilities and locating adoptive placements for their charges. Overwhelmed by heavy case loads, diminishing funds, the uncertainties associated with depending upon government financial support, and frequent worker burnout and turnover, it is all that agencies can do to attempt to effectively monitor the adequacy of ongoing foster care arrangements. In many agencies it is not uncommon to find that child clients frequently outlast their social workers. Most often agencies focus their attention on responding to crises and assuring the daily needs of children in foster care. They are unable to devote much attention to the more fundamental and longer-term needs of such children. The fragmentation of services in the child welfare field further discourages efforts aimed at securing adoptive placements.

As was mentioned in Chapter 1, there has been a phenomenal growth of interest in adopting hard-to-place children since about 1960, and particularly since 1970. Today hundreds of older, minority children with all sorts of physical and psychological limitations are being adopted yearly. In the mid-1950s such adoptions would have been unheard-of and unthinkable. The expansion of these kinds of adoptions remains to be fully documented. But what is particularly important about this emerging interest in hard-to-place children is that it has spawned a great many new organizations. The new groups that have arisen have frequently been formed by citizen advocates, most of whom are adoptive parents themselves. They have also joined together with social service professionals to pursue common social and political programs. Together they have made a number of important legislative gains in the last few years.

Citizen-advocate adoptive parent groups can now be found in every state. In some states a score or more of such organizations flourish. These groups frequently disseminate information to their memberships about available hard-to-place children in their localities. They also direct their energies to obtaining the release for adoption of children in the foster care system who are known to be eligible. They fight for legal reforms to encourage adoption at the local, state, and national levels. For example, in 1981 the prompting of adoption advocacy groups was important in changing federal tax laws, which now permit adopting parents to deduct up to $1,500 of their adoption-related expenses in adoptions of special-needs children. Advocacy groups also provide speakers for community groups who present the experiences of their members in adopting hard-to-place children.

Some adoptive parent groups have started their own adoption agencies. Many others work with the more than dozen regional social service agencies that specialize in adoptions of hard-to-place children. They help run adoption exchanges and photo listing services. As of December 1981, according to a personal communication from Ellen Weber, senior research consultant, National Adoption Information Exchange System, Child Welfare League of America, 29 states have formal adoption exchanges where information about available children and prospective adoptive parents is recorded and matched, and referrals made to agencies for facilitating adoptions of specific children; 12 other states have informal referral services; 10 states compile photo listing books of available waiting children.

In many instances these adoption exchanges are small operations where the project's office consists of someone's kitchen table and the staff is a shifting handful of volunteers. In other cases exchanges have hired a core of permanent staff members that may be supplemented by volunteers.

Many regional adoption exchanges have persisted for more than ten years; the oldest such exchange is the Massachusetts Adoption Resource Exchange, which has been in existence since 1957. Nevertheless, there is an ever-changing array of adoption exchanges as some fall by the wayside after the departure of key members, others merge, and new ones are established.

As efforts to promote the adoptions of special-needs children have surfaced at the grass-roots level, they have also been promulgated by professional social service organizations. Half of all American children receiving child welfare services are served by one of the 376 public or voluntary affiliate agencies of the Child Welfare League of America (Kahn 1979). This standard-setting organization has played a prominent role in advancing the cause of adoptions of special-needs children for some time. In 1968 it formed ARENA — Adoption Resource Exchange of North America — which sought to link waiting children with adoptive families. ARENA was instrumental in fostering the development of many local and regional exchanges that could place children closer to their original homes. More recently, to enlarge upon the goals of ARENA, the Child Welfare League of America has created the National Adoption Information Exchange System (NAIES), with a staff of 12 full-time personnel. This new organization has been mandated to carry forward earlier national adoption exchange programs and to expand its efforts to publicize the need for homes for waiting children. At the present time NAIES is also engaged in efforts to codify the objectives and practices of its national exchange program and offers training, technical assistance, and other facilitative services to persons who are involved in adoptions of special-needs children.

Perhaps the most impressive achievement of the loose federation of citizen and professional child welfare advocates was the passage of Public Law 95-266, the Child Abuse Prevention and Treatment and Adoption Reform Act of 1978. The Adoption Opportunity Act, as it is often called, earmarked $4.8 million for a variety of endeavors aimed at promoting the adoptions of special-needs children. It financed the NAIES program of the Child Welfare League of America and has also granted funds to the Urban Institute for the establishment of a uniform national data-gathering system on the numbers of children being served and the kinds of services received in the child welfare system. It also established ten regional adoption resource centers, spanning the entire country, designed to work with adoptive parents, community groups, and agency personnel to facilitate the adoptions of special-needs children. The regional centers were funded to further the development of local adoptive parent groups, establish and expand adoption exchanges, and improve the training of adoption workers.

The Adoption Opportunity Act also allocated funds for a number of research and informational projects: publicizing the needs of waiting children for adoptive and foster homes through radio and television spot announcements; developing a new curriculum for agencies to use in their training programs for staff members working with special-needs children; drafting a model state adoption law and model adoption procedures to reduce the legal barriers to adoption remaining in many states; and conducting several policy evaluation studies.

The many new efforts and programs arising from the Adoption Opportunities Act portend significant progress in the long-neglected adoptions area. A number of these programs may lay the ground-work for provision of vastly improved social services to the thousands of neglected children who are ill-served in the existing child welfare system. The ultimate success of many of these endeavors depends a great deal upon continued government funding to carry programs to more advanced stages and to maintain efforts that seem to be producing meaningful results. Unfortunately, given the drastically reduced social service expenditures of the Reagan administration, many of these programs have been severely reduced or eliminated altogether.

With the rising interest in promoting the welfare of special-needs kids there have developed new initiatives for community outreach to find homes for them. Adoption of special-needs children represents a relatively unprecedented phenomenon. Because it was never relied upon to any extent in the past, history provides little guidance. Where in the community can parents be found for the many available special-needs children? What subgroups are more likely to respond positively to the needs of the hard-to-place? Where will outreach efforts be likely to pay the greatest dividends? Does it make any sense to publicize the needs of waiting children in such publications as *The National Review*, with its predominantly politically conservative readership, or does one stand a better chance of finding homes with a notice in the leftist-leaning *Mother Jones*? Will one be more likely to find prospective adoptive parents through coverage in the *New York Daily News*, with its largely blue-collar, less educated audience, or in the *New York Times*, whose readers are white-collar and better educated? Are affiliates of any particular churches more inclined than others to be responsive to the needs of hard-to-place children? Many practical questions such as these need answers in order to promote the most efficacious results in finding homes for special-needs children. As outreach work has begun gathering momentum in recent years through growing organizational and financial support, these questions have assumed an even greater importance. It was against a backdrop of such practical matters — besides academic issues — that we were led to pursue our research questions.

THEORETICAL ISSUES

In 1976, when we began our research on this question, we found few previous studies that dealt directly with the social characteristics of those inclined to adopt stigmatized children. In one of the few published studies on the subject, Donald Chambers (1970) queried 175 applicants to four Midwest adoption agencies. The results indicated that respondents showed varying degrees of acceptance of hard-to-place children, with the greatest interest shown in Native American, Hispanic, and physically handicapped children, and the least in blacks, older (over age five), retarded, and emotionally disturbed children. A number of social background factors were linked with inclinations to adopt different stigmatized groups: father's infertility, age of mother, length of marriage, mother's interest in pursuing a career, social class, and the educational attainments of both parents. There were few explanations why these patterns prevailed.

Chambers hesitated to draw any conclusions from his results: "The author withholds judgement [*sic*] whether these data support the hypotheses that there are traits associated with the willingness to adopt children with atypical attributes. Attempts to find clusters of traits predictive of willingness responses failed" (1970, p. 278). He concluded that if agencies draw upon the largest possible audiences for finding adoptive homes, and conduct more research on this issue, the maximal results will be obtained in placing atypical children.

Given such uncertain results, we felt obliged to draw upon more general sociological theory and research, and apply it to the issue of hard-to-place children. Initially we looked to the literature on family behavior and minority/majority relations for guidance. We found sociological writings on changing American family life to be particularly helpful. It was our initial speculation that the emerging interest in adopting special-needs kids was an outgrowth of a pattern that numerous family sociologists had been discussing for some time, a trend toward increasing diversity, equality, and fulfillment of individual needs.

It is widely acknowledged among sociologists that the American family is currently in a state of transition. During the twentieth century family life has changed greatly: patriarchal authority has declined considerably; household and child care tasks have come to be more equally shared by both spouses; family size has greatly decreased; married women have entered the labor force in unprecedented numbers; interreligious and interracial marriages and divorce — once rarities — now are more common. Clearly, the traditional, role-segregated patriarchal family is rapidly changing. Members of egalitarian families feel less bound by traditional conceptions of kinship, and increasingly seek to maximize satisfaction of individual choices and personal needs (Farber 1964; Lasch 1976). The ideologies of women's liberation provide diminishing support for women's exclusive preoccupation with having and raising their own children. Bernice Lott (1973) found, for example, that women most closely identified with women's liberation are among those least committed to traditional childbearing and child rearing.

We anticipated that there would be a relationship between egalitarian patterns of family life and less conventional modes of family formation, such as the adoption of hard-to-place children. As individuals assume more flexible and interchangeable roles in their relationships with each other — less bound by traditional conceptions of the family — they may well become more receptive to a wider range of possible family members. Family theorists claim that families have become increasingly flexible about the kinds of intimate relationships they find acceptable (Keller 1971; Kanter 1974; Farber 1972). The increasing interest in adopting children racially and culturally unlike their parents appears to be consistent with, if not a derivative of, this more general pattern of accepting greater diversity and choice in family life.

As families have become more diverse and varied with increased divorce, remarriage, both parents working, and role sharing, families have become far more tolerant of others, including "unusual" families. In addition, people are increasingly using the family as a vehicle to express their innermost individual needs and to articulate their personal and social values. The same spirit that prompted many during the 1960s to form communes and other alternative family structures led others to seek minority and special-needs child adoptions as a means to give their life goals meaningful expression. We therefore expected that those most closely aligned with contemporary family patterns would be among those most willing and likely to adopt the stigmatized.

There was another line of sociological analysis that seemed relevant to us. Family values and parental behavior are deeply embedded in a matrix that includes the economic, religious, and political values of America. Traditional ideas about family life are legitimated and sustained by the traditional social institutions and political values. Bernard Farber (1972) has detailed the close relationship among religious, economic, and political ideas that prevailed in pre-Revolutionary America and the traditional structure of the American family. He argues that these ideas have continued to exert a powerful influence on American family life. Therefore, we expected that adherence to traditional religious and political values would support more conservative family practices and would be incompatible with unconventional modes of family formation, such as the adoption of minority and/or special-needs children. Two traditional supporters of the family appeared to be worth investigating: religious affiliation and conservative political views. We anticipated that those committed to established religious and political institutions would be less amenable to accepting the hard-to-place and would be more traditional in their adoption preferences — only healthy white babies.

Another line of sociological inquiry seemed to buttress these expectations. Research on intergroup relations by various sociologists (Lipset 1960; Selznick and Steinberg 1969; Stark and Glock 1968) finds that adherents of conventional religions and conservative politics tend to exhibit more intolerance toward minorities than their more secular and liberal counterparts. We expected this would be relevant in the case of adopting stigmatized or minority children, and would generally tend to preclude such adoptions. Thus, we were led to anticipate that the conventionally religious and politically conservative members of our sample would show the least amenability to adopting stigmatized children.

We were uncertain about the impact of social class on adoption attitudes. On the one hand, a large body of survey research has repeatedly demonstrated that more highly ranked, better-educated, and wealthier members of society tend to more tolerant and accepting of minorities. On the other hand, the deeper commitments of those groups to conventional religious and political institutions gave us cause to consider that they might be more deeply committed to conventional family practice, and might therefore be less willing to consider any deviations from customary actions. Other studies have demonstrated more acceptance and approval of adoption among the higher classes (Bonham 1977). Yet, Chambers

(1970) found that the higher-ranked members of his sample were significantly more unwilling to adopt retarded children. Such contradictory theory and evidence led us to suspect that social class position could be related in either way, if not remain unrelated altogether, to the willingness to adopt stigmatized children.

Although we never made this explicit, at this point of our analysis tolerance was being considered as a fundamental intervening factor. We felt that the most tolerant members of our sample would be able to accept the most stigmatized attributes; those less tolerant would in all likelihood be amenable to accepting less deprecated attributes. We expected that whatever trends would be in evidence, they would be reflected throughout the range of stigmatized attributes, with physical and psychological limitations being the most deprecated characteristics, being black in an intermediary position, and Asian and Native American attributes being those least objectionable. In other words, we surmised from our reliance on the relevant sociological literature that the acceptance of the hard-to-place was a unidimensional and cumulative phenomenon.

These were the assumptions with which we began to analyze our survey results. Looking back over our findings, we might say that in some respects many of our initial expectations proved correct; in others we learned that things were far more complex than we had originally imagined them to be; in still others we found we had been very much mistaken.

RESULTS AND ANALYSIS

Family Factors

First, we were interested in how family life changes affected willingness to adopt the hard-to-place. Among the areas investigated was the father's participation in child care, conceptualized as a divergence from traditional sex-role expectations. We explored the involvement of fathers in three areas of child care usually reserved for mothers — feeding children, supervising them at play, and diapering infants. Responding families were asked, for example, whether infants were diapered only by their mothers, mostly by their mothers, equally by mother and father, mostly by their fathers, or only by their fathers. These responses were given scores ranging from

1 (only by their fathers) to 5 (only by their mothers). Thus, scale scores ranged from a low of 3 for the three-item index to 15 for the most traditional response. For tabulation purposes this range was divided into three response categories: nontraditional (3-9), transitional (10 and 11), and traditional (12-15). Scores in the traditional group generally indicated that the three child care tasks specified were usually or always undertaken by the wife. If husbands and wives shared the three tasks, or if they were usually done by husbands, then a scale score of 9 or less resulted; these responses were considered to be nontraditional ones. Intervening responses were grouped as transitional scores. A transitional score would indicate that some of the areas of child care are the usual or exclusive province of the wife, while others are likely to be shared. Respondents were also asked to indicate how willing they would be to adopt children of various descriptions: retarded, older, black, handicapped.

Paternal participation in child care was significantly related to the willingness to adopt black children. Forty percent of nontraditional parents and 28 percent of transitionals said they could easily adopt a black child, while only 20 percent of traditionals reported they could do so. The measure of the father's involvement in child care showed similar trends in the predicted direction for the acceptance of older, handicapped, and retarded children, although the only other case that achieved statistical significance was acceptance of the handicapped. Table 2.2 indicates that 52 percent of families with high levels of paternal participation reported that they could easily or with some reservations adopt a handicapped child, compared with 37 percent and 31 percent, respectively, of families with transitional and traditional patterns of paternal participation.

Testing this hypothesis against the actual adoptions of hard-to-place children, we found that paternal participation in child care was associated with the adoption of black children. Twenty-one percent of families with nontraditional child care patterns had adopted black children, compared with 12 percent and 8 percent, respectively, of families with transitional and traditional patterns of paternal participation. A similar relationship was found for adoptions of older children, although this finding appears to prevail only under conditions of very high paternal involvement in child care. Forty-three percent of families where fathers participated in child care to a considerable degree had adopted children aged

TABLE 2.2
Willingness to Adopt a Handicapped Child and Father's Participation in Child Care

(percent)

	Nontraditional	Transitional	Traditional
Could adopt a handicapped child easily	9	5	4
Would have some reservations about adopting a handicapped child	43	32	27
Could not adopt a handicapped child	48	63	69
N	(65)	(120)	(430)

$$X^2 = 11.998; 4 \text{ df}; p > .02$$

three or older, compared with 22 percent and 24 percent, respectively, among families with transitional and traditional patterns of paternal involvement.

Another dimension of divergence from traditional sex roles that we investigated was the acceptance of maternal employment. Respondents were asked, "Do you agree or disagree with the idea that women can work and be good mothers at the same time?" Cross-tabulating these responses with acceptance of minority children revealed mixed support for the hypotheses. A statistically significant relationship occurred between attitudes accepting maternal employment and the willingness to adopt a black child. This relationship was confined to those who strongly approved of maternal employment. Thirty-eight percent of those who strongly approved said they could easily adopt a black child, compared with 18, 15, and 17 percent, respectively, of those who approved somewhat, disapproved somewhat, and disapproved strongly. This attitudinal trend was mirrored in behavior. Nineteen percent of families who strongly approved of maternal employment had adopted a black child, while only 4 percent who disapproved strongly had done so. Approval of maternal employment was significantly related to willingness to adopt an older child. No apparent trend was noted with acceptance of maternal employment and the willingness to adopt handicapped or retarded children.

The trends that were noted for approving attitudes toward maternal employment were sustained when we examined whether mothers actually worked. Working mothers were more likely to be willing to adopt blacks and older children. The differences were statistically significant. The same patterns also held for their adoption behavior.

Working mothers were no more willing than nonworking mothers to adopt handicapped and retarded children. This trend does not converge completely with the results obtained by DeLeon and Westerberg (1980). In their study it was noted that adoptive families of retarded children tended to have more nonworking mothers than families who had adopted nonretarded children. While it would seem likely that the adoption of retarded or physically handicapped children would make such heavy time demands on parents that two-career households would not be possible, we were surprised to find no association between a wife's interest in pursuing a career, her holding a job, and the reluctance to adopt such children.

Another family structural factor associated with willingness to adopt the hard-to-place was single-parent status. Compared with adoptive couples, single adoptive parents showed substantially greater willingness to adopt hard-to-place children, and these attitudes were reflected in the kinds of children they actually adopted. Seventy-nine percent would accept an older child, compared with 60 percent among adopting couples (see Table 2.3); 82 percent were willing to adopt a black child, compared with 56 percent of couples; 51 percent were willing to adopt a slightly retarded child, compared with 32 percent of couples; 40 percent were willing to adopt a handicapped child, compared with 35 percent of couples.

Although substantially similar trends in attitudes were noted for both single fathers and single mothers, fathers showed a greater tendency to actually adopt hard-to-place children. Approximately 60 percent of the fathers adopted children six years or older, compared with 23 percent of the single mothers and 9 percent of the couples. Single fathers were also more likely to adopt black children. Forty-seven percent had actually adopted blacks, compared with 30 percent of single mothers and 10 percent of couples. As a group the single parents tended to adopt children who were older. Fifty-five

TABLE 2.3
Willingness to Adopt Hard-to-Place Children, by Single-Parent and Married-Couple Status
(percent)

	Single Parents	Couples
Adopt older child easily or with some reservations	79	60
Adopt black child easily or with some reservations	82	56
Adopt retarded child easily or with some reservations	51	32
Adopt handicapped child easily or with some reservations	40	35
Adopted older child	55	26
Adopted black child	34	10

percent had adopted children over three years old; only 26 percent of couples had adopted such children.

Why do single parents show such extreme willingness to adopt the hard-to-place child? Most probably single adoptive parents are aware that their applications are viewed with much disparagement and suspicion at most adoption agencies. Most indicate great struggle and difficulty before they succeeded in getting children placed with them. Single fathers report even greater difficulty getting placements than single mothers. They know they are not likely to receive any of the few healthy babies, which are awarded to couple applicants. They know that to get any child at all, they must be willing to accept those that others may not want. Many single parents may be particularly attracted to the idea of adopting an older child. It often means less complicated child care arrangements to be coordinated with their employment. (In Chapter 7 we will probe more deeply into the experiences of single adoptive parents and into the adjustments of their adopted children.)

Another family factor linked with being willing to adopt special-needs children was fertility. Fertile couples were far more likely to be willing to accept almost all of the hard-to-place children we studied. Thirty-four percent of fertile couples were willing to adopt black children, compared with 17 percent among infertile adoptive parents. (See Table 2.4.) A similar trend appeared in the actual adoptions of black children. Thirty percent of fertile couples were willing to adopt an older child, compared with 20 percent among infertile couples. Again attitudinal trends were mirrored in behavior, with 36 percent of fertile couples adopting children over two years of age, compared with 23 percent among infertile couples. Fertile couples did not, however, exhibit noticeably greater interest in the developmentally disabled compared with their infertile counterparts: only 7 percent of fertile couples were willing to adopt a handicapped child, compared with 3 percent among infertile adopters.

The general pattern, however, is clear: fertile couples are more positively disposed to most special-needs children. When we asked both groups of couples their reasons for adoption, infertile couples usually reported that having a child that was unobtainable biologically was uppermost in their minds. Most of the reasons they gave for adoption tended to be individual and personal. As we look over their adoption preferences, we note that these more traditional adoptive parents are, for the most part, disinclined to consider the

TABLE 2.4
Willingness to Adopt Hard-to-Place Children, by Parental Fertility
(percent)

	Infertile Adoptive Parents	Fertile Adoptive Parents
Easily adopt a black child	17	34
Easily adopt an older child	20	30
Easily adopt a retarded child	4	3
Easily adopt a handicapped child	3	7
Adopted an older child (over 2)	23	36
Adopted a black child	8	16

hard-to-place. For fertile couples, by contrast, an entirely different pattern was expressed, with social and humanitarian objectives being primary in their decisions to adopt. It seems quite evident from all this that fertile couples are pursuing adoptions adhering more closely to contemporary family ideologies — expressing their personal values and goals in their adoption behavior and creating new concepts of family design — compared with infertile couples, who appear to be more closely aligned with traditional family notions and ideas about adoption. We think that the differences between fertile and infertile couples in terms of their adoption attitudes, values, and experiences are especially important for understanding how adoption is changing today. (In Chapter 3 we will examine these issues in greater detail.)

Most of our hypotheses about changing family structures seemed to confirm our expectations that these changes are linked with emerging interests in adopting hard-to-place children. It is interesting to note that three of our four hypotheses seem to be at odds with the criteria applied by most adoption agencies for prospective adoptive parenthood. Families that contain working mothers, single-parent households, and those containing fertile couples would all be viewed with varying degrees of disfavor with respect to their eligibility and suitability as adoptive parents. Yet, it is precisely these groups that show the greatest inclination to adopt the kinds of children that are available today. Adoption and child care agencies will need to put aside their traditional eligibility criteria if they hope to find homes for most of today's waiting children.

Boys: Another Hard-to-Place Group

We were also eager to explore whether our theory of changing family structures and growing receptivity to the stigmatized could be extended to another seemingly hard-to-place group, boys. An aversion to adopting males would seem very surprising today, especially considering the great shortages of healthy infants that thousands of prospective couples would be so eager to adopt. Yet, in the past, placing male children posed a significantly greater problem to agencies than did placing females. Why are females preferred for adoption?

H. David Kirk (1964) explains this most cogently in his book *Shared Fate*. He argues that infertile couples often arrive at the decision to adopt with a great many misgivings. They feel inadequate about themselves and their inability to bear biological offspring. They have fears about their impending adoption and whether their new family will measure up to the one it could have been if they had conceived children. Kirk feels that couples prefer to adopt girls in order to reduce some of their anguish and uncertainty. Males are the inheritors of family name, values, and property. If the adoption of a boy proves to be unsatisfactory, it would be perceived as a complete catastrophe. Females usually relinquish their family names at marriage. They do not represent to the community the standing and reputation of a family as much as a male would. Therefore, such infertile couples are more willing to "risk" adopting a girl because the "costs" of failure are less.

We found some evidence in favor of the continuing validity of Kirk's argument, even acknowledging today's much tighter adoption market. Although males slightly outnumber females at birth by a ratio of 105 to 100, thus leading to their slight overrepresentation among adoptees, we found the inverse pattern true for our adopted sample population. Sixty percent of our sample had last adopted a girl. Girls, then, remain slightly preferred over boys for adoption.

Yet, when we attempted to look at each of our hypotheses about family patterns and the tendency to adopt boys, we found equivocal and unconvincing evidence. Father's participation in child care was associated with the tendency to adopt boys, but the relationship failed to achieve statistical significance.

Attitudes favoring maternal employment and maternal employment itself showed no association whatever with the tendency to adopt boys. We did not see any theoretical justification for examining the hypothesis among both single parents and couples, so that analysis was not performed. When we examined the hypothesis at its most critical point, comparing fertile and infertile adoptive couples, we found no differences between the two groups. Each had selected girls over boys by the same 60-40 percent ratio. Thus, while the pattern of adopting girls remains popular, its linkages with the experience of infertility are apparently beginning to wane.

Religious and Political Factors

When it came to examining the linkages between adoption preferences and conventional religious and political affiliations, many of our original speculations proved to be mistaken. The hypothesis that religious affiliation would be inversely associated with accepting minority children was supported only in the case of black children. Thirty-nine percent of those unaffiliated with a major organized religion would readily adopt a black child, compared with 14 percent, 16 percent, and 25 percent, respectively, among Catholics, Jews, and Protestants. A similar pattern was noted for actual adoptions of black children. Twenty-six percent of those unidentified with any of the three major faiths had adopted blacks, compared with 7 percent, 7 percent, and 10 percent, respectively, among Catholics, Jews, and Protestants.

Yet, contrary to the hypothesis, persons with religious affiliations — with the exceptions of Jews — seemed more accepting of handicapped and retarded children. Table 2.5 shows the relationship between the willingness to adopt a retarded child and the wife's religious preference. Thirty-six percent of Catholics and 30 percent of Protestants said they could adopt a retarded child easily or with some reservations, while only 16 percent of the religiously unaffiliated and 21 percent of Jews felt similarly. These statistically significant figures were similar to those results found

TABLE 2.5
Willingness to Adopt a Retarded Child and Wife's Religion
(percent)

	No Affiliation	Catholic	Jewish	Protestant
Adopt retarded child easily	9	5	0	3
Some reservations about adopting retarded	17	31	21	27
Could not adopt retarded child	74	64	80	70
N =	(23)	(214)	(73)	(280)

for husband's religious preference. We believe we failed to take adequate account of the norms of charity and compassion for the unfortunate that are deeply held by the conventionally religious adherents of the Christian faith.

Data on religious participation seem to support this interpretation. Thirty-nine percent of those who participate in religious services more than once a week said they could adopt a retarded child easily or with some reservations, while only 28 percent of those who never participated said they could do so. This relationship approaches, but does not achieve, statistical significance. Adoption of a handicapped child is significantly related to religious participation. Forty-four percent of those who participated in religious services more than once a week said they could adopt a handicapped child easily or with some reservations, while only 29 percent of those who never participated said they could do so. The religiously committed appear to be more willing to accept children stigmatized by individual misfortune, but less inclined to accept those outcast by group membership, such as blacks.

Jews were found to be the least accepting of the stigmatized children included in the survey. Thirty-eight percent of Catholics and 36 percent of Protestants said they could adopt a handicapped child easily or with some reservations, but only 7 percent of Jews responded similarly. Also, 57 percent of Catholics and 64 percent of Protestants felt they could adopt an older child, compared with 43 percent among Jewish respondents. This relationship fell a fraction short of statistical significance. The reluctance of Jews to adopt handicapped and retarded children may well be accounted for by the emphasis Jews place upon achievement. Sidney Goldstein and Calvin Goldscheider (1968) observe that upwardly mobile Jews are especially conscious of the costs of child care, and often tend to defer and reduce childbearing. The absence of a missionary tradition within Judaism may account for their similar reluctance to accept black and older children (Dukel 1955).

Political conservatism was measured by the wife's political identification on a six-point scale ranging from very conservative to radical. Analyses were also made using the husband's political preference. The results of these analyses were substantially similar. Table 2.6 reveals a significant relationship between political identification and willingness to adopt a black child. Although 80 percent of the radicals and 47 percent of the very liberal said they could

TABLE 2.6
Willingness to Adopt Blacks and Wife's Political Identification
(percent)

	Very Radical	Liberal	Liberal	Moderate	Conserv.	Very Conserv.
Could adopt black child easily	80	47	29	13	11	0
Some reservations adopting blacks	0	37	40	28	34	33
Could not adopt black child	20	16	31	59	55	67
N =	(10)	(75)	(208)	(212)	(114)	(12)

$X^2 = 102.415; 10$ df; $p > .001$

easily adopt a black child, only 11 percent of the conservatives and none of the very conservatives reported they could do so.

Similar results were observed in the actual adoptions of black children. Sixty percent of the radicals and 20 percent of the very liberals adopted black children, while only 4 percent of the conservatives and none of the very conservatives did so. Political identification was unrelated to the willingness to adopt or the adoption of older, retarded, or handicapped children.

These findings suggest that the kind of child that parents choose to adopt closely reflects their values and institutional commitments. Liberal and radical parents displayed the most commitment to adopting black children. The conventionally religious, with the exception of Jewish respondents, showed the greatest interest in handicapped and retarded children. These preferences would seem to indicate that families are often making an ideological statement through their adoptions.

The ideological commitments of liberals and radicals to black children should need no explanation. The commitment of the conventionally religious to the handicapped and the retarded can be seen as a reflection of traditional Judeo-Christian compassion for the unfortunate. Yet, the charitable inclinations of Jews apparently are less readily extended to adoption than is true for those of the other major conventional faiths.

It was hypothesized that parenting stigmatized children was a unitary phenomenon. The data clearly show, however, that this is not the case. We had expected that those committed to more secular and liberal viewpoints would exhibit a greater overall willingness to adopt a stigmatized child. What we found, however, was that secular liberals differed from the conventionally religious and the conservatives not so much in their willingness to adopt stigmatized children as in the kinds of children they were willing to accept.

Social Class

When we examined the linkages between social class and adoption attitudes, we found some unclear and inconsistent trends. The most consistent pattern was noted in the acceptance of Afro-American children. Whether class was measured by occupational rank, educational attainment, or income, the higher one's social status, the more willing one would be to accept blacks for adoption. Twenty-nine percent of professional husbands could easily adopt an Afro-American child, compared with 16 percent of those doing clerical or sales work and 8 percent of those holding semiskilled jobs. Fifty-four percent of college graduates could easily adopt a black child, compared with only 13 percent among those completing high school. Both of these associations were statistically significant; in the case of income, however, while the trends showed a similar pattern, the differences failed to achieve statistical significance.

In the other groups of stigmatized children, the patterns of association are less distinct. The pattern of adopting older children showed the higher-ranked members of our sample to be more accepting. Among upper-income families — those whose annual incomes exceeded $25,000 in 1975 — 30 percent could easily adopt an older child, compared with 21 percent among those whose incomes fell below $20,000; this difference was statistically significant. Similar trends were noted for educational and occupational prestige variations, although these differences fell short of statistical significance.

When we tested for acceptance of slightly retarded children, we found the more affluent members of our sample less inclined to adopting these children. Only 17 percent of families whose incomes exceeded $25,000 yearly could easily adopt such a child, compared with two-thirds of those families whose incomes fell below $20,000. But again — as with older children — the more highly educated and those engaged in highly ranked occupations showed no statistically significant differences in their acceptance or rejection of the slightly retarded. In the last case we examined, accepting handicapped children, no statistically significant relationships were noted in any of the three important aspects of social rank.

Thus, the most pervasive effect of social class appears to be increased acceptance of some types of stigmatized children. We observed that the more highly ranked members of our sample showed greater receptivity to children who are older and who belong to minority groups. But, as we found elsewhere, acceptance of hard-to-place children is by no means a unified response. The emphasis that higher-ranked members accord to educational proficiency seems to diminish their willingness to adopt retarded children. Alfred Kadushin (1962) has claimed that the reason some studies have found more lower-status persons adopting the retarded is because such persons are marginally eligible for adoptive parenthood. Kadushin contends that agency selection processes, more than anything else, seem to produce such patterns. Yet, our attitudinal data clearly indicate that self-selection also appears to be relevant.

ADOPTING DISABLED CHILDREN: SOME UNANSWERED QUESTIONS

Back in 1976, when we first began to analyze our survey data, some nagging questions began to arise at the revelation that we had neglected to ask our respondents whether they had actually adopted any disabled children. We had no firm basis for expecting attitudes of willingness to adopt handicapped and retarded children to be linked with overt behavior. Did people who said they could easily or with some reservations adopt handicapped or retarded children actually adopt such children more frequently than those who said they could not? We were able to discern with precision the connection between being amenable to adopting older, black, and Asian children and actually having adopted such children. Here we found an extremely close correspondence. Did a similar trend prevail for physically or mentally disabled children?

It was not until our follow-up survey in 1981 that we could fully pursue this analysis. With 373 cases — 68 percent of those whom we were able to locate, who were willing to participate in this subsequent study — we found a total of 39 families (11 percent) who had knowingly adopted one or more disabled children. We wondered how they differed from the 89 percent of families who did not adopt such children, or who had done so without knowledge that the children were disabled. We were also eager to investigate whether those who seemingly were amenable to adopting the handicapped — such as fertile parents, those who share parenting tasks, highly active Christians — were any more likely than others actually to adopt handicapped children. Were there any other groups of parents who were more inclined than others actually to adopt disabled children?

Our results yielded a mixture of confirming and unexpected trends. We noted considerable convergence between parents' intentions and actions in the area of family behavior. In families where child care was shared, parents were significantly more likely to knowingly adopt disabled children. Fourteen percent of parents engaging in nontraditional patterns of child care had adopted disabled children, compared with 4 percent of transitional parents and 4 percent of traditionals. Parents' sharing of the tasks of child care seems to encourage the adoption of disabled children. Single parents were much more likely to adopt disabled children than couples. Twenty-nine percent of single parents had actually adopted disabled children, compared with 9 percent of couples. Fertile parents were significantly more likely to adopt disabled children than their infertile counterparts; 15 percent had adopted such children, compared with only 4 percent among infertile couples. All of these tendencies were supported in the attitudinal data given by our respondents.

One of the most surprising anomalies between these findings and our previous results was the absence of any association between conventional religious affiliation and the likelihood of knowingly adopting handicapped children. Christians were no more inclined than the religiously unaffiliated or the Jewish respondents actually to adopt disabled children. The Jewish respondents in our sample showed slightly less likelihood to adopt disabled children than the

Catholics, Protestants, and religiously unaffiliated; but the differences fell considerably short of statistical significance. The same pattern held for relgious participation. There was a difference of two percentage points between those who attended religious services weekly or more often and those who never went, or went fewer than four times yearly. Both religion and religious participation were associated with inclinations toward adopting handicapped and retarded children. These findings cast some doubt upon the ultimate receptivity of conventionally relgious Christians to the disabled.

Another unexpected finding was the affinity between the trend to knowingly adopt a disabled child and affiliation with an adoptive parent group. Those affiliated with adoptive parent groups and actively involved in such organizations were significantly more likely to adopt disabled children than their unaffiliated and inactive counterparts. Twelve percent of mothers who belonged to adoptive parent groups had adopted disabled children, compared with 4 percent among unaffiliated mothers. Twenty-three percent of actively involved mothers had adopted such children, compared with 6 percent among self-described inactive members. A similar statistically significant trend held for fathers.

What is somewhat surprising about these trends is that adoptive parent group affiliates and activists exhibit few differences from nonaffiliates in their attitudinal receptivity to handicapped and retarded children. No statistically significant differences were noted among these populations.

This evidence seems to suggest enormously effective social networks within adoptive parent organizations. Such networks provide knowledge about disabled children available for adoption; they offer social reward and encouragement to families who adopt such children; and they furnish substantial support, information, and counsel for dealing with the issues that parents of handicapped children inevitably confront. We doubt that many of these families, compared with other adoptive parents, share distinctive viewpoints about the acceptability of handicapped children. Rather, their experience as adoptive parents and as active members of their organizations has made them acutely aware of the potential of families to stretch their resources to provide for more children. They have also become reluctant to resist offering themselves to needy children.

One of our respondents, Sally Bradshaw, who is mentioned at the beginning of this chapter, said something to us in an informal

interview that attests to this elastic sense of family size and receptivity to stigmatized children that is nurtured in the adoptive parent
groups. Sally and Jim are extremely active adoption advocates
in their home state. We ran into Sally at an adoption conference
where this interview was conducted. We asked her how she and her
husband came to adopt so many children. Her reply was as follows:

> I don't know. I really don't know. If you told me ten years ago that
> I would have adopted these six children, I would have said you're
> crazy. When we adopted our first child, Jim and I gave a lot of thought
> to that. It seemed like the right thing for us to do then. We knew that
> illegitimate Korean children had very little to look forward to – and we
> had a lot to give. Since then we've read that social services in Korea
> have been much improved. But it is still a family-oriented society.
> And even if you're in the best orphanage in the country – it's still not
> like a real family. At that time we never could have considered adopting
> a black child like Jessie. We never could have considered Gregory then
> too. We couldn't have dealt with his need to use crutches for the rest
> of his life, much less the fact that he was obviously black. . . . We lived
> in an all-white neighborhood at that time. The neighbors would have
> made our lives miserable. And we weren't in any position to move out
> of there. . . . Our heads probably couldn't have handled it then, too –
> to be honest. Yet, as time has gone by, we've grown a lot. We've kept
> discovering that we have room for more children. You'll see after you
> adopt a child too – you begin to see that you could adopt a whole lot
> more. . . . We may have reached the limit of our family size now, but
> who knows? . . . As different as my family is today from what I may
> have expected it to be when Jim and I first got married, I couldn't
> picture us any more content as a family than we are now.

We found such families to be larger than most other adoption
families. Thirty-seven percent of families inclined to knowingly
adopt disabled children had five or more children, compared with
12 percent among those not adopting the disabled. Included in our
sample of predominantly parent group members one finds much
evidence of large family size and a receptivity to the hard-to-place.
As a group our sample seemed especially committed to having large
adoption families. Nearly half of the sample had three or more
children, which is surprisingly high when one considers the educational level of our respondents. Over 60 percent of sample members
had completed college or had a graduate school degree. In 1975
our sample had adopted a total of 1,258 children; nearly half – 48

percent — had adopted two or more children, and 18 percent had adopted three or more.

Given these statistics, it would seem that our responding parents had reached the limits of their ability to absorb additional children. Yet, six years later we found that nearly a quarter — 23 percent — of those families with two or more adopted children in 1975 had adopted even more. Among this group of 66 families, 120 additional children were adopted. Most of these children belonged to minority racial or ethnic groups, were older, or had some physical or mental disability. Clearly, participation in adoptive parent groups generates and sustains a deep and almost unreserved commitment to adopting hard-to-place children. The efforts of many to communicate to this population information on available hard-to-place children appears to be achieving substantial results.

SUMMING UP

Our results clearly show that the rapidly expanding interest in finding adoptive homes for special-needs children that has occurred since the 1960s is linked to larger changes in family and social structure. The data indicate that as the trend toward sharing work and child care roles and other modern family patterns enjoy widening social support, the numbers of families amenable to adopting special-needs children is likely to increase. Perhaps the most important practical implication of these trends is the suggestion that certain groups traditionally exempted from consideration as potential adoptive parents are among those most strongly inclined to adopt special-needs children. Fertile parents, single adults, and families with working mothers are especially disposed to adopt the hard-to-place. If agencies are to serve today's waiting children effectively, they will need to put aside traditional eligibility criteria in order to facilitate more adoptions by these and other willing groups.

Our evidence also documents that the acceptance of the hard-to-place is neither cumulative nor one-dimensional. Groups of diverse social class and religious and political orientations have varying preferences for different hard-to-place children consistent with their social affiliations and ideological interests. We have found that there is substantial acceptance for adopting blacks and other minorities, among the upper classes and the political left. The less affluent and members of adoptive parent groups seem to be more positively disposed to adopting the retarded and the handicapped. This information should be of some help to those doing outreach work in the community, for guiding their efforts and suggesting the kinds of children who are likely to be most and least appealing to different social sectors. Although the lower classes have traditionally been a group whose adoption possibilities have been greatly limited, we have found them to be very favorably disposed to accepting retarded children. This pattern needs to be fully reflected in current adoption policies. The remaining obstacles preventing them from parenting these and other children must be removed.

Last, we have found that active affiliates of adoptive parent groups represent an extremely receptive population to parenting all types of hard-to-place children. Some of these people possess nearly limitless capacities to parent special-needs children. Efforts aimed at finding homes for special-needs children have intuitively focused on adoptive parent groups as an important potential re-source. Only now can we point to some empirical evidence attesting to the fact that these affiliates are especially inclined to adopt hard-to-place children.

Taken together, the findings suggest that there may be far more homes for special-needs children than many placement agencies suspect. While our results here may reinforce some of the current efforts to find homes for special-needs children and suggest new directions for expanded endeavors, it should be clear that a great deal remains to be understood. Still more research will be necessary to better identify those amenable to parenting the stigmatized. We need to know, for example, whether parents who are not pre-disposed to adopt stigmatized children can be motivated to do so through participation in adoptive parent groups. Another set of questions we have about changing family structures and their impact upon adoptions is how they may influence people's motives to adopt, their relationships to their adopted children, and the nature and quality of life in adoptive families. These questions will be explored in succeeding chapters.

3
Preferential Adoption:
The Emerging Interest in
Adoption by Fertile Parents

Kim Ti Prewitt is typical of an increasing number of children begin adopted in America. She was born in Seoul, Korea, 11 years ago to unmarried parents of different races. Her birth mother was a native-born Korean; her father, a white U.S. soldier. Owing to a relatively effective state-run social service department, Kim Ti received good care in one of the country's numerous orphanages. Within the first ten months of her life and with the help of the Holt organization, she was adopted by David and Joan Prewitt, an American couple who lived in Wellesley, Massachusetts, a Boston suburb.

David Prewitt is a dentist, a graduate of Amherst College and the Tufts University School of Dentristry. Joan, a Boston University graduate, teaches psychology at Emerson College in Boston. The Prewitts had two biological children — Sandy, age 17, a high school senior, and Jeffrey, 15 — before they became interested in adoption. The Prewitts have another adopted child, Nicholas, a Cherokee Indian boy of 13 whom they adopted through Lutheran Social Services when he was 2.

The Prewitts typify a growing number of adoptive parents who become interested in adoption for reasons apart from infertility. David and Joan encountered no difficulties whatever in conceiving their biological offspring. They adopted Nicholas and Kim for a variety of reasons. Both parents are deeply concerned about the problem of overpopulation. They wanted to do something that would be more substantial and personally meaningful than simply writing a check or attending a conference in behalf of their cause. Adoption seemed to be the right thing to do, to make their family a living testament to their ideals. The Prewitts are very active in the Ethical Cultural Society in their community. It was their feeling that interracial adoption would lead them to live more closely to their beliefs and their deep commitment to international harmony.

The Prewitts are a very close family. The parents are deeply concerned with the pursuit of their respective careers, and much of their remaining time is spent with their children, assisting them with their studies, engaging in common leisure pursuits, and traveling together. The Prewitts have very limited association with their extended families. Detecting some indications of ambivalence toward their adoption of Nicholas from David's parents, in the intervening years they have drawn away from his family. Most of Joan's family, although receptive to their adoptions, live in California and only rarely come east. As a result the Prewitts spend most of their limited free time with each other and with their many friends, most of whom are professional colleagues, members of Ethical Culture, and transracial adoptive parents.

We might contrast Kim Prewitt and the Prewitt family with another child and family who were included in our sample, the Gerstens. Allan Gersten is 12 years old. His parents, Robert and Amy Gersten, adopted him when he was less than a month old. The Gerstens had been unsuccessfully trying to conceive a child for more than four years. Through a lawyer friend of Robert's they learned of a newborn who was to be given up for adoption in California. With great excitement and at almost a moment's notice, they eagerly packed their bags and took the next plane from Chicago to get their long-sought-after white baby.

The Gerstens were very anxious and tense during the first few months after they took Allan home. Both had nightmares during that time, fearing that their child would be reclaimed by his birth parents, and their adoption invalidated. Yet, they've never had even the slightest thought that their decision to adopt wasn't what they had always wanted.

They felt extremely gratified when another lawyer friend of Robert's was able to get them a second white child. Jennifer was four months old when the Gerstens got her. Unexpectedly, Amy Gersten found that she had many of the same jitters and anxieties when Jennifer initially joined their family as she had when they adopted Allan years earlier. She worried a lot about simple things, could not sleep well, was tense and impatient from her fatigue. Jennifer had more than her share of childhood illnesses, and there was even some question for a while of her being mildly retarded. Yet, despite their problems with Jennifer's health, the Gerstens find her winning smile and extremely pleasant disposition an almost constant source of joy and satisfaction.

In his modest suburban home in Chicago, Robert Gersten occasionally feels slight tinges of regret at the enormous expense of his private adoptions and their frustration of his hopes of ever moving to the more luxurious home in the fashionable suburb of Evanston that he and Amy have long talked about. He is happy with his work as an accountant. Well paid for his services, and very much on his own in decision making, he is especially glad for the opportunity his work has offered to make valuable contacts with lawyers. Such contacts have made it possible for him to have the family life he always dreamed of.

Amy was an office manager before they started raising a family. Now she is a full-time housewife. She is very happy with her routine of looking after the children, cruising the malls in search of bargains, playing tennis once in while, and cooking good food for her family. Both she and Robert have close and continuing associations with their extended families. Both sets of relatives were extremely supportive and helpful when the Gerstens adopted their children.

Recalling the questions we raised in Chapter 1 and probing these particular families, we are led to wonder about families like the Prewitts and how common such families are among adoptive parents. Why do such families as theirs — fertile couples — join the ranks of adoptive parents? What prompts people like David and Joan Prewitt to want to adopt children like Kim and Nicholas? What leads them to pursue such transnational and transcultural adoptions?

A great many other questions arise when we compare and contrast such "newer" adoption families as the Prewitts with more "traditional" infertile adoptive couples like the Gerstens. We may wonder about people like the Prewitts, who pursue adoption in response to more general social and humanitarian motives: How do they fare as adoptive parents? Do their children adjust as well as, better than, or worse than the children of more traditional infertile couples like the Gerstens? Are such generalized and more abstract motivations sufficient to provide for the very demanding tasks of parenthood? And what if people like the Gerstens — infertile adoptive couples — in their great eagerness, even desperation, to become parents were led to adopt transracially or transculturally? Many have been, such as the Ragusas; they adopted a Colombian child. Many others have adopted children from Korea or Vietnam, American-born blacks, and children from many other national and racial groups. Is their great eagerness to assume the parental role adequate to the exacting job of raising the transracially or transculturally adopted child? How do such parents compare with fertile adoptive parents like the Prewitts in raising their transculturally adopted children? Also, we may wonder how the adjustments of these children — of fertile and infertile adoptive parents — change over the years.

Another question that arises, given the different motivations and interests in adoption of such families as the Prewitts and the Gerstens, is how they vary in the ways they bring up their children. Do their differing outlooks and attitudes about adoption have a substantial impact on their children's behavioral patterns and adult behavior? For example, would their children be any more or less inclined to search for their birth parents as a consequence of their particular socialization experiences? What, if anything, may be said about how differently and how well they prepare their transculturally adopted children to live in American society?

Many studies reveal that infertile adoptive couples like the Gerstens often have a great deal to come to terms with in accepting their infertility. They often feel a sense of inadequacy, and it sometimes takes a long time before parents fully adjust to this perceived inadequacy. We wonder whether these feelings affect how they perform their roles as adoptive parents and how they raise their adopted children. Do they bring up their adopted children in the same way, or do they face any distinctive problems when they are compared with fertile adoptive parents? What, if any, particular concerns emerge from their experience of infertility that influences how they treat adoption with their children? Such are the concerns of this chapter, comparing families like the Prewitts and the Gerstens. We are also concerned with the particular needs of both fertile and infertile adoptive parents for social services. What kinds of assistance will each type of adoptive parents require?

Before we can proceed any further, we will need to offer some definitions. Fertile couples like the Prewitts, for want of a better term, will be called preferential adopters. Such families are often inspired by religious, social, or humanitarian motives to seek adoption of a child in addition to their biological offspring. Those like the Gerstens will be called infertile adopting couples. Three factors were used in the classification of families as infertile adopting couples: either spouse indicated that infertility or subfertility played a part in their decision to adopt a child; there were no biological children in the family; and the wife indicated it was difficult for her to accept that she probably would not bear a child. All other families were grouped as preferential adopters. It was noted in our 1975 survey that 431 families (60.5 percent) consisted of traditional infertile couples, and 281 (39.5 percent) were preferential adopters.

SOCIAL CHARACTERISTICS OF PREFERENTIAL ADOPTERS

The social characteristics of preferential adopters in our sample showed fundamental convergence with the results of other studies of transracial adoption (Nutt and Snyder 1973; Grow and Shapiro 1974; Falk 1970; Fanshel 1972; Simon and Altstein 1977; Ladner 1977). Forty-seven percent of the husbands were 35-44 years old, 35 percent were 34 or younger, and 18 percent were over 45. The group differed significantly in age from traditional infertile adopters, who were noticeably younger. Half of traditional husbands were 34 or younger. Wives, however, were comparable in age with more traditional wives. Fifty-two percent were 34 or younger, 35 percent were between 35 and 44, and 13 percent were over 45.

Both groups tended to be suburbanites (67 percent). Yet, preferential adopters were more likely to describe themselves as farm residents, and fewer regarded themselves as urban dwellers than was true of traditional couples. (Nine percent of the preferential adopters lived on farms, compared with 3 percent among infertile couples; and 15 percent of fertile couples were urbanites, compared with 22 percent among the traditionals.)

Incomes tended to be higher among the preferential adopters. Forty-five percent reported annual incomes exceeding $25,000, (in 1975), compared with 35 percent among traditional adopting families. Eighty-four percent of preferential adopter husbands were in white-collar occupations, compared with 77 percent among traditional husbands. In regard to educational attainment, 80 percent of preferential adopting wives had completed college, compared with 77 percent among traditional wives, a difference that fell short of statistical significance. Husbands' educational attainments showed a similar pattern.

The religious affiliations of preferential adopters were varied: Protestants accounted for 48 percent; 28 percent were Catholics; 10 percent were Jewish; 9 percent had other religious membership; and 5 percent were unaffiliated. Traditional adopters included significantly more Catholics (36 percent) and fewer Protestants (41 percent). Both groups of sampled families showed fairly high levels of religious participation. More than 53 percent of the wives reported attending religious services once a week or more frequently.

The political affiliations of preferential adopters tended to be liberal and left-of-center. Fifty-two percent of preferential adopters described themselves in this way, compared with only 44 percent among traditional adopters. In terms of political party attachments, 44 percent of the wives described themselves as Democrats, 14 percent as Republicans, and 36 percent as independents, 6 percent did not profess any political identifications, much the same as the attachments expressed by traditional adopters. Husbands' political preferences and ideologies showed much the same pattern.

Preferential adopters had less extended family affiliations than was true of traditionals. Thirty-nine percent reported that they got together with relatives a few times a month or more frequently, compared with 47 percent among traditional adopters.

Preferential adopters tended to have larger families. Seventy-nine percent of the nontraditional families had three or more children, compared with 26 percent among traditional adopters. Although the majority of families had adopted one child, infertile couples were somewhat more likely to adopt two children (32 percent, compared with 20 percent among preferential parents).

MOTIVATIONS FOR ADOPTION

What distinguishes preferential adopters from infertile couples, more than anything else, is their reasons for adopting. Mary McClosky, one of our preferential adoptive respondents, told us why she adopted:

> We had no infertility problem, but we chose to adopt. We thoroughly enjoy children, and we wanted to make our home available to a child who didn't have the advantages of family life.

Betty Lacey, another respondent, gave somewhat a different reason for her preferential adoption:

> We felt a moral obligation toward American-Vietnamese orphans. We felt these children were innocent victims of an American intrusion in Vietnam. Before anyone else, we wanted to adopt a Vietnamese-American child.

Thomas A. Nutt and John Snyder's transracial adoption research (1973) found that motivations for transracial adoption assumed a bifurcated pattern. On the one hand, they found families who emphasized social and societal reasons for their interest in transracial adoption; most of these families included biological children. On the other hand, there were families that emphasized personal reasons for their adoptions. These families did not usually include biological offspring. By and large our data closely conformed to the same pattern. Infertile adopters tended to emphasize personal considerations in their decisions to adopt: completion of desired family size, companionship for family members, success with a previous adoption, and family pressure to have children. In every case significantly greater numbers of traditional adopters gave these as important reasons in their adoption decisions. Similarly, in transcultural adoptions traditional adopters placed significantly greater emphasis on the unavailability of suitable American children, excessive delays in domestic adoptions, and the high cost of domestic adoptions.

Significantly more preferential adopters tended to emphasize social and humanitarian reasons in their decisions to adopt. They cited provision of a home for a needy child, religious convictions, the promotion of international brotherhood, and interest in a particular culture. One interesting exception to this trend of universalistic concerns was that preferential parents were more likely to cite the opportunity to choose the sex of a child as a very important motive for adoption (22 percent versus 5 percent). We considered the possibility that this association was an artifact of the overrepresentation of first-time parents among traditional adopters. Yet, when first-time parents were excluded from the analysis, the relationship remained undiminished. This indicates a conscious effort on the part of preferential adopters to use adoption to control family composition. Conversely, the traditional adoptive parents more closely adhered to the socially conventional model of procreation in which the sex of the child remains unknown and beyond human influence.

What accounts for this emerging interest among fertile couples in adopting children? We think that it is not merely coincidental that just as fertile couples began to appear on the adoption scene, there was a rise in the adoptions of hard-to-place children. The reader will recall the connection that was established in Chapter 2 between those most inclined to adopt hard-to-place children and fertile adoptive parents. We think that both these novel adoption trends are linked with changing American families and the development of egalitarian and shared role patterns.

It should also be noted that as ideas about what is appropriate in family life have changed, so have the standards that adoption agencies use to determine which families are acceptable as adoptive parents. Agencies have slowly shifted from the idea that only infertile, affluent, conventional families should be eligible to adopt a child. As those in the child welfare field have come to understand that there are other appropriate motives for adopting a child beyond infertility, fertile parents — and other less conventional families — have been permitted to adopt.

Our data suggest that preferential adoptive parents show a much closer identification with modern conceptions of family role sharing and sexual equality than do traditional adoptive couples. Preferential wives were more likely to pursue careers than were their traditional counterparts. Thirty-seven percent of traditional wives were neither working nor looking for work, compared with only 26 percent among preferentials. Preferential wives also indicated far greater agreement with the view that women can work and still be good mothers.

There also was a trend that showed preferential parents to be more likely to share child care tasks than was true for infertile parents. This pattern, however, fell short of statistical significance. We suspect that since most of the scale's questions apply to younger children, this may not have been the most appropriate test. (Preferential parents are more likely to adopt older children.) In our survey we also included another scale of sex role traditionalism. The items used came from Blood and Wolfe's (1956) study. An abbreviated eight-item scale was presented to respondents, covering such matters as repairing things around the house; grocery shopping; doing the dishes; deciding on what car to buy, where to live, family food expenses, and where to go on vacation; and keeping track of the family's money and bills. Respondents were asked whether these decisions and tasks were shared or done by husbands or wives exclusively. Responses were scored on a five-point scale with the following intervals: always done by husband, mostly done by husband, equally, mostly done by wife, always done by wife. When scale scores were computed, it was found that 48 percent of infertile couples showed high levels of sex role traditionalism, compared with 37 percent among preferential adopters. Thus, our preferential adoptive parents appear to be more closely aligned with modern family notions of sharing household and occupational roles.

These new types of adoptive parents see adoption as a means to extend and express personal social values and to create kinship bonds with children of sharply different racial and cultural characteristics. They tend to be people whose own life-styles are increasingly autonomous and independent of traditional family norms and roles. Thus, our evidence suggests that as parents come to possess more flexible and interchangeable conceptions of husband and wife roles, they also tend to become far more open-minded to alternative modes of family formation, such as adoption, and to adopting the hard-to-place. The increasing presence of preferential adopters portends more placement opportunities for many waiting hard-to-place children.

PARENTAL ADAPTATIONS TO ADOPTION

H. David Kirk (1964) has analyzed the many factors with which adoptive parents must come to terms in their decisions to adopt. They must accept that American culture tends to denigrate adoption. When they are infertile, adoptive parents must cope with a sense of inadequacy in their failure to bear biological offspring. They also must cope with the stigma of their child's likely illegitimate birth and allegations regarding the child's inferior heredity. Thus, adoptive parents are presented with a role handicap that leads them to be particularly sensitive to the responses of others.

Kirk pinpointed a number of stressful areas likely to be associated with the adoption process. He asked adoptive parents whether they had difficulties in depending on the assistance of outsiders in getting a child, having to prove to authorities that they were suitable parents, having no dependable timetable for how soon the child would arrive, and dealing with the discovery that, among one's family and friends, there are those who are ill-informed about adoption. He found women to be more sensitive and to have greater difficulties accepting the role handicaps associated with adoption than men.

We investigated the above four aspects of role distress associated with becoming an adoptive parent, and expected that infertile adopters would be subject to a greater sense of role handicap than would be likely among preferential adopters. These expectations were substantiated to some extent by the following trends: 27 percent of traditional adopters had difficulty in depending on the assistance of outsiders in getting a child, compared with 16 percent among preferential adopters; and 28 percent of traditional adopters had difficulties proving to authorities that they were suitable parents, compared with 16 percent among preferential adopters. In the other two aspects — having no dependable timetable and discovering that among your friends there are those who are ill-informed about adoption — no differences were noted between the two populations.

Other researchers, who include E. E. LeMasters (1957), Everett D. Dyer (1963), and Daniel F. Hobbs (1965), have documented the existence of a crisis that parents usually confront on the birth of their first child. Although researchers differ in their judgments of how severe the crisis of parenthood is, all seem to acknowledge that this event is a disruptive one that necessitates a reorganization of roles and relationships within the family and, once confronted, usually dissolves with the addition of each subsequent child. We included eight items from the LeMasters report pertaining to the following areas: money problems, increased emotional tension, excessive work, added fatigue, problems from changing plans, interference from in-laws, decreased sexual response, and reduced contact with others. It was expected that traditional adopters, more often as first-time parents, would be subject to stress similar to that found among first-time birth parents. This appeared to be supported: 25 percent of infertile husbands reported three or more problems in the eight surveyed areas, compared with 16 percent among preferential husbands. Forty-nine percent of infertile wives reported three or more problems, compared with 40 percent among preferential adopters.

As a control we added the number of other children in the family, in the expectation that the differences between traditional and preferential adopters would dissolve when both groups were similarly matched in excluding first-time parents. Surprisingly, the differences persisted. One of our respondents, Robert Gersten, commented:

> When Jennifer came, things were even more chaotic than they were when we adopted Allan — our first child. The house was a sea of dirty diapers and bad tempers. We love our kids and each other, but I sometimes wonder how we lived through it.

Among those with other children in the family, 28 percent of infertile husbands experienced three or more problems associated with the addition of their latest child, compared with 17 percent among fertile husbands. And 50 percent of traditional wives experienced three or more problems, compared with 40 percent among preferential wives. The persistence of these trends suggests that first-time parenthood may be a less critical factor than the role distress associated with accepting adoptive parenthood. This interpretation is further supported by other convergent findings.

Kirk's research on adoption stress included an analysis of the subtle and obvious disparaging remarks that others make, which contribute to a sense of personal inadequacy and marginality among adoptive parents. Such statements include "They are those unselfish people with the adopted child"; "It surely takes a special gift to love someone else's child as your own"; "How lucky you didn't have to go through all the troubles of pregnancy and birth like I did"; "Do you know anything about your child's background?"; "Your child is certainly lucky to have you for parents"; "Isn't it a shame you couldn't have children of your own?" Although there is no way of knowing how frequently these statements may be made in the general population, it is assumed that infertile and preferential adopters would be more or less equally likely to hear such remarks.

Yet, 32 percent of traditional adopters heard three or more of these remarks frequently, compared with 28 percent among preferential adopters. This difference is statistically significant. Thus, infertile adopters seem to be more troubled by the role handicaps associated with accepting adoptive parenthood than preferential adopters seem to be. The evidence suggests that their role handicap anxieties tend to recur with the addition of each adopted child to their families.

GIVING ADOPTEES GENEALOGICAL INFORMATION

Another matter we investigated was the way parents responded to adoption search issues. Did parents offer their adopted children correct and complete information about their genealogical origins? Did they tell their children early in life that they were adopted? How did they respond to the general idea of adult adoptees seeking out their birth parents? What help, if any, did they plan to offer (or had they already offered) their adopted children who asked questions and sought information about their birth parents? Did parents feel that their adopted children would ultimately seek their birth parents? These questions seemed pertinent to ask our respondents, not only for their intrinsic value but also for what they may show about how comfortable and secure parents feel in their roles as adoptive parents. Betty Jean Lifton (1979) suggests that adoptive parents with biological children (preferential adopters) seem less threatened by the search and are likely to be more willing participants in their child's searching efforts. She implies that because fertile adopters are biological parents, they find it easier to empathize with the connection between birth parents and their adopted children.

We suspected that traditional infertile parents would exhibit the most reticence in this area; because of a sense of shame and embarrassment about their own infertility, we felt they would be more inclined to "forget" or postpone telling their adopted children about their genealogical origins. We believed that since the issue of searching is more likely to be personally disruptive and difficult, they would tend to be more opposed to it, and to discourage it insofar as it might be possible to do so. One of our respondents, John Shulweiss, a 35-year-old electrical engineer who, with his wife, adopted an American-born male infant nine years ago, after three years of futile attempts to conceive, commented:

> I'm very uneasy about the whole idea of telling our son about his background. We're his parents, and I think it would be very upsetting for him to have to deal with the idea of two mothers and two fathers. Who would he think of as his real parents? He's only talked about it once — and in a kind of roundabout way — I felt it was best to just change the subject.

Comments such as these suggest the ambivalence of many infertile adoptive parents toward acknowledging their children's birth parents.

H. David Kirk (1964) talks about two fundamentally different responses to adoption that parents are likely to make. On the one hand, parents may "reject the difference" — that is, assume wherever possible that adoption is the same as or equivalent to biological parenthood. Or, on the other hand, parents may "acknowledge the difference," recognize that adoption is distinctive and fundamentally different from biological parenthood. It was our suspicion that infertile parents, in their haste to rid themselves of their anxiety and discomfort about not being able to bear biological offspring, would be more inclined, in Kirk's words, to "reject the difference." We would expect infertile parents to explicitly discourage their adopted children from searching and to offer their children genealogical information with reluctance. By contrast, we anticipated that preferential adopters would be more inclined to readily acknowledge the difference between adoption and biological parenthood; consequently, we felt they would be inclined to offer adoptees as much genealogical information as was available and the fullest support possible.

By and large, most of our expectations were sustained by the data. Preferential mothers and fathers were significantly more approving of the idea of adoptees making contact with their bioparents. Sixty-four percent of preferential fathers approved of the trend among today's adoptees to learn about their birth parents and in some cases make contact with them, compared with only 48 percent of infertile fathers. We asked our respondents an extensive battery of questions regarding whether they would favor the opening of adoption records and the conditions under which they would approve of such a policy change. The pattern of responses was consistent throughout, although in a few instances the differences failed to achieve statistical significance; preferential parents were considerably more willing to have adoption records opened and made available to all concerned parties. The differences that were found between preferential and infertile fathers were noted in mothers' responses to a comparable degree.

We also investigated parents' actual willingness to help adopted children acquire genealogical information about themselves. Among those families with at least one adopted child 16 or older, we found that 73 percent of preferential fathers had offered all the information that they had, compared with 64 percent among infertile fathers. A similar trend was noted for mothers. Both these patterns approached, but failed to achieve, statistical significance. Parents were also asked whether they thought their oldest child would be likely to search for his or her birth parents. Among this same group of parents with older children, searching was significantly more likely to be anticipated among preferential parents; 21 percent, compared with 8 percent among infertiles, anticipated that their child would probably or definitely search for his or her bioparents.

There was only one area in which our expectations remained unrealized by the data. No trends or significant differences were noted between preferential and infertile parents in time at which parents told their children they were adopted. Both groups of parents told their children they were adopted at approximately the same age levels. Sixty-two percent of nontraditional parents told their children they were adopted before they were 3 years old. This compared with 60 percent among infertile adoptive parents.

ADJUSTMENTS OF ADOPTED CHILDREN

Initially it was expected that the adjustments of the children adopted by infertile parents would be more difficult than those adopted by preferential adopters. It seemed reasonable to anticipate that the greater problems of accepting the stigmatic conditions associated with adoptive parenthood would be extended into the realm of child care. Yet, this expectation was not sustained by our initial findings; in fact, the opposite trend was more nearly approximated.

The adoptive parents were asked a number of direct and indirect questions pertaining to their child's adjustment. They were asked to describe their child's difficulties in a number of areas — emotional adjustment problems, growth problems, other unspecified problems — and to rate the child's behavior on a four-point scale indicating whether the child had difficulties never, rarely, sometimes, or often. They were also asked to rate their child's overall adjustment on a comparable four-point scale. Two indirect measures were included: parents were asked how much time had elapsed before their adopted child became "their own" (entitlement) and whether they would recommend adoption to others.

All of the adjustment items appeared to be interrelated, and all showed the children of preferential adopters to have significantly more adjustment difficulties than the children of infertile parents. Thirteen percent of preferential adopters reported emotional adjustment problems often, compared with 6 percent among traditional adopters; 9 percent reported growth problems often, compared with 4 percent among traditionals; 18 percent reported other problems often, compared with 14 percent among infertile couples; and 15 percent of preferential couples listed difficulties in three of the four surveyed areas, compared with 9 percent among preferentials. Seventy-four percent of infertile couples described their child's adjustment as "satisfactory in every possible aspect," compared with 59 percent among preferential adopters. Eighty-seven percent of traditional adopters said it took a month or less for their adopted child to become their own, compared with 74 percent among preferentials; 89 percent of infertile couples unreservedly recommended adoption to others, compared with 79 percent among nontraditional adopters.

An Empirical Assessment of Adjustment
Problems in Preferential Adoption

What accounts for the seemingly poorer adjustments found among children of preferential adopters? One possibility might be the different kinds of children generally selected by preferential adopters. We have already observed that fertile adopters are more receptive to hard-to-place children. We found that whereas 36 percent of preferential parents adopted a child over two years of age, 23 percent of infertile couples did so. Although 91 percent of the preferential parents studied adopted a child of a different race, only 63 percent of traditional parents adopted similarly. Adoptions of older children have been noted to present more adjustment difficulties because a child's personality development is already well under way before joining his or her adoptive family (Kadushin 1970).

Similarly, transracial adoptions, although generally sound, involve additional adjustments to reconcile and integrate the child's differing racial or ethnic identity and to deal with the hostile responses of outsiders. Conceivably a racially different or older child should present greater adjustment difficulties than one might encounter from adopting an infant of the same race and ethnic group. Yet, our initial controls for age and race seemed to indicate that these factors only partly account for the observed differences.

When controlled for age, the data indicated that the relationship disappeared among those adopting older children, but remained undiminished among those adopting infants. Among those adopting infants, 67 percent of preferential adopters described their child's adjustment as satisfactory in every possible aspect, compared with 78 percent among traditional parents. This pattern was consistently demonstrated on all adjustment indicators. Thus, the preferential adopters encounter greater child adjustment difficulties than do matched infertile couples.

This pattern may be associated with differing levels of support and approval shown toward the adoption by social intimates. Elsewhere, we have found that the responses of kin and close friends are associated with children's adjustments (Feigelman and Silverman 1977). Where extended family and friends respond negatively to the adoption, there is poorer adjustment on the part of the child. This pattern was exhibited in the present case; 56 percent of traditional adopters encountered uniformly positive responses from kin and friends to their infant adoptions, compared with only 30 percent among preferential adopters. On the other hand, when traditional and preferential adopters selected older children, responses among social intimates generally were similar. Thus, the preferential adopter, as a family innovator, encounters substantially less approval and encouragement from close associates when adopting an infant. Intimates apparently express reservations: "Why did you adopt when you could have given birth to biological offspring?" Conversely, traditional adopters find substantially more positive responses and approval, thus supporting and enhancing children's adjustments.

Multiple Regression Analysis of Children's Adjustments

One of the most serious obstacles to assessing the impact of preferential adoption on children's adjustments is the fact that it is so closely associated with other factors that critically influence adjustment. As we have already noted, adopting transracially, adopting an older child, and encountering opposition from family and friends are all closely linked to both the fertility of the adopting parents and the adjustments of their adopted children. In order to sort out the relative impact of all of these variables — and, most critically, to evaluate the impact of preferential adoption — we conducted a multivariate analysis of children's adjustments employing multiple-regression techniques.

We constructed a scale of children's adjustments by adding together the responses given to our questions dealing with the frequency of emotional problems, growth problems, and parents' overall evaluations of their children's adjustments. Using this scale as our dependent variable, we examined the simultaneous impact of the child's age, race, age at adoption, and the response of the parents' family, friends, and neighbors to the child's adoption. We also examined the impact of the stress experienced by each parent in response to the adoption: whether mothers and fathers reported difficulties in assuming their parental roles, such as money problems or interference from in-laws. When the influence of all of these factors on each other was held constant, we found results that were much closer to our original expectations.

Our most critical finding was that when all of the other variables in the equation were held constant, preferential adoption was positively associated with children's adjustments. With all the other factors adjusted for, preferential adoptive parents reported somewhat better adjustments among their adopted children than was true for infertile adoptive parents. The variable "preferential adoption" had a beta weight of .141, a value that achieved statistical significance.*

---

*For those unfamiliar with multiple regression, the beta statistic may be thought of as a measure of how closely two variables are associated when all of the other variables under consideration have been taken into account. The first beta weight mentioned above describes the association between the parents' fertility status and adjustment when the effects of the child's age, age at adoption, race, and the other variables in the equation have been considered. In this example the beta weight of .141 tells us that the association is relatively modest.

Surprisingly, the race of the child had no independent impact on the child's adjustment. The betas for adopting a black child and adopting an Asian child were negligible, and did not achieve statistical significance. Apparently the impact of these of variables in our earlier-mentioned cross-tabulation analysis seems to be interwoven with the influence of the response of family and friends to the child, the child's age, and age at adoption. Child's age had a beta of .165, and child's age at adoption had a beta weight of .166. Both were, therefore, modestly influential in predicting children's adjustment scores. Family response had a beta of .113, and friends' and neighbors' response had a beta of .094. These variables, therefore, were somewhat less useful in predicting children's adjustments, although both beta weights achieved statistical significance.

Apparently the most influential variable in our regression equation in predicting children's adjustments was mother's stress; this factor had a statistically significant beta weight of .235. Father's stress, by contrast, had a negligible beta that failed to achieve statistical significance. The fact that mother's stress was the most significant of all variables suggests that when mothers are overwhelmed with anxiety in assuming their parental roles — experiencing problems from interfering in-laws or limited economic resources, overwhelmed by fatigue — it seems to impair their children's adjustments. We would imagine that there is a mutual interdependence between these two variables. Since children's behavior may require extraordinary parental involvement and concern, we suspect this would induce stress among parents, especially mothers.

In theory beta weights may vary from .000 to 1.000. A beta of 1.000 would indicate that two variables are identical. A beta of .000 would indicate that two variables are not at all related. In practice, most social science researchers find that beta weights range from .001 to .500. A beta weight of less than .100 indicates that two variables have only the most minimal association. A beta weight of .100 to .200 has a modest impact, indicative of a meaningful association. Beta weights greater than .200 suggest stronger associations between variables. Those familiar with the statistical usage of multiple regression will, of course, realize that our explanation departs from the strict statistical meaning of the beta weight or standardized regression coefficient. What we have attempted to do here is to present a very simplified definition of the beta weight to our readers who are not versed in multivariate statistics so that they can follow our discussion. Readers who wish a further explanation of the beta weight or multiple-regression techniques should consult Hubert Blalock, *Social Statistics*, 2nd ed. (New York: McGraw-Hill, 1972).

We also examined whether there was an interaction effect between mother's stress, infertility, and child's adjustments. When we excluded mother's and father's stress from the multiple regression equation, we found that preferential adoption had virtually the same impact on the child's adjustment. Therefore, we were obliged to conclude that each of these factors has independent influences on children's adjustments.

These data seem to suggest paradoxical trends – the findings that were evidenced in the simple cross tabulations are reversed in the multivariate analysis. Yet, this is not all that surprising, on further reflection. We began our multivariate analysis because we knew that many of our independent variables were closely interrelated, and we had reason to suspect that our original results might be statistical artifacts. The results of the multiple regression suggest that preferential adoption has an identifiably positive impact on the adjustment of adopted children. These findings are congruent with both our general line of reasoning and the many other studies that have found most transracially adopted children to be well-adjusted in their adoptive homes.

Comparative Transracial Adjustments

Another of our questions concerned the adjustments of minority children adopted by infertile parents. We wondered whether children adopted by these more traditional parents possessed the same adjustment advantages as those adopted by fertile couples. We were also concerned with how infertile parents handled their experience of transracial adoption: Did their more personal and self-oriented adoption interests provide sufficient motivation for them to succeed in raising their adopted children, compared with their counterparts among preferential couples? How did such parents meet the challenge of community and family opposition commonly experienced by many transracial adoptive parents? Did stigmatization of infertile parents – for adopting and for adding a racially or culturally different child to their family – pose a distinctive problem to this group of parents? It seemed likely to us that the most stress and child adjustment difficulties would be encountered when parents had to deal both with the stress associated with infertility and that linked with transracial placement. We anticipated that among those adopting children of the same race, fewer adjustment problems would be encountered.

In our discussion of the multiple-regression analysis of children's adjustments mentioned above, we see the answer to at least one of our questions. Whether one adopts a black, Asian, or white child appears to have no significant impact on the variations in children's adjustments. These results point to the conclusion that variations in adjustments are not affected by transracial or same-race placement, per se. What remains to be understood is the differential impact of preferential adoption among transracial and same-race adopters. In order to examine this question, we repeated our regression of children's adjustments among families who had adopted only white children and among those who had adopted transracially.

The data suggested that preferential adoption had its greatest impact on the adjustment of transracially adopted children — those black or Asian children in our sample who were adopted by white parents. When we computed a multiple regression of children's adjustments among those families who had black or Asian children, we found that preferential adoption had a statistically significant beta weight of .151. On the other hand, when the regression was calculated among white families adopting white children, the Beta weight for preferential adoption was −.019. Here the beta weight did not achieve statistical significance. This suggests that preferential adoption has its greatest impact when nonwhite children are adopted by white parents; it also indicates that infertility has a limited impact on children's adjustments — if any association whatsoever — when parents adopt white children.

These findings, based upon our multiple-regression analysis, seem to be at odds with an earlier examination of these questions that we undertook with cross tabulations. In that analysis (Feigelman and Silverman 1979) we found there were no significant differences in the adjustments of black children who were adopted by either preferential or traditional parents; the data also showed that the preferential parents of Asian children reported significantly more adjustment problems than their traditional counterparts. Our evidence also showed substantially greater approval and support from community and kin for infertile adoptive parents. We attributed the poorer adjustments of preferential children to the diminished social support available to them. Yet, these observed trends did not effectively control for all the other associated factors with the same precision and completeness that is possible with multiple-regression analysis. When all the potentially important variables were simultaneously controlled for, we noted that the children of traditional infertile parents showed statistically significant poorer adjustment scores than their preferential counterparts.

These findings are consistent with our earlier expectations about the impact of infertility on the behavior of adoptive parents. There are a number of possible explanations that may account for this trend in our data. One possibility is that infertile adopting parents regard their transracially adopted child not only as the solution to their problems of infertility, but also as the visible reminder of it. For this reason the greatest numbers of infertile adopting parents want a child as similar as possible to one that would have been born to them. When infertile parents adopt a visibly different child, their uneasiness about their failure to reproduce appears to be aggravated. Such increased levels of tension appear to be manifested in poorer adjustments among their adopted children.

Another possibility is that the infertile parents, more often as first-time parents — and possibly lacking confidence and self-assurance in their parental roles — may be more easily overwhelmed by the behavior of their transracially adopted child, and more likely to regard their child's behavior as difficult. Still other explanations may be needed to account for these findings. Further studies, involving in-depth interviewing, would seem to be called for, to explain why this group of respondents has somewhat greater adjustment problems with their transracially adopted children.

Another question we investigated concerned whether the problems that infertile parents initially had with their transracially adopted children would persist over time. We felt that it was probable that as infertile parents became more comfortable in their roles as adoptive parents, they would be less likely to convey their unease and anxiety to their adopted children. A multiple regression of children's adjustments in 1981 — six years after the first questionnaire was completed — suggested that the preferential/traditional dichotomy was no longer an influential one. This variable failed to achieve significance with our 1981 survey data, suggesting that as time passes, the fertility status of adoptive parents becomes inconsequential in influencing adjustment outcomes.

Another interesting finding that emerged from this analysis was recognition of the persistent influence of the response of friends and neighbors on children's adjustments. All the other previously statistically significant variables — mother's stress, age, age at adoption — no longer were important in accounting for variations in adjustment outcomes in 1981. The only one to achieve statistical significance, with a beta value of .137, was friends' and neighbors' responses. Such results suggest that the attitudes of support or rejection by friends and neighbors continues to be important in determining longer-term adjustment outcomes.

EMPHASIZING CULTURAL BACKGROUNDS IN RAISING TRANSCULTURALLY ADOPTED CHILDREN

We also investigated another potentially important aspect of the socialization of transculturally adopted children — how parents deal with their child's birth culture. It seemed to us that there were two possibilities: either parents could emphasize their child's different culture and consider it to be important facet of that child's existence, or they could minimize it and ignore it. Moreover, we believed that, depending upon what parents do — and the emphasis they accord to the child's birth culture — transculturally adopted children will be encouraged to take interest in their ethnic affiliation and experience a sense of pride in their background or, if parents deemphasize the birth culture, transculturally adopted children will be likely to be disinterested in their own birth group and more likely to feel ashamed and uncomfortable about their affiliation to this "alien" community.

We suspected that preferential adopters would give more emphasis to their transculturally adopted child's birth group than would infertile adoptive parents. Considering their social and group orientations in their reasons for adoption and their predilection, in Kirk's terms, to "acknowledge the differences," we felt preferential adopters would be inclined to take an active interest in their child's birth culture and to pursue it from a positive standpoint. By contrast, infertile couples, as they pursue their more personal and self-directed interests in adoption, and with their role discomfort about adoption and their failure to procreate, would be led to minimize or ignore the birth cultures of their adopted children. As traditional parents may be inclined to "reject the differences" between adoption and biological parenthood, they would similarly be inclined to reject or diminish the importance accorded to their child's birth culture; we felt they would especially likely to "Americanize" their transculturally adopted child, obliterating from memory any connection the child may have had or been capable of having with his or her birth group.

To some extent the results seemed to conform to our expectations. Respondents were asked to describe their interest in the culture of their child's birth. Significantly more preferential adoptive parents expressed some or considerable interest in their adopted child's birth culture — 74 percent, compared with 65 percent among traditional adoptive parents. Among those parents adopting nonwhite children, preferential families were more likely to live in integrated communities than their infertile counterparts. Twenty-eight percent of fertile parents lived in communities where nonwhites could be found in substantial numbers, compared with 22 percent among traditional adoptive parents. This trend was particularly pronounced in the families that had adopted black children. Eighty-five percent of the preferential families who adopted blacks lived in integrated communities, compared with 38 percent among traditional parents. Yet, despite their apparent overtures to the birth cultures of their adopted children, preferential parents did not describe themselves as emphasizing their child's birth group any differently from traditional parents. When both groups of parents were asked if they ever talked to their child about the child's racial or cultural background, substantially similar responses were given by both sets of parents.

Even more surprising results were found when we investigated children's interest and pride (or shame) in their birth cultures. The children of preferential adopters were described as no more interested in their birth cultures, no more proud of their group affiliations, not possessing any greater sense of shame or discomfort about their appearance than children of infertile adopters. Although differences were noted on some of the above dimensions between the two sets of parent groups, they were neither consistent or statistically significant. Thus, from our analysis so far, it appears that parents' interests and integrated community living arrangements have a minimal effect in engendering a sense of interest and positive feeling for a transculturally adopted child's ethnic identity. In Chapters 4 and 5 we will explore these matters more fully, assessing their impact on each other and how they contribute to shaping adoptive adjustments.

IMPLICATIONS FOR SOCIAL WORK PRACTICE

These findings demonstrate the presence of a new pattern of adoptive parenthood that appears to coexist with more conventional and traditional adoption patterns. Preferential adopters actively select adoption over biological parenthood, and their emergence seems to be associated with fundamental changes in the structure of American family life. The interest and willingness of these people to assume parental responsibilities, and their overall success in parenting offer agencies new resources for dealing with hard-to-place children. The motives, experiences in adoption, and needs for social services of these parents differ considerably from those of more traditional infertile adoptive couples. As they become more numerous, their presence offers a profound potential for further revolutionizing adoption by reducing the stigma surrounding adoptive parenthood.

Inasmuch as preferential adopting parents are not confronted with the personal crisis associated with accepting their own infertility, they are less troubled by the subtle condemnation of adoptive parents and the role stress linked with adoptive parenthood. A substantial majority experience few serious difficulties in raising their adopted children. Yet, compared with traditional adoptive parents, their children show more adjustment problems.

The more frequent child adjustment difficulties found among preferential adopters appears to be associated to some extent with the kinds of children they tend to select. More inclined to adopt older children and children of different racial heritage — as well as disabled children — they must deal with the more demanding, distinctive features attendant upon these kinds of adoptions. These problems appear to be compounded by an overall lack of support for and encouragement of their adoption by extended family and friends. Being innovators in family behavior, they appear to be subject to the disapproval that those in the vanguard of any social movement are likely to experience. Their social and humanitarian orientations toward adoption provide an important counteractive influence to sustain them during troubled periods. Since many of their problems are created by social disapproval, preferential adoptive parents may find peer support extremely important in coping with their difficulties. Adoptive parent groups may prove especially helpful in offering the kind of support needed.

Since these parents are more likely to adopt children with serious mental or physical problems, the services of child care professionals may be most relevant to helping these families deal with their children's problems. The shared experiences of other adoptive parents may also provide aid and comfort to families facing difficulties.

Traditional infertile adopting couples appear to require different social services. Their problems — the recognition and acceptance of infertility, then deciding to find and adopt a child — may point to a need for adequate preplacement and onset family counseling services. Our results, indicating that parental crisis and trauma are recurrent phenomena, suggest that the need for these kinds of services is unsatisfied. Our data also suggest that the anxiety and uncertainty generated by the crisis of infertility are communicated in many cases to the adopted children and adversely affect their adjustment. This seems to be particularly true in the adoption of black and Asian children. The intrapsychic nature of their problems would clearly seem to call for the kind of therapy and counseling resources available from psychiatric and social service professionals. Human service professionals will need to bring to the forefront a cognizance of the social psychological meanings of adoption and infertility, if they are to offer these clients effective therapy and counseling.

Although our multiple-regression analysis has shown that the adopted children of infertile couples tend to be more poorly adjusted than those of preferential adopters, we think it would be quite mistaken to conclude that such families would be overall poorer placement risks. Although the regression coefficients were statistically significant, they were modest in size. More important, perhaps, we found that in considering the adoptions of white children and longer-term child adjustments, the importance of fertility status diminishes in affecting adjustment outcomes. Taking into account the high levels of extended family and peer support usually received by these families, and their deeply felt individual and personal orientations to succeed as adoptive parents, we find sufficient resources that will help them function effectively as adoptive parents.

Our data also suggest that infertile adoptive parents are likely to oppose genealogical questioning and searching for biological relatives by adoptees; they are also less likely to recognize and give any emphasis to the cultural backgrounds of their transracially adopted children. The significance of these orientations — and their implications for adoptive adjustments — remain to be analyzed in later chapters of this work.

This chapter has demonstrated that the status of adoptive parenthood continues to be deprecated in American society. This seems to be particularly clear in the case of infertile adopters who find the advent of adoptive parenthood an especially stressful period. Such stresses seem to have an especially adverse impact on the well-being of children adopted by infertile parents. Much effort remains to be expended by social service professionals and citizen advocates to dispel adoption's disrepute, creating for adoptees socialization opportunities equivalent to those enjoyed by birth offspring. There is a need to look beyond the immediate questions of placement and adjustment to the larger issues of attitudes toward adoption in the population-at-large.

This chapter has begun to raise a great many questions about the elements in the adjustment process and the significant forces that lead some adoptees to be poorly adjusted and distressed in their adoptive homes while others flourish. Our results demonstrate that the fertility or infertility of parents is one of a number of factors that is of some importance in influencing adoptive outcomes and adjustments. Other factors have also been suggested here, such as the age of children at adoption, their racial or ethnic affiliation, and the support families receive from extended kin and other associates. In the next two chapters we will focus more directly on these other elements and gauge their overall significance in affecting adoptive adjustments.

4
The Adjustments of
Black Children
Adopted by White Families

INTRODUCTION

Paul Dinitz is one of the children in our sample. His experiences typify those of many of the black children adopted by white parents. At two years of age he was placed by Catholic Charities with Matthew and Mary Dinitz. Their second adopted child, he is now 12 years old. The Dinitzes have four children: Amy, their firstborn, is now 15; their birth son, Matthew Jr., is 13; their older adopted child, 13-year-old Carol, was born in Korea. The Dinitzes live in a modest ranch house in a suburb of Columbus, Ohio.

After their adoption of Paul, the Dinitzes gave serious thought to relocating from predominantly white Hillsdale to a more integrated area. However, after hearing frequent comments about the inferior quality of the junior high school in the nearby integrated neighborhood, they decided to remain in Hillsdale. The Dinitzes realized that they had grown comfortable living in Hillsdale; it is an easy commute to Matthew's job, and the family has a lot of friends there. They are very close to a good shopping center and, most important of all for their children, the schools are considered to be the best in the county.

It hasn't always been easy for Paul to grow up in an all-white community. Althought the Dinitzes haven't been victims of many overt incidents of racial bigotry, they are aware of an undercurrent of disapproval from some of their white neighbors. As transracial adoptive parents they have become sensitive to the many subtle ways in which people can be rejected and mistreated. Incidents such as the time when their water main burst, and none of their neighbors took the trouble to call either Mary or Matthew at work, made a strong impression upon them. They were never sure if no one had noticed it; but with all that water flowing in front of their house, it hardly seemed possible to miss. Paul has been the target of occasional racial epithets at the school playground. Despite these difficulties, their immediate family has drawn especially close.

Paul, at age 12, seems to have positive feelings about himself. He gets along very well with his brother and sisters. He is a very even-tempered and mild-mannered child. Outgoing and friendly, he has a great many friends in his class at school. However, Paul is not an especially able student. Although he is in little danger of failing or being left back, his schoolwork is below average. Paul shows little interest in his studies; he does his work hurriedly in his eagerness to play with his friends. In his predominantly white neighborhood he has had very little contact with other black children. With his light skin coloration he considers himself to be a biracial child. He doesn't feel that he is missing anything by not having much contact with blacks; he has come to identify being black with being poor. He is very happy and content with his present friends.

The Dinitzes are active in their local Catholic church. Both Matthew and Mary grew up in homes where religion was considered especially important. Ever since they married, they have found their church involvement to be especially gratifying and meaningful. Matthew has been active in the local Catholic Interracial Council. In fact, they consider their interest in transracial adoption to be partly an extension of their deep religious commitment. When the Dinitzes first adopted Paul, they thought they would make an effort to do things that would help him become connected with the black community. Yet, as time went on, they began to recognize their limitations in communicating the black experience to their child. They knew and felt most comfortable with their own Eastern European Catholic origins; the idea of projecting anything other than this to their children left them unsettled. They felt a deep and unwavering commitment to their Catholic beliefs; they felt confident that their children would obtain similar benefits from their faith. They were gratified to see Paul adapt so readily to their religious community; he has several friends from the church. He thoroughly enjoys singing in the youth choral group. The Dinitzes' only reservation about their church involvement comes sporadically, usually following thoughtless and irritating remarks made by some of their fellow parishioners regarding Paul.

Paul's experiences raise many questions about the quality of life available to black children adopted and raised by white parents. How deeply do the occasional instances of racial hostility affect Paul? Do they affect his overall adjustment in any measurable way? Is his transracial placement in any way related to his difficulties in school? Are there any other personality disturbances that may be linked with his transracial placement? Is Paul's sense of himself affected by his isolation from other blacks? Are the Dinitzes unusually isolated from black families, or are their experiences common among white families who adopt black children? Is Paul's marginal commitment to the black community a typical or unusual response to transracial adoption? Would Paul's overall adjustment be better if the Dinitzes maintained closer ties to the black community? How much of his marginal commitment to the black community is related to his relatively light skin coloration? We will attempt to address these questions in this chapter.

We are particularly interested in probing how transracially adopted children fare in white homes, in terms of both their immediate and their longer-term adaptations. We are also concerned with identifying the kinds of experiences that are likely to be associated with optimal adaptations. We wonder, for example, whether parents' efforts to positively emphasize the child's birth culture — to live in integrated communities, to have close friendships with many blacks, and the like — affect adjustment outcomes. We are especially interested in trying to identify in which homes and in which families we will be likely to find the best- and least well-adapted transracially adopted children. These are the concerns of the present chapter, and they will carry through to the next two, in which we discuss the patterns of adaptation of Colombian and Korean-born children adopted by American parents.

Our analysis here is based on the 58 families in our sample who had adopted black children in 1975. Whenever it seemed appropriate to do so, these families were compared with the 96 families who had adopted white children born in the United States. Many, if not most, of the questions we explored here are based upon our follow-up study sample. That investigation was based on the 47 families who had adopted blacks and the 65 families with white adopted children who were resurveyed in 1981. Our adoptive families with black children in 1981 tended to have children who were generally preadolescents. Thirty percent of the families had children who under ten years of age. The largest number, approximately 60 percent of our respondents, had children who were between the ages of 11 and 16. The remaining 10 percent had children who were over 17 years old.

Eighteen of our families (31 percent) had only one child in 1975 — their adopted black son or daughter. Twenty-three additional families had other adopted children. Nineteen of these had adopted other nonwhite children; eleven of these families had other black children. Thus, a third of the children had nonwhite siblings. In all, 40 of our 58 families (69 percent) had other adopted or birth children. At the time of our 1975 study, 37 of these children (61 percent) had been in their adoptive homes for three years or more. The majority of these black children grew up in families where they had transracially adopted brothers or sisters. By the time of our 1981 follow-up survey, only seven of our black transracial adoptees (2 percent) did not have siblings.

The practice of transracial adoption is an extremely controversial one. Its more extreme critics denounce it as a form of kidnapping and cultural genocide. In discussing the adoption of Asian and Latin American children by white American or European parents, some critics have conceptualized the process as one in which Third World peoples are taken from their homelands and stripped of their connection to their communities and cultures. They see this practice as one that diminishes the size, strength, and vitality of the cultures from which the children are taken. More moderate critics see it as psychologically crippling to the children involved, leaving them in a cultural no-man's-land where they are never fully accepted in the majority culture and maladapted for effective participation in the culture of their birth. Few advocates of transracial adoptions would prefer them to adoptive placement within the child's indigenous group, yet they do not see the practice as necessarily damaging to the children affected; they see adoption as providing vastly better opportunities for these children's welfare than would otherwise be available in most Third World countries. A similar debate can be observed with respect to the adoption of American-born black children by white parents.

In the 1970s the adoption of black children by white American parents came under severe criticism from many black Americans. Even the most restrained critics, who accepted the good intentions of those attempting to place black children in white families, argued that the process might be dangerous for the child's development (Chestang 1972). A position paper approved by the National Association of Black Social Workers stated the matter in even stronger terms:

> Black children should be placed only with black families whether in foster care or for adoption. Black children belong physically, psychologically and culturally in black families in order that they receive the total sense of themselves and develop a sound projection of their future. . . . Black children in white families are cut off from a healthy development of themselves as black people. . . . [We must] go back to our communities to end this particular form of genocide. (Simon and Altstein 1977, p. 45)

Clearly, this statement and the efforts that emanated from it had a substantial impact on reducing the number of black children adopted by white families in the United States. In 1971, 2,574 black children were adopted by white families. By 1976, the last year for which comparable data are available, the number had dropped to 1,056 (Opportunity 1971-76).

During these years of fewer adoptions of black children by white families, considerable progress has been made in the placement of black children in black homes. Many of the obstacles that effectively blocked black families from adopting through agencies have been diminished. Agencies such as Homes for Black Children in Detroit have achieved remarkable success in placing more black children within the black community (Day 1979).

Such efforts notwithstanding, black children still form a disproportionate number of those lacking permanent homes (Fanshel 1978). The Child Welfare League of America suggests that the number of nonwhite children free for placement far exceeds the number of nonwhite homes approved for placing them (Haring 1976). A 1979 study by the Citizens Committee for Children in New York City indicated that 56 percent of the adolescents entering the city's emergency foster care program were black; 29 percent were of Hispanic background. The study also revealed that many of these adolescents

> . . . are in a holding pattern, circling endlessly from family to agency, back to family, back to another agency, accumulating sheaves of paper and emotional scars. (Kihss 1981, p. 36)

Studies such as these suggest that the problem of creating permanent placements for minority children is by no means resolved.

One of the important issues in studying transracial adoption is the absence of a sufficient number of black adoptive homes for those black children who need them. At least some in the social work and child care profession believe that black families are somehow reluctant to adopt. Recent research, however, casts doubt on this explanation. Gordon Scott Bonham has demonstrated that black families adopt with roughly the same frequency as whites (Bonham 1977). This fact is particularly surprising and impressive when one considers that black families are much more likely than white families to be poor or working class. The social characteristics more widely shared among blacks are those that would lead agencies to discriminate against them as potential adoptive families. Black families not only must overcome the barriers imposed by racial stigma, they must also confront the obstacles imposed by such patterns as working wives, greater employment instability, renting rather then owning their homes — attributes that are likely to lead to their disqualification by middle-class-value-dominated social agencies.

Biases still remain in the ability of blacks to qualify as acceptable adoptive parents. Dawn Day's careful study has demonstrated the impact of agency values and practices upon the placements of black children (Day 1979). She found that the more professional the agency, the less likely they were to place black children.

The research of Carol Stack (1975) and other students of Afro-American family life reveals the ability of black kinship networks to care for children even in communities with minimal economic resources. Informal adoption, or "child minding" as Stack refers to it, has been a feature of Afro-American life for some time. In the light of this resourcefulness and concern for children in the black community, it seems more than likely that the generally deteriorating economic circumstances in the black community over the last two decades must be of some relevance in accounting for the rising numbers of black children who come to the attention of formalized child care agencies. Under the impact of what has become a relatively permanent economic depression, the minimal economic and social stability required to maintain informal systems of "child minding" are no longer possible for many low-income blacks. The extending reach of the contemporary welfare bureaucracy and rising interests in personal need satisfaction are other trends that must be considered in understanding the large numbers of minority children who cannot be placed within their respective ethnic communities.

It seems probable that if the policy of restricting or eliminating transracial adoption is continued, substantial numbers of nonwhite children will remain without permanent adoptive homes. Thus, it is reasonable to ask whether the arguments against transracial adoption can be sustained by social research. If, on the contrary, social research can establish that the transracial placement of black children does not contribute to their maladjustment — or at least is substantially less injurious than the consequences of transitory placements or institutional care — then there would be a cogent argument for its continuance.

GAPS IN THE RESEARCH ON TRANSRACIAL ADOPTIVE ADJUSTMENTS

The bulk of the research examining the adjustment of transracially adopted children refers to Asian and Native American children as well as to black children adopted by white American parents. Nearly a dozen studies consistently indicate that approximately 75 percent of transracially adopted preadolescent or younger children adjust well in their adoptive homes (Fanshel 1972; Grow and Shapiro 1974; Davis 1961; DiVirgilio 1956; Simon and Altstein 1977; Kim and Reid 1970; Keltie 1969; Kim 1977; Fricke 1965; Rathbun, DiVirgilio, and Waldfogel 1958; Falk 1970; Nutt and Snyder 1973; Zastrow 1977). In studies that refer directly to the adjustment of black children in white homes, similar trends are evident (Grow and Shapiro 1974; Fricke 1965; Simon and Altstein 1977; Zastrow 1977; Falk 1970; Nutt and Snyder 1973).

Ideally, one should compare the adjustments of transracially adopted black children with those of inracially adopted children, specifically with white children adopted by white parents and black children adopted by black parents. Unfortunately, the number of studies of this kind is very limited.

Among studies that take a comparative approach is an investigation by Lawrence Falk (1970), which was based on 186 transracially adopted children and 170 inracially adopting white families. This study provides some indication that transracially adopted children are more likely to have difficult adjustments than their inracially adopted peers. Transracially adopting parents anticipated that their black children might experience more difficulties in school, dating, and getting jobs. These differences may or may not indicate adjustment difficulties as much as they may reflect realistic parental assessments of societal prejudices. The study found that fewer transracially adopting parents would be willing to recommend adoption to others or to adopt if they were to do it again. These differences could indicate less satisfaction and poorer adjustments for transracially adopted children. It might also suggest that white parents face unusual difficulties in integrating their nonwhite adopted children into their families and communities. It could be argued from these findings that transracial adoptions are inherently problem-filled. Is this is indeed the case?

In contrast with Falk's data, other studies suggest that transracial placement in and of itself has no detrimental effect on the psychological adjustments of black transracial adoptees. Indeed, there is even some evidence that transracially adopted black children may be likely to enjoy superior adaptations, compared with other black children.

Charles Zastrow (1977) found that white parents of black adopted children and white parents of white adopted children did not differ, either in their rating of their child's adjustment or in their satisfaction as a whole. Interestingly, the adoptive parents of black children commented that they had experienced far fewer problems with racial hostility and antagonism than they had expected. Zastrow's study, however, leaves open the question of how well transracially adopted black children adjust when compared with black children adopted by black parents.

A study by Ruth McRoy goes part of the distance to answer this question. Hers has been the only research, to our knowledge, to examine the adjustments of black transracial adoptees with a comparable population of black children of similar age who were adopted by black parents (McRoy 1981; McRoy, Zurcher, Lauderdale, and Anderson 1982). Data derived from standard psychological inventories indicated substantial similarity in the adjustments of both groups of adoptees. Yet, considering the limited numbers of families included within McRoy's sample — 30 in each group of transracial and inracial adoptees — one must evaluate these findings with a certain measure of caution.

Simon and Altstein's research (1977) dealing with attitudes of racial awareness and identification found that transracially adopted children tended to develop a sense of racial consciousness sooner and to possess more positive attitudes toward being black than comparable groups of nonadopted black children. Sandra Scarr and Richard Weinberg (1976) also obtained data showing that transracially adopted black children outperformed black children raised in black homes on standardized school achievement tests, demonstrating superior intellectual functioning. Scarr and Weinberg also found that as a group they tended to possess healthy self-attitudes. While these two studies are somewhat tangential to the question of overall psychological adjustment, their implications are clear; transracial adoptees are likely to be at least as well adapted psychologically as their inracially adopted counterparts. Thus, when we consider all of this evidence — Falk's results suggesting more adjustment problems, and those of other scholars showing no damaging consequences — the question remains open. Is race consequential in affecting a child's adjustments? And, if so, how important is it?

TRANSRACIALLY ADOPTED BLACKS: ARE THEY REJECTED BY THE DOMINANT COMMUNITY?

A frequent argument against transracial placements is that the hostility of the families and friends of white adopting parents will adversely affect the adjustment of the adopted child. Leon Chestang states:

> The white family that adopts a black child is no longer a "white family." In the eyes of the community its members become traitors, niggerlovers, do-gooders, rebels, oddballs, and most significantly, ruiners of the community. Unusual psychological armaments are required to shield oneself from the behavioral and emotional onslaughts of these epithets. (1972, p. 105)

There is a plausible quality to this stance. The prejudice and discrimination aimed at black Americans have often had negative and devastating effects on their personal adjustments (Kardiner and Ovesey 1951; Karon 1958). It is less clear, however, that prejudice and discrimination aimed at black adopted children are of such magnitude that they lead to serious personality problems.

One of the more interesting features that emerges from the few studies of transracially adopted black children is the absence of the kind of unremitting hostility that Chestang and others expect. Rita J. Simon and Howard Altstein (1977) report that less than 10 percent of their sample of transracially adopting families reported any resistance by their friends and neighbors to the adoption. Families offered a bit more opposition to the adoption of black children. Thirty-seven percent of the sample reported that their families (grandparents, uncles, and aunts) continued to oppose the adoption. Yet, seven years after their original study, Simon and Altstein (1981) reported that extended family opposition had diminished, affecting 12 percent of transracial adoptive parent respondents. The data obtained in the Simon and Altstein study are by no means isolated. Zastrow (1977) also found that most parents encountered a good deal less hostility and opposition than they had expected.

Our own data showed that parents adopting black children tended to encounter a generally positive response from extended kin, friends, and neighbors. Approximately half of most relatives and neighbors, and as many as 90 percent of friends, responded positively to their adoptions. Yet, when adoptive parents of black children are compared with those of white children, we observe markedly less positive responses among the social intimates of transracial adopters. In most instances − with the exception of friends − we noted that transracial adoptive parents received 30 percent fewer positive responses than their inrace adoptive counterparts. Table 4.1 shows the percentages of different intimates reacting favorably to our sample members' adoptions.

There is no doubt that transracial adoptive parents receive far less support and encouragement of their adoptions than do inracially adopting parents. It seems reasonable to anticipate that the hostility toward transracially adopted black children must

TABLE 4.1
Family and Friends' Responses to the Adoption
(percent responding positively)

	Transracial Parents	Inracial Parents
Husband's parents	56	79
Wife's parents	48	86
Other relatives	43	74
Friends	89	87
Neighbors	51	85

have some negative effect on the childrens' adjustments. As we have found elsewhere, extended family and community support — or its absence — exerts a measurable impact on adoptive adjustments (Feigelman and Silverman 1977). The question is, how much of an effect? And it remains to be measured just how significant this factor is in affecting children's adjustments, compared with other likely adjustment influences.

ASSESSING THE EFFECTS OF DELAYED PLACEMENT

On the other side of the adjustment equation, the influence of delayed placement has yet to be considered. Students of child development — Selma Fraiberg, Anna Freud, John Bowlby, and others — recognize the importance of continuity and stability in a child's environment, particularly during the early years (Fraiberg 1977; Freud and Burlingham 1973; Bowlby 1952). Joseph Goldstein, Anna Freud, and Albert Solnit (1977) have placed such a critical emphasis on the need for permanence and continuity that, when at issue, they claim it should take precedence over the links between birth parent and child. The absence of a stable and enduring parental relationship is seen as devastating and traumatic to a child's development.

The desirability of early, permanent placement is generally accepted as axiomatic within the social work profession (Lawder et al. 1969). It is well documented by Alfred Kadushin (1970a) that the later the child is placed, the more serious and lasting the adjustment problems that accompany adoption. In David Fanshel's

(1972) study of Native American children adopted by white families, he found that a child's adjustment was negatively correlated with age at placement. His research also indicates why delayed placement may be so significant for the child's ultimate well-being. Not only is it a matter of disruption and discontinuity but, with delayed placement, the child is more likely to suffer from a hazardous environment. Fanshel points out that children who are adopted later are often exposed to poverty, mental illness, disease, and alcoholism among their parents.

We undertook to assess the effects of delayed placement, and to compare it with other sources of maladjustment for the black transracially adopted child. Did race difference and racial isolation in an alien community pose a more potent determinant for a child's adoptive adjustment than the discontinuities and hazards associated with delayed placement? Or did the ever-shifting and unsettled conditions associated with late placement exert overshadowing consequences on the child's development?

The focus of our investigation begins with examining these different views concerning the adjustment of black transracially adopted children. We hope to help resolve a very perplexing policy dilemma: Should a black child be placed in another racial group, thereby subjecting him or her to a position of marginality? Or is one more likely to risk doing serious psychological damage to the child by delaying placement until same-race adoptive parents can be found? Indeed, given the existing realities of placement opportunities for black children, excluding the possibility of transracial adoption could eliminate the likelihood of adoption altogether. Such questions underscore the need for a better understanding of the relative significance of each of the many factors that contribute to a child's overall adoptive adjustment. Once a better grasp of the relative importance of each factor is obtained, social policies and practices can be formulated with a more realistic assessment of their probable impact.

EXPLAINING INITIAL ADJUSTMENTS

First, we were interested in assessing the adjustments of our black transracial adoptees. How did their adjustments compare with those of black transracial adoptees in earlier studies? We were also concerned with how black transracial adoptees compared with white inrace adopted children.

Our data revealed the following: 45 percent of the black adoptees were described as having problem-free adjustments; 50 percent were described as mostly well-adjusted, with some problems; the remaining 5 percent, as having frequent or severe adjustment problems. These trends are most consistent with the results of previous studies, which have found the majority of black transracial adoptees well adjusted in their adoptive homes.

When we looked at the description of specific problems, we found that 67 percent of the white parents of black adopted children in our sample reported few or no physical health problems among their children. Fifty-four percent of these parents indicated that their children had few, if any, emotional adjustment problems; only 27 percent said that their black adopted children had more than occasional growth problems.

A factor analysis of these four questions revealed that three of them — the parental estimate of overall adjustment, the frequency of emotional problems, and the frequency of growth problems — were closely related. We therefore combined them to form a single scale of children's maladjustment.

The principal factor underlying the three variables employed in the index accounted for 60 percent of the variation in those variables. For a given respondent the index had a maximum possible score of 12 (very maladjusted) and a minimum score of 1 (not at all maladjusted). No child received a score of more than 8, and the majority of children received a score of 3 or less. A score of 8 meant that a child often encountered difficulties in two of the three problem areas. A score of 3 meant that child sometimes experienced problems in one of the problem areas.

Carol Henderson, one of our respondents, described her nine-year-old black adopted daughter Jennifer as sometimes having emotional problems; she said the adoption itself was working out well, with some problems. In her comments to us at an adoptive parents' meeting, Mrs. Henderson described Jennifer as

> . . . not an easy child. She has more than her share of tantrums. We worry sometimes because Jenny can settle an argument with her fists if she loses her temper. . . . [In school] Jenny is very restless and easily

bored. Her teachers find her a problem, but she's never had any serious trouble in the classroom.

Jenny had an overall scale score of 7.

Paul Dinitz was described by his parents as having only occasional emotional problems. Matthew Dinitz described his son's adoption as working out well in all aspects. Neither of Paul's parents felt that he had any physical or growth problems. His father had only one reservation:

> I sometimes worry that Paul isn't aggressive enough in dealing with his problems. He'd rather run away from things than face them. If he'd just stand up to some of the kids at [the parish school] who tease him, they'd stop. Carol — our Korean daughter — wouldn't anyone let get away with calling her names behind her back. She's spent some time in the principal's office because of it, but there's no more teasing. Paul has to learn to do some of that.

Paul received a scale score of 1 on the index of children's maladjustment.

Similar scales have been used by a number of students of adoptive adjustments, including Fanshel (1972), Zastrow (1977), and Grow and Shapiro (1974). Fanshel's scale was significantly correlated with his measure of overall adjustment, which employed assessments made by interviewers and psychiatrists as well as parents' reports. Zastrow also reported close agreement between the ratings made by parents of their adopted child's adjustment and those made by interviewers.

A similar scale was constructed to assess family opposition to the adoption. The adopting families were asked whether the husband's parents' response to the adoption had been positive, mixed, indifferent, or negative. Similar questions were posed about the responses of the wife's parents and other relatives. The responses to these three items were then added to form a scale of family opposition. Scores on the index ranged from a minimum of 3 (no opposition) to 12 (a great deal of opposition). No family received a score of more than 9, and the majority of the families had scores of 4 or less. The principal factor underlying the three variables employed in the index of family opposition accounted for 50 percent of the variation in these items.

When we compared our black transracial adoptees with white inracially adopted children, the results indicated that transracially adopted children were less well-adjusted. The cross tabulation of the adopted child's maladjustment scores by background, presented in Table 4.2, clearly demonstrates an association between transracial adoption and maladjustment. Forty-five percent of white inracially adopted children fall into the least maladjusted category, while only 27 percent of the black transracially adopted children received such scores. These data tend to support the arguments made against transracial adoption. It is worth noting, however, that less than a third of the transracially adopted children received the highest maladjustment score.

Table 4.2, however, does not necessarily demonstrate the source of the maladjustment. Is this maladjustment inherent in the trans-racial relationship, or is it an artifact of the child's preadoptive experience and his or her present stage of development? Black children are more likely to be adopted after infancy and to have been exposed to hostile preadoptive environments. Transracially adopted black children are often older than comparable white adopted children. Black children, then, may be reaching more complex and difficult stages in their personal development than a comparable group of younger white adopted children.

The data in Table 4.3 indicate that there is a clear association between age at adoption and maladjustment. The older the child

TABLE 4.2
Maladjustment Index Score, by Child's Race: 1975
(percent)

| Index Score | Race | |
	White	Black
1-2	46	27
3-4	32	42
5-8	22	31
Total	100	100
N	93	55

$$X^2 = 4.687; 2 \text{ df}; p > .05$$

TABLE 4.3
Maladjustment Index Score, by Child's Age at Adoption
(percent)

	Index Score		
	1-2	*3-4*	*5-8*
Less Than 2 yrs.	82	74	41
2 yrs.-2 yrs., 11 mos.	6	0	0
3 yrs.-3 yrs., 11 mos.	2	6	13
4 yrs. and Over	10	20	46
Total	100	100	100
N	52	51	52

$$X^2 = 26.47; 6 \text{ df}; p > .001$$

is at adoption, the higher his or her maladjustment score. These data could be taken to support the hypothesis that preadoptive environment, rather than transracial relationship, is critical for the adjustment of the black adopted child.

Table 4.4 shows that adjustment of all adopted children in the sample declines as they grow older. These data are compatible

TABLE 4.4
Maladjustment Index Score, by Child's Age
(percent)

	Index Score		
	1-2	*3-4*	*5-8*
Less Than 2 yrs.	20	2	0
2 yrs.-4 yrs., 11 mos.	31	36	17
5 yrs.-9 yrs., 11 mos.	36	36	50
10 yrs. and Over	13	26	33
Total	100	100	100
N	55	50	36

$$X^2 = 22.61; 6 \text{ df}; p > .001$$

with the argument that as a child grows older, his or her increasingly complex developmental patterns will lead to more problems, irrespective of race differences between parents and child. These trends are also compatible with the hypothesis that the problems in transracial adoptions will become apparent only as the child grows older and is exposed to an increasingly hostile world outside of his or her family.

In order to sort out the equally plausible arguments suggested above, it was necessary to subject the data to multiple-regression analysis. The results of this analysis are presented in Table 4.5. The regression equation looks at the impact of each of the variables under scrutiny while controlling for all of the others. The association between a child's race and maladjustment, present in Table 4.2, disappears in the regression equation. The regression coefficients for adopting a black rather than a white child are negligible, and do not remotely approach statistical significance at the .05 level. That datum suggests that transracial adoption, in and of itself, does not have a negative impact on the initial adjustments of black children.

The resistance of family members, as expected, has a negative impact on the adjustment of adopted children. The regression coefficients for "family opposition" are positive, modest in size, and statistically significant. This finding is consistent with the arguments of those opposed to transracial adoption. Yet, the impact of family opposition is not nearly as great as would be suggested by transracial adoption's critics. Given the arguments of these critics, "family opposition" should have been more sizable than was observed. When "family opposition" was excluded from the analysis in Table 4.5, the regression coefficients for the other independent variables remained virtually unchanged. This finding would suggest that opposition to the adopted child is not based on race alone. Whatever differences exist in family opposition associated with race, they are not sufficient to create variations in the child's initial adjustment.

The age of the adopted child at the time of the study also had an impact that was, to some degree, congruent with the position of those critical of transracial adoption. The older the child, the greater the child's maladjustment. The regression coefficients for the variable "age" showed some trend of association; the coefficient for age approached but did not achieve statistical significance ($p > .066$). This finding was in the direction predicted by the critics. The fact that the level of hostility has been adjusted for would seem to rule

TABLE 4.5
Regression of Child's Maladjustment on Selected Characteristics Among Families Adopting Whites or Blacks

Independent Variables	Regression Coefficient	Standardized Regression Coefficient
Constant	1.609	
Black adopted child (white adopted child excluded)	.066	.018
Age	.079	.148
Age at adoption	.210*	.333*
Family opposition	.229*	.211*
R^2 .209		
N 153		

*p > .05.

Age at adoption = adopted child's age at time of adoption (0 = 1-11 months; 1 = 12-23 months; 2 = 24-35 months; etc.).

Age = adopted child's age at time of study (0 = 1-11 months; 1 = 12-23 months; 2 = 24-35 months; etc.).

Family opposition = index of extended family opposition to adoption (3 = least opposition; 12 = most opposition).

Black adopted child = U.S.-born black child.

White adopted child = U.S.-born white child.

out the claim that maladjustment increases because the child is the target of increasing age-linked hostility. The maladjustment linked to being older may result from the simple increase in the child's developmental capacities or, as has also been suggested, from problems of racial identity unrelated to overt hostility.

An analysis of white, American-born adopted children and children born in Colombia was conducted, employing the set of independent variables used in Table 4.5. In this analysis the variable "age" also had a modest positive impact on maladjustment. It should be noted that Colombian children are not the targets of racism, either direct or subtle, in anything like the proportions encountered by black Americans. Thus, it would seem likely that the impact of increasing age has more to do with the child's development than with transracial adoption.

Clearly, the most consequential variable in the present analysis is the child's age at adoption. The regression coefficients for "age at adoption" are moderate in strength and statistically significant. This finding is consistent with the claims of those who argue that it is the child's preadoptive environment that is most crucial in his or her adjustment.

The standardized regression coefficient for "age at adoption" is larger than those for any of the other variables in the equation. Central to this analysis is the fact that it is larger than the standardized regression coefficient for "family opposition." The regression of the variables in Table 4.5 indicates that the age at adoption accounts for more of the variance explained in the index of child maladjustment than any of the other variables considered here. Of the 20.9 percent of the variance explained by the four variables, "age at adoption" accounts for 15.1 percent.

Similarly, when the intercorrelated ($r = .51$) variables "age" and "age at adoption" are excluded from the regression equation in Table 4.5, the entire equation loses significance. If the equation including only "family opposition" and "black adopted child" had achieved statistical significance, it would have accounted for 3.5 percent of the variance. Thus, it should be abundantly clear that the most decisive element influencing children's maladjustment scores is age at adoption.

The data presented above have potentially dramatic policy implications. They suggest that the deleterious consequences of delayed placement are far more serious than those of transracial adoption. The findings imply that when a choice must be made between transracial placement and continued foster or institutional care, transracial placement is clearly the option more conducive to the welfare of the child. The conventional wisdom of social work, that the earliest permanent placement is most desirable, is amply supported by these results.

PATTERNS OF INTEGRATED LIVING AND
TRANSRACIAL ADOPTIVE ADJUSTMENTS

Some researchers of transracial adoption suggest that if it is to succeed from the black child's standpoint, it is important that adoptive parents live in integrated communities. They contend that in order for the child to have a healthy and positive sense of self — in order to adjust well psychologically — there is need to have close access to blacks and to the black community.

Joyce Ladner takes such a position, based upon her own and others' transracial adoption research:

If white parents are permitted to adopt black children . . . they should certainly have a lifestyle that will permit their family to have sustained contacts with other blacks on an equal basis. . . . These parents must also live in integrated neighborhoods and be willing to send their black child to an integrated school, preferably where there are a large number of blacks. This will prevent the child from being the lone black, where special attention is drawn to him or her. The parents should also become involved in institutions and organizations (churches, neighborhood associations, etc.) in which there are other black members.

White parents who adopt black youngsters must also be willing and able to identify not only with their black children but also with blacks generally. They cannot be permitted to isolate their child and view him or her as "different" from other blacks, but rather they must perceive their child to be an extension of other blacks.

To adopt a black child means that these parents have forfeited their rights to be regarded as a "white" family. They cannot try to continue to fit the role of the idealized white middle-class nuclear family who happen to have a black adopted child. Therefore, they will never be able to successfully retreat into their previously protected all-white enclaves without risking psychological harm to their child, to their biological children and to themselves. . . .

It is important that white parents expose their black children to a variety of role models in all walks of life. It is necessary for these black youngsters to see black "success" models, as well as people functioning in ordinary roles. Children should be exposed to and interact with blacks — adults and children — instead of being aware of their existence vicariously, through children's story books on black heros, eating "soul food," and . . . other indirect ways. (Ladner 1977, pp. 245-246, 254-255)

Although Ladner presented no systematic empirical data on the psychologically healthful benefits of integrated living for transracial adoptees, her views on this subject are very explicit.

Ruth McRoy maintains a similar position. Although she, too, presents no specific quantitative data, it is her impression from evaluating her research results that integrated living patterns are essential to the psychological well-being of the black transracial adoptee.

> This study suggests that transracial adoptions require special efforts on the part of adoptive parents and children. Parents ideally should be able to realistically perceive the child's racial identity as being different from their own and be willing to make changes which are conducive to the child's development of a positive racial identity. Black children who have an opportunity to interact with black role models and have relationships with black peers tend to be more accepting of their racial heritage than those who are relatively isolated from other members of their racial groups.
>
> Therefore, although most white families applying to adopt a black child would be able to provide a loving home for a child, only certain families will be able to fulfill the child's needs to feel positive about his racial group identity. Agencies should exercise a great deal of care in the selection of transracial adoptive families, and must be willing to adapt their case study procedure to include an investigation of not only the prospective family but of the total milieu in which the child will be socialized. A commitment, as well as a practice and policy emphasis on the importance of racial identity, is necessary. First preference should be given to families who are able to demonstrate their abilities to understand racial dynamics through a history of social relations with blacks in the community, school, church and other institutional settings of which their family is a part. Families should reside in mixed or black areas, children should be attending racially integrated schools, and families should have associations with both blacks and whites. Thus, interracial living must have already been firmly established as a way of life for all members of the family long before they decide to adopt. A black child adopted by such a family can more easily blend into the neighborhood and can feel more comfortable in acknowledging his or her black heritage than if living in an all white community.
>
> Second priority should be given to families who are willing to move to [a] racially integrated school and develop social relationships with blacks. Agencies should require that workers do a complete assessment

of the neighborhood and community in which the family resides and
. . . talk with the family's black friends in order to better ascertain
whether or not black role models would be provided for the child.
(McRoy 1981, pp. 306-308)

Earlier studies of transracial adoption have marshaled limited
evidence on the psychological benefits of integrated living patterns.
Grow and Shapiro (1974) found that integrated residence was
unrelated to the child's psychological adjustment. They did discover,
however, that parents who lived in integrated neighborhoods
expressed greater satisfaction with their adoptions than those living
in all-white communities. McRoy (1981) found no significant associations between the level of community or school integration and
black children's self-esteem scores. Although she noted that the
black children adopted by white parents often lived in predominantly white communities — where black children could be subjected
to racial harassment — such instances were relatively rare. It is
important to note here that Professor McRoy's data do not seem to
confirm her arguments about the importance of racial integration
for the self-esteem of transracially adopted black children.

Some studies among nonadopted black children have found that
those raised in racially segregated communities have less self-esteem
than those growing up in integrated communities. Rosenberg and
Simmons (1971) found, for example, that black children who
attended racially segregated schools where they were in the minority
tended to have lower self-esteem scores than black children from
racially integrated schools. Such patterns, however, have not been
consistently demonstrated. A review of 25 studies of school integration and black self-esteem found no consistent pattern (St. John
1975). The reviewer found nine studies showing negative relations
between desegregation and black self-esteem; four showed positive
relations; the other studies showed no or mixed relations.

Our own data showed the following patterns: transracial adoptive parents, for the most part, maintained close contact and association with the black community. Sixty-eight percent indicated
that they lived in places where blacks were found in substantial
numbers or were the majority group in the community. Thirty-nine
percent reported having a significant number of close friends who
were black. Two-thirds indicated that blacks were represented in
substantial numbers at their children's schools; 48 percent indicated

that their children had large numbers of blacks among their close friends.

When we cross-tabulated each of these four integration variables with the tendency to have a poorly or well adjusted child, we found no association. Parents who lived in integrated neighborhoods, whose children attended racially mixed schools, who had many black friends, and whose children were said to have many friend-ships with blacks were no more likely to have well-adjusted children than their racially segregated and isolated counterparts.

Integrated life-styles, however, did seem to influence a number of other important dimensions of children's adjustments that we investigated. We found an association between integrated residence patterns and the tendency to have an adopted black child who was proud of being black, more deeply interested in his or her Afro-American heritage, and less ashamed of that heritage. Integrated life-styles were also linked with the pattern of black or biracial identification. We divided our respondents into two groups: children who identified with being black or biracial, and those who identified only with being white. Children residing in integrated communities were more likely to identify themselves as black or biracial. Only 9 percent of the transracially adopted children identified exclusively with the Afro-American community. Fifty-four percent aligned themselves with both white and Afro-American communities. On the other hand, 30 percent identified only with their white adoptive parents; the remaining 7 percent were unsure of their identities.

Table 4.6 documents the trends among the four forms of com-munity integration and the child's tendency to be proud of and interested in his or her racial group, the child's sense of shame at belonging to that group, the child's racial identification, and whether the child feels any discomfort about his or her appearance.

Table 4.6 clearly demonstrates an affinity between the pattern of residential integration and the tendency to have a black trans-racial adoptee who is both interested in and proud of his or her racial group. Integrated residence is also positively linked with black identification. Community integration seems to be slightly less closely associated with a sense of being ashamed of one's mem-bership group. There does not appear to be any consistent asso-ciation between integration and the tendency to have a child who feels uncomfortable about his or her appearance.

TABLE 4.6
Community Integration, Race Pride, and Identification
(percent)

	Living in Integrated Community		Parents Have Bk. Friends		Going to Integrated School		Child Having Many Black Pals	
	Yes	No	Yes	No	Yes	No	Yes	No
Expresses race pride sometimes or often	75	54	88	56	77	53	85	52
Very interested in race group	79	65	81	69	75	73	90	59
Is never ashamed of birth group	74	50	80	58	69	60	68	64
Identifies with being black or biracial	75	50	75	63	75	50	85	50
Never feels discomfort about appearance	33	29	29	33	41	13	24	39

Among all the variables that we are examining, only one turned out to have a significant impact upon children's adjustments: discomfort about appearance. We found that 60 percent of those transracially adopted blacks said to be well adjusted never experienced any discomfort about their appearance, compared with only 22 percent among those said to be poorly adjusted.

These results suggest that the sense of race pride, interest, and identification, and the absence of a sense of shame, among black transracial adoptees are all linked to the experience of integrated living. These factors seem to comprise a separate and important area of the transracial adopted child's adaptation. When adoptive parents live in integrated environments and carry out their social lives at least partly within the black community, this seems to have decisive results in promoting a positive sense of identification and pride among their black adopted children. Yet, this dimension appears to be distinct from and unrelated to the child's overall adjustment as it is conceived by the child's adoptive parents. One of the more interesting possibilities that these findings open up is that the adjustment of transracially adopted children may be unrelated to their racial identification or their interest in the black community.

THE IMPACT OF PARENTS' EFFORTS TO INSTILL A SENSE OF RACE PRIDE AND IDENTIFICATION AMONG ADOPTEES

As earlier studies (Grow and Shapiro 1974; Ladner 1977; McRoy 1981) have suggested, the attitude of white adoptive parents toward black culture can be critical in their child's development of a sense of race pride, race interest, and racial self-identification. As we've noted above, when parents live in integrated neighborhoods and they have friendships in the black community, there is an identifiable impact on the development of an Afro-American consciousness within the child. It also reduces the likelihood that the child will be ashamed of being black.

Yet, it remains to be demonstrated empirically whether parents' conscious efforts to cultivate these attitudes in their children — through didactic actions — produce the intended results. We investigated this matter to see if such actions were in any way linked with the development of the child's racial pride and consciousness, and overall adoptive adjustment. In 1981 we asked parents if they had recently read any materials dealing with their adopted child's birth group, and if they encouraged their children to read about their Afro-American heritage. We also wanted to know whether parents talked to their adopted children about being black. Further, parents were asked how frequently they went to museums or attended special cultural events that dealt with Afro-American life and culture.

The results did not indicate statistical significance in every instance, but they did show a consistent pattern. Where parents emphasized the child's cultural connections, there was an associated positive racial identification. Among the parents who occasionally or often read materials dealing with Afro-American culture, 73 percent of their children identified themselves as black, compared with 38 percent of the parents who rarely, if ever, read about their child's group. Those parents who occasionally or often encouraged their child to read about blacks were more likely to have children who positively identified with being black; 68 percent had children who identified as black or biracial, compared with 50 percent among those who rarely encouraged such reading among their children. Of the parents who often or occasionally talked with their child about being black, 75 percent of the children identified themselves as black, compared with 33 percent among the parents who rarely had such discussions with their child. Those parents who fostered their children's links with Afro-American culture by going to museums and cultural events had children who more often identified themselves as being black: 74 percent of the children identified themselves as black or biracial, compared with 59 percent among those who never engaged in such activities.

The pattern was unmistakable. Much the same trends were found when we examined each of these four variables' associations with the child's sense of racial pride, racial interest, and the reduced likelihood that the child would feel ashamed of being black. Yet, when we investigated the impact of each of these four variables on children's adoptive adjustments, we found no association between any of these behaviors and how well children were felt to be adjusted.

It is important to raise the question of whether the impact of these deliberate attempts to foster a sense of connection to the black community is independent of the child's social contact with the black community. What impact does taking a racially isolated black adopted child to an exhibition of black folk art have — if it can be said to have any independent impact in and of itself? Can it have a meaningful influence in the absence of continued interaction with other black people? Since we know that activities such as talking to a transracially adopted black child about Afro-American history and culture are closely related to living in integrated settings, it is important to see if the impact of these deliberate forms of socialization have an independent influence. If they do, then such activities may be especially relevant for the black child who is racially isolated. In order to examine the impact of these two sets of variables — racial integration and deliberate socialization — a regression analysis was completed.

To facilitate the multiple regression, a scale of deliberate socialization was constructed. Each family received a score of one to four points for each of the four deliberate socialization activities

— talking to the child about his or her Afro-American background, reading to him or her about Afro-American culture, taking her or him to Afro-American cultural events, and making explicit efforts to gain information about black culture. A family received a score of 4 if it engaged in the activity often, 3 if it engaged in the activity occasionally, 2 for once or twice, and a score of 1 if the family never participated in that activity. Scores for each of the four items were then added. A family's score could range from 16 (extensive deliberate socialization) to 4 (no efforts at deliberate socialization).

A similar additive scale was constructed for racial integration. Four measures of racial integration were included: the presence of blacks in the community, the number of black friends that the parents had, the presence of black children in the neighborhood schools, and the number of black friends the child had. A family received a score of 4 if blacks were the largest group in the community or the child's school, or the preponderant group among the parents' or child's friends. A score of 3 was given if blacks were not the largest group, but a substantial minority. A score of 2 was given if there were only a few blacks present, and if no blacks were present, a score of 1 was given. The scores ranged from 16 (living in a predominantly black community and social circle) to 4 (living in a community and social circle where no blacks were present).

Our measures of racial pride and racial interest were combined to form a third additive scale: an index of racial pride and interest. A factor analysis of the four measures of racial pride, racial interest, shame about racial background, and discomfort about appearance indicated that questions on racial pride and racial interest represented a single factor. If children expressed pride in their racial background often, they received a score of 4. If pride was expressed sometimes, a score of 3 was given. When pride had been expressed only once or twice, a score of 2 was given. If pride was never expressed, a score of 1 was appropriate. Expressions of racial interest were scored similarly. The scale of racial pride and interest ranged from a maximum of 8 (frequent expressions of pride and interest in being black) to 2 (no expressions of pride or interest).

The regression equation that examined the impact of both racial integration and deliberate socialization indicated that both of these activities had a significant independent influence on the child's pride and interest in his or her racial background. Although we expected that the impact of racial integration would be significantly greater than that of deliberate socialization, our results indicated otherwise.

When we ran the regression equation without the index of deliberate socialization, the equation failed to achieve statistical significance. In and of itself, our integrated living scale did not determine a greater amount of variation in the responses of racial pride and interest than would be expected by chance occurrence. Yet, when the index of deliberate socialization was included in the equation, a statistically significant result was obtained. Together, these variables offered greater-than-chance predictive power to account for some of the variations in racial pride and interest.

The influence of such deliberate socialization techniques as reading to the child about Afro-American culture and museum visits was greater in generating racial pride and an interest in the black community than was racial integration. The beta weight for the scale of deliberate socialization was .474, while the beta weight for the scale of racial integration was .305. Together these two scales explained 35 percent of the variance in the scale of racial pride and interest. Thus, our data suggest that when parents give emphasis and reinforcement to the idea of their child's membership in the black community, they are likely to produce children who have more pride in being blacks and are more interested in their black heritage.

Judy Gold, the mother of an 11-year-old black transracial adoptee, told us:

Long Island is not a very integrated place and there aren't very many blacks in [our community]. About the only black people that Greg sees are two of the other women workers in my unit at [a social service agency] and some of the kids whose parents belong to [an adoptive parents' group]. Unfortunately we don't get to see these kids very often. We're not entirely happy about this, but it's not easy for us to change the situation.

Howie and I do try to make a conscious effort to talk to Greg about being black — not so much in general terms, but as it affects him in little ways from day to day. My dad gave him a little chemistry set on his last visit and told Greg that he would be the next George Washington Carver — Dad's not very subtle. So Greg and I had a little talk about who George Washington Carver was — and then another discussion about why Dad mentioned Carver and not someone who was white. I think it's things like this that keep Greg on an even keel about himself. . . .

Since we're always running into Manhattan to go to museums and art galleries, it's not hard to find exhibitions that have black or African themes — and since we're always taking the children to these things anyhow, it's not difficult to get Greg to go. What this does for his sense of being black — I don't know. I sometimes think it's a lot less useful than talking to Greg — or even his poring through a book about Martin Luther King. . . .

What it all seems to convey to him is that we all think it's a good thing to be black, that black people do things that are important, and that he has every reason to be proud and nothing to be ashamed of. It all seems to be working out well — as far as we can tell.

Mrs. Gold's comments seem to converge with our data. Her sense that talking and reading are more important than museum visits was borne out by our analysis. A factor analysis suggested that most of the variation in our scale of deliberate socialization was accounted for by the questions on talking to one's children about their Afro-American heritage and their reading patterns.

Our findings here have interesting implications for the transracial placement of black children — especially in light of the arguments made by Ladner (1977) and McRoy (1981) about the importance of integrated living. The data suggest that transracial adoptive parents not living in integrated communities may be capable of fostering the development of a sense of racial pride and interest in their adopted black children. They imply that the attitudes of adoptive parents are crucial to their black children's racial indentification.

THE IMPORTANCE OF SKIN COLOR FOR RACIAL PRIDE, IDENTIFICATION, AND ADJUSTMENT

Earlier studies of transracial adoption have suggested that skin color is an important element in influencing the outcomes of transracial adoptions. Grow and Shapiro (1974) found in their study that children who were judged by their interviewers to be of darker skin color were more likely to feel uncomfortable about their appearance. Such children were also reported to have been adopted at older ages and to have been more frequent targets of cruelty. Grow and Shapiro also found that the most successful transracial black/white placements were those in which the child's color was obviously black. They speculated on the reasons for this association between darker skin color and successful adjustment. They contend that such differences make it easier for parents to develop the ego strength to deal with the challenges of child rearing, and to recognize and accept the differences inherent in transracial adoption. Less obvious physical differences foster denial. The patterns they observed, while discernible, were by no means overwhelming.

In their study of nonadopted children, Rosenberg and Simmons (1971) found that their black respondents tended to associate attractiveness with lighter skin color. But there was little relationship between the subjects' judgment, their own skin color, and their self-esteem.

Our data indicated that nearly two-thirds of our black transracial adoptees were obviously black in appearance. A comparison of lighter and darker children suggested that the obviously darker children were more likely to be poorly adjusted. While 36 percent of black transracial adoptees with fair complexions were described as free of adjustment problems, only 16 percent were described similarly among more obviously black adoptees. None of the fair-complexioned children had received professional care for problem behavior, compared with 25 percent among darker transracial adoptees; more than twice as many − 57 percent compared with 23 percent − of the more recognizably black transracial adoptees showed higher scores on the Conners hyperactivity scale. These results contradicted those of Grow and Shapiro, but there seems to be no easily available explanation of why this should be so. Our own sample of transracially adopting families is quite similar in most of its characteristics to Grow and Shapiro's sample (Silverman 1980).

Otherwise, appearance seemed to have no other discernible impact on adoptive adjustments. Darker children were no more likely to identify with being black; they were no more likely to feel proud of or interested in their race group membership; they were no more likely to feel discomfort or shame about their appearance.

We investigated the likelihood that age or age at adoption might be a confounding variable in producing these associations. The many studies of transracial adoption suggest that social workers apparently feel reluctant to place darker black children with white families; they are inclined to do so only as a last resort, when no other apparently better options may be available. This generally means that darker black adoptees are more likely to be placed in white homes when they are older. Our cross-tabulation results also showed that darker black adoptees were somewhat older than their lighter counterparts and were significantly more likely to have been adopted at later ages. Two-thirds of the darker transracial adoptees were over two years of age when they were adopted, compared with 43 percent among those whose skin color was lighter. It is altogether possible that the poorer adjustments of darker transracial adoptees could be attributable to their older ages or their placements at later ages — factors that we have found to be negatively associated with adjustment. Our question, then, is whether it was the child's age or age at placement — or the response to darker color — that was producing this association with poor adjustment.

We conducted a regression analysis with our index of maladjustment as a dependent variable and with skin color, age, age at adoption, and our index of family opposition as independent variables. The results of this regression approached, but failed to achieve, statistical significance. The negligible beta weight for "skin color" (.036) and the much more substantial ones for age (.218) and family opposition (.268) suggest that these variables do account for the influence of skin color on the adjustment of transracially adopted children. It does not appear from our data that skin color is likely to be of major importance in accounting for the adjustment of transracially adopted black children. Whatever influence skin color appears to have on adjustment outcomes seems to be a by-product of the older ages at which black children with darker coloring become available for transracial adoptions.

BLACK TRANSRACIAL ADOPTEES AND THE SEARCH

Previous studies have had little to say about the likelihood that black transracial adoptees would or would not be inclined to pursue the search for birth kin. It has been suggested by the National Association of Black Social Workers that black transracially adopted children will find the search for birth kin more than usually traumatic:

> Many adoptees are trying to re-establish their roots by searching for their biological parents. Black children raised by white families must suffer an even greater identity crisis as they have been cut off not only from their biological parents but from a whole race and culture that was their heritage. (Neal 1979)

We investigated this potentially important area with our respondents, and attempted to ascertain whether black transracial adoptees were any more or less likely to embark upon the search for genealogical kin than white adoptees. The evidence suggested that black transracial adoptees were seen as more eager to seek their birth kin. They also were more likely to ask to see their adoption records and to ask more frequent questions about their genealogical origins. Among the parents of black transracial adoptees, 39 percent anticipated that their child probably or definitely would search for birth relatives, compared with 21 percent among the parents of white adoptees. Sixty-three percent of the parents of adopted Afro-Americans had children who asked for information about their genealogical origins sometimes or often, compared with 48 percent among those with white adoptees. Among black adoptees 26 percent had asked to see their adoptions records, compared with only 10 percent among white adoptees.

The parents of black adoptees also seemed to be far more encouraging and supportive of their children's searching efforts. Seventy-eight percent of fathers had offered their black transracial adoptees all the information they had about the child's background, compared with 61 percent among the fathers of white U.S.-born adoptees. Only 8 percent of black transracial adoptive fathers had limited the genealogical information they had given their children, compared with 27 percent among the fathers of white adoptees. Why is there such a tendency to withhold genealogical information among the parents of white U.S.-born adoptees? And why are the parents of transracially adopted black children willing to share this knowledge? We think this pattern has a great deal to do with the way parents view their adoptive relationships as a whole. This, in turn, is influenced in important ways by the role of infertility in the decision to adopt. As we mentioned in Chapter 3, preferential adoptive parents — those most inclined to adopt transracially — are more likely to approve of and cooperate with the search efforts of their adopted children. In Chapter 8 we will discuss the reasons for these patterns in more detail.

TRANSRACIAL ADJUSTMENTS SIX YEARS LATER

At the time of our follow-up survey we were interested in evaluating the adjustments of our black transracial adoptees after they had been in their adoptive placements for at least six years. We wanted to see how adjustments evolved over this time period and how they compared with those of white adoptees.

In 1981, 30 percent of our Afro-American adoptees were described by their parents as having problem-free adjustments; 47 percent were described as mostly well-adjusted with some problems. The remaining 23 percent were judged to have frequent adjustment problems. For whites the comparable figures were 46 percent extremely well-adjusted, 33 percent somewhat well-adjusted, and 22 percent with frequent adjustment problems. While the black transracial adoptees were less likely to be rated as well-adjusted as their white counterparts, the differences fell short of statistical significance. Parents were asked if they had ever wanted to get − or had actually received − the help of professionals with their children's behavioral problems. Approximately similar proportions of both groups − about 20 percent of each subsample − reported wanting such aid for their child's behavior. Substantially similar percentages of transracial and inracial adoptees were reported as having difficulties in getting along with their peers, approximately a quarter of both groups indicating such problems occasionally or more often.

It is interesting to compare these evaluations with the ones given by both sets of parents in 1975. At that time comparatively fewer parents indicated that children were having serious adjustment problems. Less than 5 percent indicated that children were having frequent adjustment problems; by 1981 close to 25 percent were experiencing such difficulties. These trends testify to the pattern mentioned earlier of the increasingly difficult adjustments of older children.

Since all of the adoptees were of school age, we thought it advisable to evaluate their school adjustments. None of the Afro-American adoptees were judged to be doing below-average school work; 57 percent were described as average students, and 43 percent were considered to be doing above-average work. These evaluations showed close comparability with the white adoptees, 6 percent of whom were described as doing below-average school work, 46 percent as doing average work, and 48 percent as doing exceptionally well.

Black adoptees seemed to trail behind the whites in their scholastic motivations; here the differences approached, but did not attain, statistical significance. While 52 percent of the white adoptees were judged as possessing exceptional interest in school, for blacks the comparable figure was 40 percent. Thus, the adoptive adjustments of our black transracial adoptees did not demonstrate them to be significantly more maladjusted when they were compared with white adoptees. Although the black adoptees showed somewhat greater problems on a few of our adjustment indicators, by and large the differences were insubstantial.

Our data strongly suggest that six years after our initial survey there was no consistent pattern of differences in adjustment between inracially adopted white children and transracially adopted black children. This is confirmed by a regression of our 1981 maladjustment index on the variables of child's age, child's age at adoption, the opposition of family members to the adoption in 1981, and the race of the child. Both white and Afro-American children were included in this regression. The race of the child had no meaningful impact on adjustment. This regression is identical to that calculated for children's adjustments in 1975. Only the data for the family's opposition in 1981 and the child's maladjustment score had changed. This finding would seem to imply that six years — or more — of transracial placement had not led to serious problems for black children. The implications of this pattern diverge from the expectations of some critics of transracial adoption. They contend that as black transracial adoptees grow older, they are likely to encounter increasing racial antagonism — and a growing sense of their racial isolation — that likely will impair their adaptations. Our data do not support such arguments.

The last part of this investigation consisted of a multiple-regression analysis of our 1981 index of children's maladjustment. We were interested in establishing which, of all the variables we have been analyzing in this chapter, contributed most significantly to explaining the variations of reported child adjustments. For our dependent variable, respondents were asked the same set of questions in 1981 that they had been asked in 1975 about their children's growth, and emotional adjustment problems and overall adjustments. As independent variables we employed almost all of the variables that have been mentioned in this chapter: the child's age, age at placement, family opposition (1981), a scale of integrated living, a scale of deliberate socialization to black culture, a scale of racial pride and interest, child's skin color, and the child's adjustment in 1975.

To a great degree the findings concurred with many of results that have already been discussed. A number of factors that have been hypothesized as potentially important elements affecting adjustment outcomes were not found to have any significant influence. Whether families lived in integrated environments, whether parents took actions to encourage identification within the black community, whether children felt great pride and interest in being black, variations in black children's skin coloration – none of these variables had any measurable impact on the likelihood that children would experience adjustment difficulties.

Two variables were found to have a significant impact in determining adjustment outcomes: the child's maladjustment score in 1975 and the opposition of extended family members to the adoption in 1981. The more significant of the two, clearly, was the child's prior level of maladjustment. This produced a beta weight of .507, accounting for 19 percent of the variations in adjustment scores. Family opposition accounted for a modestly significant amount of the variance, with a beta weight of .273, explaining 7 percent of the differences in the range between optimal and poor adjustments.

These findings suggest that the most important factor affecting black transracially adopted children's adjustments in 1981 – after they've been in their adoptive families for at least six years – is the level of their previous adaptation. Earlier in this analysis it was mentioned that the child's initial adaptation was significantly affected by age at placement. As the preadoptive experiences of the child helped shape his or her initial adaptation, it apparently continues to have power over the longer term. Those children having preplacement histories of uncertainty and frequent change – those who had been through the mill of longer exposure to foster and institutional care – were likely to have been more poorly adjusted during the earlier years of their adoptive placements. Adjustment difficulties that may have arisen from those early years continue to affect the present. We may also speculate that, under these conditions, the child begins to develop a reputation in the adoptive family as a problem child. That reputation or role may shape parental expectations that outlive the child's disruptive behavior, thus casting a die for the future.

Our finding that extended family opposition has a statistically significant association with poorer later adoptive adjustments contains several implications. It suggests that some of the critical contentions about transracial adoption's damaging consequences on black adoptees could be justified. Our evidence confirms the assertion that as the child grows older and experiences continuing antagonism from the extended kin group, there is an association with poorer adjustment. Yet, it remains to be documented — by more than isolated cases — that black transracial adoptees are generally likely to experience psychological harm from this experience. Our evidence did not show this sample of black transracial adoptees to be significantly different or inferior in their adjustments than a group of inracially adopted white children, despite their reduced extended family support.

It seems altogether plausible that as the black transracial adoptees grow older, they may be subject to increasing exclusionary treatment and to psychologically damaging consequences. Future research will find it useful to explore these issues in samples of black transracial adoptees among adolescent and postadolescent populations.

SUMMARY AND IMPLICATIONS FOR
SOCIAL WORK PRACTICE AND POLICY

The practice of transracial adoption continues to evoke much controversy. Its detractors have succeeded in substantially reducing the numbers of black children being placed with white parents. While more black children are finding homes in the black community than ever before, there remain substantial numbers of black and other minority children who are not so fortunate. In our estimation, for these children transracial adoption continues to be a viable policy option.

Critics of transracial adoption point to a variety of damaging social and psychological consequences that are likely to result from a black transracial adoptee's growing up in a white home. Our research evidence suggests, however, that the adverse adjustment consequences owing to delayed placement are more serious than those associated with the rejection that black transracial adoptees are likely to encounter when growing up in a white family. The multiple-regression analysis of early adoptive adjustments showed the child's age at placement was more influential in determining variations in adjustment outcomes than the opposition or support their adoptive parents received from close relatives and friends.

As measured by our updated index of children's maladjustment, the adjustment of transracially adopted black children in 1981 — six years after our first survey — was largely a product of their adjustment in 1975. This adjustment, in turn, was most critically influenced by the preadoptive experiences of these children. Their experiences all too often included years of transiency and turmoil. Although the attitudes of the extended kin were also important influences on the children's adjustments in 1981, these feelings were secondary to what happened to the child before he or she was finally placed.

After transracial adoptees had been in their adoptive placements for a minimum of six years, we found no significant differences in the range of adjustments between inracially adopted white children and black children adopted by white parents. Such findings attest to the possibilities of raising black children in white homes without inflicting lasting injury or harm upon them. In fact, our data suggest that transracial adoption may be a significant means of promoting the well-being of black children without permanent homes.

Some analysts of transracial adoption have emphasized the need for immersion in the black community to assure the psychological health and well-being of the black transracial adoptee. Our research findings did not provide confirmation of this viewpoint insofar as it refers to the overall adjustments of black transracial adoptees. We did, however, find evidence that transracially adopting families living in integrated social environments were likely to foster the development of racial pride, interest, and identification among their black transracial adoptees. We also found that where parents are resolved to socialize their black transracial adoptee as a member of the black community and where they engage in concrete activities to bring this about, they are likely to be even more successful at fostering black identification among their black adoptees than by immersion in the black community alone. The results further suggested that parents' commitment to familiarize their black children with Afro-American culture was a more important determinant than their pattern of integrated living for fostering a sense of racial pride and interest.

Our findings raise questions for future research on the linkages among the sentiments of racial pride, interest, and identification, on the one hand, and adoptive adjustments, on the other. It seems obviously desirable — among black transracial adoptees — to foster the development of a sense of racial pride and identification. Such attributes would seem to be valuable for the development of self-esteem and optimal psychological functioning. Yet, we were unable to find any connection between the possession of black self-identification and a variety of indicators suggesting optimal social and psychological adaptation.

Black transracial adoptees possessing black self-identifications were no less likely than others to have adjustment problems, to show evidence of hyperactivity, to receive professional care for problem behavior, to have problems in getting along with siblings or peers, to be doing well academically, or to be motivated to perform scholastically. It is entirely possible that these represent independent dimensions of social and psychological life. It may be that a transracial adoptee can be well-adjusted and identified with the black community, white society, or both. Obviously it remains for future research to further unravel the interconnections between adjustment, feelings of race pride, and race identification among black transracial adoptees.

In recommending transracial adoption as a policy option, it is important to recognize that there is some receptivity to the idea within the black community. A study of black child care professionals conducted by Elizabeth Herzog, Cecilia Sudia, and Jane Harwood (1971) indicated that black social workers were by no means uniformly opposed to transracial adoption. Herzog found that the attitudes of black social workers tended to vary with their contact with the practice. Workers who had substantial contact with transracial adoption generally favored it. Black professionals who had no contact were much more critical.

Research on community rather than professional attitudes toward transracial adoption, conducted in a midwestern black community by Alicia Howard, David Royse, and John Skerl (1977), found that nearly 57 percent of the sample were generally receptive to the idea of transracial adoption, while only 7 percent of those questioned were totally opposed. Even more significant was the feeling expressed by 81 percent of the respondents that a black child would be better off in a white adoptive home than in foster care or an institution. Both of these studies suggest that there is a measure, perhaps a considerable measure, of support for transracial placement within the black community.

In conclusion, our findings support the position that transracial adoption remains a viable option for the placement of black children. If policy makers and social workers fail to consider it as a possibility for homeless nonwhite children, then they are likely to condemn those who cannot be placed in black homes to significant and lasting psychological harm.

5

The Adoption of Colombian-Born Children By U.S. Families

Fred and Phoebe Goodman spent more than two years visiting adoption agencies, talking to lawyers, following up elusive rumors in their attempt to create a family by adoption. Married for more than eight years, the Goodmans' attempts to conceive a child ended in failure and miscarriage. Frustrated by several years of temperature charts, doctors, adoption agencies, and lawyers, they turned at last to a Colombian-based adoption agency known for its large number of adoptive placements with North American families.

Within six months their application had been processed and accepted. A month later they arrived in Bogotá to adopt twin seven-month-old girls. In 1982 the Goodmans and their twin daughters, Amy and Jennifer, now seven, lead unremarkable lives in a Long Island suburb of New York City.

Phoebe Goodman commented:

We had almost given up . . . I can't tell you what it was like. Fred and I had been to every agency in driving distance of [their home community], talked to everyone who might know anything about an available child, gone to at least one meeting of every adoptive parent group on Long Island. Finally we heard about a couple who had adopted a child in Colombia and then we were on our way. . . .

There were a lot of false starts at first, but once the paperwork got moving, we had the feeling it would all turn out . . . and it did. In May we sent our first notarized documents down and in January [the agency] told us to fly to Bogotá. And we've been flying — so to speak — ever since!

It hasn't always been the dream we imagined it to be, but our home has been so much richer since the twins came into our lives. We've had no unusual problems. Only the girls' health at first. They were so tiny and weak. During those first few years we worried a lot about their frequent illnesses. But then don't most parents worry a lot about their babies' health? But now, as the children have grown older, we worry less about them. We are a bit concerned about Amy, though; she doesn't seem to be doing nearly as well in school as we know she is capable of. That still concerns us a great deal.

Parents like the Goodmans are increasingly common among the families that are created every year through adoption. Of all foreign adoptions from countries in North and South America, adoptions from Colombia now surpass those completed anywhere else by four to one. Since 1976 Colombia has become the second most common among all foreign sources for U.S. adoptive parents. There have been spectacular increases in the numbers of adoptions of Colombian children by American parents since the mid-1960s. In 1969 fewer than 50 adoptions from Colombia took place. In 1980 — the last year for which data are available from the Department of Justice — 653 Colombian children were adopted by American parents (U.S. Immigration and Naturalization Service 1983).

Although there has been some discussion of this phenomenon in the news media, there has been little research documentation of this flow of children to the United States. Adoptions such as the Goodmans' raise a number of questions of broad interest to policy makers, adoptive parents, and social scientists. It is clear, for example, that many of the parents who adopt Colombian children first attempt to adopt in the United States. Why are they unable to do so? A very common impression is that these parents are willing to adopt only white infants: children who are generally unavailable for adoption here and now. Parents who adopt Colombian children, the argument runs, are unwilling to adopt the older, non-white, handicapped, or retarded child. Is this the case? Or are the parents who adopt Colombian children a potential resource for the thousands of waiting children in the United States?

Many descriptions of the children of Colombia and their biological parents stress their poverty-striken condition. Much of the population of cities like Bogotá consists of poor peasants. Like the peasants of many Third World countries, most Colombians are less than a generation removed from tilling the soil in the countryside, chronically underemployed, and inadequately nourished (López de Rodriguez and Rueda 1979). Parents who adopt Colombian children frequently mention the physical disabilities of their adopted children. Jean Nelson-Erichsen describes a recently adopted Colombian child as follows:

> I visited the B's a few days ago after their return from Colombia. Rita was (and is) a pretty child, with curly chestnut hair and an olive complexion. Symptoms of her second degree malnutrition were evident: pale skin, streaks of carrot color in her hair, bloated tummy and leg muscles so weak she could not run or climb stairs easily. (Nelson-Erichsen and Erichsen 1981, p. 44)

Younger children are often described as suffering from malnutrition and a variety of diseases. Are such conditions frequently found among the Colombian children adopted by American parents? Do such inadequacies have a lasting effect on the children as they grow older? What impact do such deprivations have on the adjustment of the children and the experiences of their adopting families?

Still another issue about adjustment is raised by the question of the transracial nature of many of these adoptions. Many, if not most, of the Colombian-born children have recognizable Indian or African ancestry. What response do family and friends have to the introduction of a child with a different racial background? How do these responses affect the adjustment of the child and the experiences of the parents?

Both adopting parents and adopted child have the choice to reinforce or ignore the child's links with another society and culture. Obviously, what parents choose to do will influence their children a great deal, but it is not clear that both will make the same choices. Although adopted Colombian children will grow up far from Bogotá and substantial Colombian populations, citizens of Hispanic descent make up the largest single minority in the United States. The relationship of adopted Colombian children to both American Hispanics and Colombia could be a significant issue for them and for their families. The growing interest among adoptees in their preadoptive pasts and biological kin is likely to raise this as an important question for these families.

In this chapter we will discuss the motives of this group of adoptive parents and their postplacement experiences with their children. We will also describe the characteristics of these adoptions and the adjustments of the children. To answer these questions, we will systematically compare the families who adopted Colombian children with other adoptive parents. We are especially interested in the contrasts between families adopting Colombian children and those adopting U.S.-born white children, Korean children, and Afro-American children. In 1975 our sample contained 46 families who adopted at least one Colombian-born child; they were compared with the 298 families that adopted one or more Korean child, the 96 families who adopted one or more white U.S.-born child, and the 58 families who adopted Afro-American children. In 1981, at the time of our follow-up survey, we were able to locate 19 of our parents of Colombian children, 65 of our families with white children, 161 who had adopted children born in Korea, and 47 who had adopted Afro-Americans.

CHARACTERISTICS OF PARENTS AND CHILDREN, AND THEIR EXPERIENCES IN COMPLETING THEIR ADOPTIONS

Fred and Phoebe Goodman, in their infertility, their history of futile attempts to adopt in the United States, and their relatively brief wait for a child, are typical of the families in our sample who adopted in Colombia. Seventy-six percent of the parents who adopted Colombian children cited their infertility as an important motive in their decision to adopt. This is very similar to the 78 percent of parents who adopted white American-born children, but considerably more than the 44 percent of those who adopted Korean-born children. By contrast, among the adopters of Afro-American children, only 23 percent cited infertility as a reason that led them to adopt. Interest in Colombia per se was critical in the decisions of only 14 percent of the parents adopting from Colombia. By contrast, interest in Korea was an important consideration for nearly 28 percent of the families adopting Korean children.

Sixty-seven percent of the parents who adopted from Colombia had made previous attempts to complete this adoption, somewhat more than the 58 percent of parents who adopted white American-born children and substantially more than the 38 percent of those who adopted Korean-born children. Our data, therefore, suggest that there is some accuracy to the notion that American parents are adopting in Colombia because of their inability to complete an adoption in the United States. This picture is reinforced by the finding that 87 percent of the parents who adopted Colombian-born children reportedly did so because there was no suitable American child available for adoption. These trends are comparable with the findings obtained in another study of adoption in Colombia by Americans (Resnick and Munoz de Rodriguez 1982).

One of the more remarkable features of the Colombian adoptions is the relatively brief period that agencies required to respond to applications. In nearly all of our cases — 88 percent — the application of the adopting family was approved in less than three months. In no case did the process require more than six months. In contrast, families adopting Korean children waited up to 29 months for approval. One family who adopted an American-born white child waited 24 months. Most of these families, however, did not wait that long. Forty-four percent of the families adopting from Korea and 61 percent of those adopting in the United States were approved within three months.

Families who adopted Colombian children were also less likely to endure prolonged periods of waiting once they were approved. Seventy-one percent of our families who adopted Colombian children brought their adopted child into their home within three months of being approved. Only 11 percent of the parents adopting Korean children and 32 percent of the parents adopting white American children experienced such rapid placements. Given the prior difficulties of most of our parents who adopted Colombian children, this must have been a very pleasant and satisfying experience.

Despite the relatively short period of time it took our adoptive families to bring their Colombian children home, these families were less pleased with the agencies with which they had worked. Eighty-five percent of the families adopting white American-born children and 83 percent of the families adopting Korean children found the agencies through which they adopted to be "very helpful." Only 59 percent of the families who adopted through Colombian agencies held this opinion. Forty percent of the families who adopted Colombian children found the agencies they worked with only "somewhat helpful" or "unhelpful." This relatively negative picture extended to the lawyers employed by American families in Colombia. Forty-seven percent of the families found their Colombian lawyers "very helpful," in contrast with 92 percent of parents of Korean children who regarded their Korean lawyers similarly.

Comments made by the American parents who adopted in Colombia suggest that their problems may have arisen in the necessity for them to work at long distances with agencies whose requirements were often imperfectly understood. Confusion and misunderstandings were also generated by the multiplicity of public and private agencies in the United States and Colombia that had some involvement in the adoption. The adoption of Colombian children by U.S. citizens is subject to the simultaneous supervision of private agencies in Colombia, the national courts of Colombia, the Colombian welfare department, the U.S. and Colombian immigration authorities, and the courts of the states in which the adopting parents live. No single body coordinates these adoptions; at this time there is no agency that provides information on all of the diverse requirements with which adoptive parents must comply. As one of our respondents said:

Adopting through [a Colombian adoption agency] was much more difficult than we had expected. We first learned about adopting in Colombia from [a local adoptive parent group president and adoption activitist]. . . . She was really our only source of information at first, and although most of what she told us was correct, there was a lot she didn't know. We also got a lot of misinformation from the Colombian consulate. They led us to believe that if everything went smoothly with the adoption agency, we could expect to take care of all the immigration things in three to four days. As it was, it took us nearly three weeks to take care of all the immigration matters. There were times when I thought we'd never get out of there with our child. If we weren't so lucky, we might still be there now, waiting to get our visa to bring [our child] home. I can't begin to tell you how confusing all the bureaucracy was — not only with the Colombian government, but also with American immigration. To this day I still can't even explain what we had to do to complete our adoption.

The people at the orphanage meant well. I suppose if it weren't for them, we wouldn't have [our child] now. But they should have known better . . . how to get our adoption processed. After all, we weren't the first Americans to adopt there. I don't know how many days we sat around in their lobby waiting for them, waiting to get our paperwork straight. They never gave us much information about [our child's] background and health either, only the vaguest answers whenever we asked them. . . . We ran ourselves ragged all over the city of Bogotá trying to get medical exams and forms filled out so that we could get our exit visa. In retrospect, I think the agency should have helped us more with this. After all, they had doctors coming in almost every day to care for the children.

Our lawyer was the pits. He was recommended to us by the adoption agency. He was, I was told, from one of the leading families of Bogotá, supposedly thoroughly familiar with all the foreign adoption requirements. Yet, you would have thought we were his first . . . American adoption. He was also handling several other cases of Americans while he handled ours. At least we had the satisfaction of knowing that he didn't single us out for mistreatment. All of us had the same problems with him.

There were five American couples like us — adopting Colombian children — that stayed at a pension that was recommended to us. Almost every evening one of us was sitting around waiting for [our lawyer] to come or call with information about some important document necessary for the adoption decree or for immigration. Half the time he never showed up. Whenever you called his office, you never could be sure if he got the messages. It was simply terrible; everything seemed so disorganized and so much in flux. You could never get a straight answer out of him about what needed to be done. We all felt like prisoners. None of us thought we'd ever get out of there. If it weren't for the man who ran our little guest house helping us out, I don't think any of us would have ever left the place.

We may wonder why the parents of adopted Korean children were so much more satisfied with the agencies and lawyers with whom they came in contact. After all, they too were dealing with a foreign country with language barriers and different cultural expectations. The answer may lie in the fact that most often parents adopting Korean children deal with an American-based agency that coordinates most aspects of their adoption and is familiar with the requirements. Also, Korean social services have been heavily influenced by American models. Korean social service professionals are frequently American-trained. Many Americans working in this field are closely acquainted with Korean social services and professionals. By contrast, in Colombia child welfare programs are not as heavily influenced by American practices. Links between Colombian and American social service workers are also not as close or as frequent.

Most adopted Colombian children were not newborn infants when they were placed in their adoptive families, but they were younger than most of the other adopted children in our sample. Sixty-eight percent of the Colombian children were adopted before they had reached the age of two. Forty percent of the white

American-born children were older than six when they were placed, as were 20 percent of the Korean-born children. But only 5 percent of the Colombian-born children had reached this age when placed. Again, our results were closely comparable with the findings of Resnick and Munoz de Rodriguez (1982).

Colombian-born children not only were younger than most other adopted children in our sample, but also were likely to be perceived as racially similar to their parents. Twenty-seven (59 percent) of the 46 Colombian children were designated as white; three were described as having "Indian" features; and the remainder were described as "Latin" or "Hispanic" when a racial designation was asked for. None of the children were described as wholly or partly black. When asked if they could have considered adopting a black child, a much older child, or a special-needs child (handicapped or retarded) when they adopted their Colombian-born child, most parents said that they could not have done so. Seventy-four percent of these parents could not have considered a retarded child, and 50 percent would have rejected a child eight years or older. In all of these instances the responses of the parents who adopted from Colombia were very similar to those of the parents who adopted white American-born children. By contrast, parents who had adopted Korean children were much more open to the adoption of older, black, and special-needs children.

The data presented up to this point would seem to suggest that parents who have adopted Colombian children are not potentially available to adopt hard-to-place children. Resnick and Munoz de Rodriguez suggest that the preferences of Americans who adopt Colombian children may lead to problems:

> . . . parents adopting Colombian children are white and are seeking children who have features similar to theirs. This may eventually bring about problems both in Colombia − leaving behind children "hard-to-place" because they do not have white features − and in the U.S. (Resnick and Munoz de Rodriguez 1982, p. 132)

The data in Table 5.1, however, suggest that the attitudes of these parents are not as inflexible as many suspect. Parents who were unwilling to adopt an older, nonwhite, or special-needs child at the time of their adoption of a Colombian child are more prepared to do so afterward.

As one father said to us:

> We were very frightened before Karen came to us. We were fearful of a lot of things at that time — of never having a child, of being too old to be good parents, that our families would not approve of our adoption, that everyone would know we adopted. Without really admitting it to ourselves, we were anxious not to adopt a child with black or Indian features. We wanted our kid to look like our kid. . . .
>
> We've put all that behind us now. We want to adopt again, and I know that we won't be as fearful as we were before. Adopting a black child, or a kid with a deformed leg — like a lot of those street children we saw in Bogotá — doesn't scare us now. When we first adopted, we were thinking entirely about what we needed — a child, a family. Now Joan and I see ourselves as having something important to offer, a home and a future to a child who might not have one.

At the time of their adoption only 7 percent of the adopting parents could have easily accepted an older child; if they were to adopt again, 33 percent could easily do so. Seventy-two percent of the parents who adopted Colombian children would not have considered adopting a handicapped child at the time of their adoption; but if they were to adopt again, 63 percent would reject handicapped children. Similar changes were noted in the responses to our questions about adopting black and Asian children.

Table 5.1 also suggests that the parents adopting Colombian children may well be representative of families who would be especially willing to adopt some of today's waiting children. They could be amenable to accepting some of the thousands of mixed-race Asian children, fathered by American servicemen in Vietnam and elsewhere, who now occupy positions of marginality and extreme deprivation in their homelands. At the time of their adoption of a Colombian child, 59 percent of these parents could have easily adopted an Asian child; subsequently some 70 percent of these parents felt that if they were to adopt again, they could easily accept an Asian child. These attitudes compare closely with the feelings of the families who adopted white children born in the United States, who also showed sharply rising acceptance of Asians subsequent to their adoptions. At the time of their adoptions only 32 percent of the parents who adopted white children said they could have easily accepted an Asian child. Later a noticeably greater number —

TABLE 5.1
Willingness to Adopt Hard-to-Place Children at the Time of the Adoption and Afterwards

(percent)

	Parents of Colombian Adoptees		Parents of White U.S. Adoptees		Parents of Korean Adoptees	
	Before	*After*	*Before*	*After*	*Before*	*After*
Willingness to adopt Asian children	59	70	32	46	98	95
Willingness to adopt blacks	26	37	29	32	61	64
Willingness to adopt older children	50	70	53	68	60	83
Willingness to adopt handicapped children	28	37	30	30	34	41

46 percent — could have easily accepted an Asian child. Yet, there are substantial differences between these groups; adopters of Colombian children show greater interest in adopting Asian children than adoptive parents of white children.

The above data show that most parents adopting Colombian children initially indicated considerable reluctance to adopt American-born children who are older or nonwhite, or have special needs. There is, however, a substantial minority who would be willing to adopt nonwhite or handicapped children, about one parent in four. If there is a serious concern about recruiting parents to adopt nonwhite Colombian children, they might well be recruited from the ranks of these parents.

The results also suggest that parents' attitudes are far from immutable. The more noticeable changes in increasing amenability to adopt various hard-to-place groups — compared with adoptive parents of white children — indicate that this group is an especially receptive one to meeting the needs of today's waiting children.

RESPONSES OF FAMILIES AND FRIENDS
TO COLOMBIAN ADOPTIONS

Another of the areas we investigated was how the immediate associates of our adoptive parents reacted to their adoptions of Colombian-born children. We wondered whether these parents were subject to disapproval similar to that encountered by white parents of black adopted children. The results showed, rather clearly, that parents of Latin-American children are likely to encounter minimal social antagonism.

Table 5.2 shows the positive responses of extended family members, friends, and neighbors to the adoptions of white, Colombian, Korean, and Afro-American children. Parents of Colombian children received just about as much social support and approval — or slightly more positive responses — as were likely to be encountered by adoptive parents of white U.S.-born children. Parents of Korean children received intermediary levels of positive response. The least support and approval were experienced by the parents of black adoptees.

Table 5.2 shows considerable stability over the period of our study. Community response — among both kin and personal acquaintances — shows general approval and positive response to the white American parents who adopted Colombian children.

Considering the above findings, we expected that parents of Colombian adopted children would be unlikely to anticipate difficulties for their children because of prejudice and discrimination. We also expected that the parents of Colombian children would be among those least likely to incur community disapproval. As was shown in Table 5.2, parents of black children were likely to receive the greatest social disapproval; parents of Colombian children, the least. More than 70 percent of the parents of Afro-American adoptees received negative comments about their children, compared with 55 percent among the parents of Korean-born children. Those with Colombian adoptees experienced even less social disapproval, with 46 percent hearing negative remarks made about their children. Whites, of course, were least likely to be subjected to this kind of criticism: only 8 percent of the parents of white U.S.-born adoptees heard negative remarks about their child's racial or ethnic affiliation.

TABLE 5.2
Positive Response to the Adoption of a Child Among Family, Friends, and Neighbors

(percent)

	Parents of Whites	Parents of Colombians	Parents of Koreans	Parents of Blacks
Wife's				
parents (1975)	92	93	75	46
(1981)	86	95	73	48
Husband's				
parents (1975)	79	86	61	44
(1981)	79	89	63	56
Other				
relatives (1975)	80	87	66	40
(1981)	75	79	69	43
Friends (1975)	91	96	92	79
(1981)	89	95	90	87
Neighbors (1975)	78	78	72	54
(1981)	85	84	76	51

The findings show that the parents of Colombian children are not completely sheltered from racial antagonism. Forty-six percent of our responding families had experienced some level of condemnation. Marge Freeman, mother of 11-year-old Michael — a Colombian-born adoptee — told us about the negative remarks she had heard from members of her family when she told them that she was awaiting the adoption of her child:

I can remember my family's response to our adoption of Michael. There really was not much of a negative reaction to his foreign birth and to his Indian or mestizo heritage. Most everyone in the family knew that Harvey and I had been trying to conceive a child unsuccessfully for years — they were almost as glad for us as we were. But my aunt gave me a hard time. Because of the way she reacted then, I can't find it possible to have any kind of a relationship with her now. When she was told that we were adopting a child from Colombia, she gave me some "friendly advice," as she called it. Her point was that considering the poverty and poor health of many of the children in Colombia, Harvey and I would be sure to end up with a child who was likely to be some kind of basket case. She warned me we better be prepared to spend the rest of our lives in doctors' waiting rooms; she was certain that our child would be a mental retard. As I'm told by some of my cousins, even now she still thinks Michael has "bad blood" in him — whatever that means.

Seeing how healthy our Michael is, I can really laugh at this now. Yet, at the time she really had me worried. And she wasn't the only one; even my brother, who is a psychiatrist, gave me a whole business on how poor and hungry children are likely to have brain damage. It's all statistically true, I suppose. But I'm not so sure that these reservations that people in my family have had to our adoption don't contain some kind of put down to Colombia and to all the Colombian people, that they belong to some kind of inferior race or something. . . .

Even my own mother said something critical about our adoption. She said this to me at one point and never repeated it again. She said that if I couldn't have a child of my own, how could I ever really treat another woman's child as my own. I told her I saw no problem in that. And that was the extent of her opposition.

The experiences of racial antagonism by parents of Colombian children were said to be rare, with only 9 percent indicating that they had encountered such negative comments sometimes; in most instances — 37 percent of the cases — such remarks, if they existed at all, were said to occur rarely.

Few parents of Colombian children thought that the extent of racist sentiments against their child would cause them much harm. None of the parents of Colombians thought social rejection would interfere with their children's getting along with others at school. Only 11 percent saw it as a possible impediment to their child's dating; none of the parents thought it would interfere with their child's efforts to get or keep a job. Again, our findings were very consistent with the trends shown in Table 5.2. Parents of Afro-American children anticipated the most social difficulties, and parents of Korean children fell into an intermediate position. Twenty-three percent of the parents of blacks saw obstacles interfering with their child's efforts to get work; 46 percent thought their child would have problems in dating; and 18 percent expected that their Afro-American adoptee would have problems getting along with peers. For the parents of Korean adoptees the respective percentages were 7, 33, and 9.

When we consider all these results, it appears that the parents of Colombian children do not generally incur much disapproval as a result of having adopted a child racially or culturally different from themselves. In fact, of all the groups of transracial adoptive parents, these parents appeared to encounter the least prejudice and discrimination.

EMPHASIZING THE RACIAL AND CULTURAL HERITAGE OF COLOMBIAN ADOPTEES

Another of the issues we explored with our data was how the parents of Colombian adoptees treated the cultural heritage of their adopted children. Parents had the choice of making their child aware of their Latin American background, living among the American Hispanic community, and projecting to their child a positive vision of Hispanic culture. Parents could also pay little conscious attention to their child's origins. They could promote the child's identification entirely with white American society and not accord much, if any, significance to the child's culture of birth.

As we saw in Chapter 4, adoptive parents of Afro-American children generally tended to emphasize their child's and their family's connection to the black community. Most parents were interested in acquiring information about Afro-American life; they usually shared this information with their black adopted children. They often talked with their black adoptees about being black; they were also inclined to participate in Afro-American cultural activities. Such families were also likely to live within integrated communities, to have many friendships with blacks, and to do everything possible to encourage their children to be closely affiliated with the black community. Such endeavors, our evidence showed, often resulted in feelings of racial pride and interest, and black or biracial self-identifications among their adopted children.

We were uncertain whether similar patterns would be found for our families with Colombian children. As these parents have been shown to have a limited interest in the culture of their adopted child, and inasmuch as infertility was an important reason for their decision to adopt, we anticipated that the parents of Colombian children would be especially eager to minimize the differences between them and their adopted children. Since Colombian adoptees are often described as "white" and are less likely to be targets of racial hostility, we did not expect their parents to promote pride in their Hispanic backgrounds as a social and psychological defense.

The findings confirmed these expectations. Compared with parents of Korean and Afro-American children, parents of Colombians showed the least interest in familiarizing their children with their Hispanic heritage. Table 5.3 shows that the parents of Colombian children are less interested than others in encouraging transracially and transculturally adopted children to identify with their birth culture.

The pattern is clear and consistently demonstrated; parents of Colombian children give the least emphasis to their child's cultural heritage. Parents of black children are at the other end of the continuum, showing the greatest support of their adopted child's membership group. Considering the greater racial prejudice perceived

TABLE 5.3
Parents' Efforts to Familiarize Transracially Adopted Children with Their Background
(percent)

	Parents of Colombian Child	*Parents of Korean Child*	*Parents of Afro-American Child*
Parents read things about child's group often or occasionally	42	46	77
Parents give reading material to child about child's group often or occasionally	32	39	83
Parents talk often or occasionally about child's background	79	87	94
Parents go often or occasionally to museums and cultural events dealing with their child's group	26	37	52

by the parents of Afro-American children, it is not surprising that they offer counteractive information and support in behalf of their child's group. The responses of the parents of Korean children, again, seem to take an intermediate position.

We also investigated the patterns of families living in integrated communities. When we consider the larger numbers of blacks and Hispanics in American society — compared with the numbers of Asians — it is obviously far easier to live amid blacks and Hispanics than to live among Asian-Americans. These patterns were reflected to some extent in our results. Again, our results showed parents of black American adoptees to be the most inclined to live in integrated communities, and parents of Colombian children to be the least disposed to do so. Table 5.4 shows the patterns of each group of parents.

Thus, Table 5.4 shows that the adoptive parents of Colombian and Korean children show very limited interest in living in integrated surroundings; by contrast, parents of black adoptees generally assume decidedly integrated living patterns. As Chapter 4 indicated, families emphasizing the black experience and living in integrated

TABLE 5.4
Integrated Family Life-styles and Child's Origin
(percent)

	Parents of Colombian Child	Parents of Korean Child	Parents of Afro-American Child
Parents live in integrated setting where child's group is found in substantial numbers	11	17	73
Parents have many friends of the same group as their child	11	4	40
Adopted child goes to a school with many others of his/her group	11	9	67
Adopted child has many close friends of his/her race or ethnic heritage	11	4	50

environments tend to raise children who are more likely to be proud of and interested in their racial heritage and more closely identified with it. We anticipated that the parents of Colombian children, by their general disinterest in their child's group, would encourage their children to have little connection with their Hispanic affiliations. The data conformed to our expectations, as Table 5.5 demonstrates.

We were also concerned with whether Colombian adoptees displayed interest in their birth parents and their background. Given the generally low level of emphasis accorded to their children's heritages by the adoptive parents, we anticipated that Colombian children would not be encouraged to search for their birth parents. Also, considering the high proportions of infertile adopters among the parents of Colombian children, we thought that infertility, too, would reduce the support they received from pursuing their interest in their birth parents. We suspected that when parents are anxious about their relationship to their adopted children — as infertile parents often are — they are frequently uneasy about the personal meaning of their children's curiosity about their birth

TABLE 5.5
Ethnic Pride, Interest, and Identification, by Child's Origin
(percent)

	Parents of Colombian Child	Parents of Korean Child	Parents of Afro-American Child
Child sometimes or often is proud of his/her race or ethnic group	50	57	70
Child never is ashamed of his/her race or ethnic group	58	59	67
Child sometimes or often shows interest in his/her race or ethnic group	58	64	76
Adopted child identifies only with white society	59	52	36

parents. Such uneasiness could readily be communicated to their adopted children and serve to inhibit their inclination to ask about their background. In Chapter 8 we examine the search issue in greater detail, explaining at length why infertile parents are more likely to have children who do not search for their birth parents.

Our results were consistent with these expectations. Compared with other adoptees, Colombian children showed the least inclination to search of all the groups of adoptees. Thirty-two percent of the Colombian adoptees had never asked for any information about their birth parents. This was similar to the percentages found among each of the other groups of adoptees. However, none of the Colombian adoptees in our sample had ever asked to see their adoption records. This compared with 10 percent of white adoptees, 15 percent of Korean adoptees, and 26 percent of the blacks.

The largest disparity between the responses of Colombian adoptees and the other groups of children was noted when parents were asked to evaluate whether they thought their adopted child would ever search for birth kin. None of the parents of Colombian children anticipated that their child would do so. This contrasts sharply with the responses of the other groups of adoptive parents: 21 percent of the parents of white adoptees, 14 percent of the parents of Korean children, and 39 percent of the parents of blacks anticipated that their children would one day seek their birth relatives. It might seem that the relative youth of the Colombian adoptees would make the search a more remote prospect to their adoptive parents. Yet, our data in Chapter 8 show that the age of the child has relatively little influence upon genealogical curiosity. It is clear from our data that the parents of Afro-American adoptees are most likely to anticipate that their child will eventually seek his or her birth parents.

ADJUSTMENT OF ADOPTED COLOMBIAN CHILDREN

One of the most important questions about the Colombian children adopted by American parents revolves around their adaptation to their adoptive homes. We were particularly interested in probing the numerous reports of Colombian adoptees with serious health problems. We wanted to know how frequently such problems were encountered among our respondents. We wondered what impact such health difficulties might have on the overall adjustment of Colombian adoptees.

Another issue we wanted to investigate was the influence of the Colombian children's sense of ethnic identification and pride on their adaptation. Considering the minimal emphasis accorded by parents to their children's Hispanic heritage, we also wondered about the consequences of this upon their children's overall adjustment.

Our results did indeed suggest that Colombian children were more likely than other adopted children to be suffering from serious physical health problems. This was reflected in our finding that Colombian children in 1975 were more likely to require extensive medical treatment at the time of their adoption or shortly thereafter than was true for other adopted children. Twenty-four percent of the Colombian children in our sample required hospitalization or extensive medical treatment, compared with 9 percent of the white children born in the United States, 12 percent of the adopted Korean children, and 14 percent of the Afro-American children.

We suspected that children who received extensive medical care would be more likely to have poor overall adjustment. It seemed plausible for us to anticipate that when such physical health difficulties existed, they would weigh heavily on all family members and impair the quality of the child's overall adaptation to the adoptive family. Surprisingly, our findings did not confirm this expectation. The results suggested that children reported as having such extensive medical care were no more likely to be less well adjusted. Among Colombian children who received extensive medical care, 73 percent were reported as having fully satisfactory adjustments, compared with 74 percent among those not having physical health difficulties. The more serious physical health difficulties of these children — most often owing to the poverty, inadequate nutrition, and poor medical care available in their country of birth — did not seem to exert an observable impact on the quality of their psychological adjustment.

Interestingly, when we examined this question among all our groups of adoptive parents, the results showed that children with serious health difficulties were more likely to be more poorly adjusted. Among all groups of adoptees, only 69 percent of those who received extensive medical care were reported as being well adjusted, compared with 80 percent among those not having such difficulties. For Colombian children, by contrast, no such trend was found.

Why was it that the physical health problems of the Colombian children cast such a slight shadow over these children's adaptation? We suspected that the trend had a great deal to do with the younger ages of the Colombian children. The Colombian children in our sample were considerably younger than the other children for whom we reported data. Sixty-seven percent of the Colombian children were less than two years of age in 1975, compared with only 27 percent of the Korean children, 23 percent of the white children, and 14 percent of the Afro-American children.

Other studies have demonstrated the enormous adaptive capacities of younger transracially adopted children to transcend experiences of earlier environmental deprivation (Rathbun, DiVirgilio, and Waldfogel 1958; Rathbun et al. 1965; Winick, Meyer, and Harris 1975). These studies have shown that the vast majority of children exposed to moderate-to-acute deprivation during early infancy were able to recover rapidly when placed in their enriched adoptive homes. When adopted relatively early in life, these children could surmount many of their initial limitations and obstacles. Later comparisons between them and nonadopted children in their adoptive families showed little evidence of learning difficulties or impaired psychological adjustment (Winick, Meyer, and Harris 1975). Our findings corresponded to these earlier studies.

Our results suggested that the impact of such serious physical health difficulties was insignificant on the short-term and longer-term adaptations of the Colombian children. Neither our 1975 nor our 1981 measures of child adjustment were influenced by the need for extensive medical care or hospitalization. When we compared the adjustments of the Colombian children with those of the other groups of adoptees, these children were shown to have no noticeably greater adjustment problems. When asked to consider the growth, emotional adjustment, and overall adjustment of their children, parents of Colombian children reported no greater frequencies of difficult adjustments than other adoptive parents. Most parents considered the adjustment of their children to be more than satisfactory. Table 5.6 shows the reported adjustments for 1975 among each group of children. Table 5.7 dislays adjustments among all the groups of adoptees six years later.

Tables 5.6 and 5.7 show that of all the children included here, Colombian children were reported as having the fewest psychological and overall adjustment problems. We may wonder why the

TABLE 5.6
Children's Adjustments, by Child's Ethnic Origins: 1975
(percent)

	Parents of White U.S. Child	*Parents of Colombian Child*	*Parents of Korean Child*	*Parents of Afro-American Child*
Child received extensive medical care or hospital- ization	9	24	12	14
Child has emotional adjustment problems*	44	15	34	45
Child has growth problems*	18	11	15	26
Child's adjustment described as fully satisfactory	75	74	65	46

*Reported sometimes or often.

Colombians show up so favorably when compared with the other groups of adoptees. Here again, we suspect that the youth of these children has a great deal to do with their more favorable adaptations. At several points in our text we have demonstrated that younger children tend to have fewer adjustment problems.

To conclude our analysis of adjustment, we turned our attention to the ethnic identification of the Colombian children. The results indicated that most of our Colombian adoptees identified themselves exclusively with white society; 59 percent thought of themselves only as whites. Parents of Colombian children tended to pay scant attention to their children's Hispanic affiliations. Compared with other transracial and transcultural adoptive parents, these parents played the smallest role in acquainting their children with their cultural heritage. Parents of Colombian adoptees also tended to live outside Hispanic communities. We wondered about

TABLE 5.7
Children's Adjustments, by Child's Ethnic Origins: 1981
(percent)

	Parents of White U.S. Child	Parents of Colombian Child	Parents of Korean Child	Parents of Afro-American Child
Child has emotional adjustment problems*	40	26	37	54
Child has growth problems*	4	5	13	7
Child's adjustment described as fully satisfactory	43	73	53	19
Child shows discomfort about appearance	16	11	26	38
Child has received professional care for problems	25	0	10	16
Child receives above-average school grades	48	58	58	38
Child has above-average interest in school	48	79	59	28
Child is in frequent conflict with brothers and sisters	10	0	16	19

*Reported sometimes or often.

the effects of this dissociation of Colombian children from their cultural origins upon their adaptations.

The results suggested that children's adjustments in 1981 seemed to have little to do with their affiliations to the Hispanic community. Whether children lived in Hispanic communities, whether their parents positively emphasized being Latin American, whether children felt a sense of ethnic pride and identification seemed to have little if any association with Colombian adoptees' adjustments. The same trends that were found for the Afro-American adoptees were found among the Colombian children. Like the Afro-Americans, when parents of Colombians lived in Hispanic communities, when parents took measures to acquaint their children with their Hispanic heritage, they were more likely to have children who had Latin American or biracial self-identifications and were proud of their cultural group. Only one-third of Colombian adoptees who lived in all-white communities were biculturally identified, compared with 63 percent among those living in mixed or Hispanic communities. Fifty-seven percent of the parents who actively promoted their child's Hispanic affiliation had biculturally identified children, compared with only 30 percent among parents who tended to deemphasize their child's ethnic membership. Eighty-seven percent of the parents who took an active role in cultivating their Colombian child's Hispanic identification had a child proud of his or her Latin American heritage, compared with only 25 percent among parents who tended to deemphasize their child's ethnic affiliation.

Parents who stressed their child's ethnic affiliation – either by consciously making efforts to cultivate an ethnic identity in their transculturally adopted child or by living in an integrated community – were likely to raise transracially adopted children who identified positively with their ethnic group. Yet, their children appeared to be no more likely to be any better adjusted than the adopted children of parents who placed little significance on these matters. These trends were much the same as those we had found among the families with Afro-American adoptees. This evidence gives further reinforcement to the trends discussed earlier. But since the results presented here are based upon only 19 families with Colombian adoptees who were resurveyed in 1981, we advance these patterns tentatively.

SUMMARY AND IMPLICATIONS FOR
SOCIAL WORK POLICY AND PRACTICE

This analysis of families who adopted children from Colombia has revealed a number of interesting results. The findings are consistent with the expectations of many who claim that adoptive parents of Colombian children are generally likely to be infertile couples who have been unable to find white infants for adoption in the United States. The implication that some have drawn from this pattern, that parents of Colombian children are generally unreceptive to adopting hard-to-place children, remains in doubt from our findings. Parents of Colombian children, it seems, show considerable change in their attitude toward the hard-to-place after having adopted a Colombian child. They may, indeed, be receptive to providing adoptive homes for many of today's waiting children, both in the United States and abroad. We suspect that among these parents there may be considerable interest — especially among those who have already adopted — in providing homes for hard-to-place children from Colombia and elsewhere.

Compared with the parents of Afro-American children, parents of Colombian children encounter relatively little opposition and hostility to their adoptions of racially and culturally dissimilar children. Although parents of Colombian children do experience some levels of antagonistic response from the community, the intensity of the hostility is so slight that parents are provided with very little impetus to positively emphasize the cultural heritage of their adopted children. Since most of the children appear to be racially "white," the most pervasive response among their adoptive parents was to bring up their children as white Americans and to accord minimal positive value to their Hispanic background. Adoptive parents also seemed little disposed to live among Hispanics, and most Colombian adoptees were likely to grow up in relatively homogeneous white communities.

Our investigation has shown that adopted children from Colombia adjust remarkably well to their American homes. Although they were more likely than any of the other groups of adoptees to come to their adoptive families with serious health problems, their difficulties appeared to be short-lived and did not seem to impair their overall adjustments. Most of our Colombian children were relatively young at the time of our 1981 follow-up study; almost all (94 percent) were under 12 at that time. We see an important link between the relatively younger ages at which these children were adopted and their overall positive adaptations. For the time being, the results suggest that the needs for social services among adoptive parents with Colombian children appear to be rather minimal.

Whether these children will feel troubled because of their estrangement from Hispanic culture when they reach their adolescent and young adult years is difficult to say. In Chapter 6 — based upon our analysis of the many adoptive parents of older Korean children — we should be better able to speculate on this important question. Should the question of the relationship of these children to their Hispanic background arise, it can be observed that Colombian adoptees will hardly be isolated in dealing with such issues. They, like many of the millions of other Latin American migrants to the United States, will be engaged in the process of fusing these cultural tranditions into a viable ethnic identity.

The general pattern of infertility among most adoptive parents of Colombian children seems to influence how they raise their children in several important ways. Infertility appears to color parents' responses toward "rejecting the differences" between adoption and biological parenthood. Specifically, we found adoptive parents of Colombian children were inclined to place minimal importance on the cultural origins of their children. While we have found that this pattern did not appear to influence the quality of adjustments per se, it did seem to diminish the sense of ethnic pride and identification that adopted Colombian children eventually develop. Adoptive parents of Colombian children were also less likely to encourage and to recognize the genealogical questioning of their adopted children. Whether these patterns will ultimately create difficulties for these parents in relating to their children, and whether children will be psychologically impaired by this pattern of rejection, remains to seen. At this time we can not discern any ill effects arising from parents' unwillingness to relate to their adopted children's backgrounds. Given the relatively young ages of their adopted children, we cannot demonstrate whether any such difficulties will be likely to emerge.

6
The Adaptation of
Transracially Adopted Adolescents:
The Case of Korean-Born Adoptees

Jennifer Gold is one of the adoptees in our sample. Born in Inchon, Korea, she looks far different from most other American Jewish middle-class adolescents. She is the adopted daughter of Herb and Miriam Gold and lives in a comfortable, but by no means spacious, house in the Boston suburb of Brookline. Herb Gold, her adoptive father, is free-lance photographer. While assignments for Herb were always plentiful in the past, lately he's been finding it difficult to get assignments. Ever since the Golds became adoptive parents, Miriam has been at home caring for the children. She worked as an elementary school teacher before children came into their lives. Lately, the Golds have been discussing Miriam's return to work as a substitute teacher.

The Golds were one of the first members of their adoptive parent group to adopt through the Holt program in 1973. Ever since then, they have given adoption advice to many other couples. In 1977 they adopted again. Wendy also was a Holt baby, born in Korea.

Jennifer was adopted when she was six years old. At that time the Golds were apprehensive about her age. They were doubtful that any child of that age would accept them as parents. A younger child would have been preferable; but they were also concerned about the amount of time they would have to wait for another placement. The Golds were concerned that their age would be a handicap in the eyes of placement agencies. Herb was 42 at the time and Miriam was 39. Considering their relatively advanced ages for first-time parents, they felt lucky to be getting a child at all. They reasoned that had they been able to bear natural offspring, they probably would have had children of Jennifer's age and older.

Their uneasiness about Jennifer unfortunately proved to be correct. During the first years she was plagued by nightmares and often had to be given sedatives in order to sleep. She was extremely fearful, and it wasn't until she had been with Herb and Miriam for six months that she would let Herb near her without showing fear. She often tested Herb and Miriam, asking them when they planned to return her to the orphanage. Three years passed before she began to trust them and accept their love. She now has a very close relationship with her parents, perhaps a more intimate one than most children of her age. Jennifer has a sly sense of humor and shares many private jokes with Herb and Miriam.

Her close relationship with her parents suffered a brief setback when the Golds adopted Wendy. Even now she remains distant from her sister. Jennifer has never been a particularly attractive child. Now that she is an adolescent, her lack of physical beauty is beginning to weigh heavily upon her. She responds to this by crash diets, bouts of depression, and rage.

Wendy has always been a striking contrast to Jennifer. From early infancy Herb and Miriam remember her as almost always confident, assertive, and ready to try new things. Now that Wendy is seven years old, they are finding her to be a child who makes friends easily, is well liked, bright, and inquisitive. In contrast with Jennifer, she has always been a beautiful, fascinating-looking child. Her good looks have elicited comment from people. There has always been a deep sibling rivalry between the two girls.

Herb and Miriam Gold are concerned about Jennifer. From the earliest days of her adoption, their daughter's life has been difficult. They attribute their problems with her to the fact that she was adopted at a relatively late age, and that she had been through a great deal of uncertainty and hardship during her preplacement years. They have been to see the school psychologist on several occasions regarding her poor academic record. They feel certain that in a supportive setting Jennifer could thrive and demonstrate her intellectual capabilities. Herb and Miriam have made some substantial sacrifices to provide private psychotherapy for Jennifer. Miriam thought that with the right professional help, Jennifer might resolve some of her conflicts and anxieties, and apply herself to her schoolwork more effectively.

Adoption has never been a particularly sensitive subject around the Gold household. Although Herb and Miriam were greatly disappointed when they learned they would never be able to conceive a child together, they arrived at the decision to adopt without much difficulty. In the back of their minds they had always thought of themselves as positively disposed to the idea of adoption. Perhaps, even if they could have raised birth children, they would have still wanted to adopt, to make a home for a child. Both Herb's and Miriam's families have been generally supportive, although when they first heard that Herb and Miriam were adopting a Korean child, there was some surprise and concern.

The most significant question close family members raised was whether they intended to raise their adopted daughter as a Jew. Both Herb and Miriam come from traditional Jewish homes. While they themselves had moved some distance from the Orthodox religious practices of their parents, they wanted to affirm their Jewish identities. They decided to join a Reformed temple in their neighborhood. When they first joined, they were uneasy about an environment that was so different from the Orthodox synagogues of their youth. Yet, as time has passed, they have become very active members of their congregation.

The girls are actively involved in the congregation, too. Jennifer was Bat Mitzvah three years ago and continues her affiliation with the temple's junior youth group. One of the more positive elements in her life is her warm friendship with the youth group director, who seems to have a special empathy for her. Wendy has just begun to go to Sunday School, and eagerly looks forward to her own Bat Mitzvah. There have never been any overt negative remarks made about either of the girls in any of the temple activities. There are two other foreign-born adopted children among congregation members. The most irksome response to their international family has been thoughtless question they often hear asked: "Are the girls actually sisters?" This question continues to unsettle Herb and Miriam. They feel that it suggests a lack of acceptance of their adoption. It implies that the absence of a biological tie between the girls diminishes their relationship.

Jennifer seems to have a great deal of difficulty in accepting her Asian features. She has remarked to Miriam on more than one occasion that she would like to have an operation to change the shape of her eyelids. Miriam and Herb have been deeply disturbed by these remarks. They have always taken pains to convey to the children positive feelings for their Korean heritage. Until recently they have been active members of their adoptive parent group. They have often read the children stories about Korea; they attended slide shows that were given by a few adoptive families who had traveled to Korea. They keep in close touch with a number of the members of the parent group who adopted Korean children. For a number of years, every Christmas they used to go with several members of their adoptive parent group to a Korean church in metropolitan Boston for special holiday blessings for the children and a feast. Herb and Miriam have been very troubled and disappointed by Jennifer's great uneasiness about her Korean heritage.

Herb and Miriam don't know what to do. They feel that they have very few options left to them. As Jennifer is getting older, she seems to be becoming more and more estranged from her peers. Her fits of temper have become more frequent and more vitriolic; there seems to be self-destructiveness in many of her actions, particularly in her long and stringent diets. Herb and Miriam are beginning to worry a great deal about whether Jennifer will ever have a normal social life.

The concerns of the Golds provide a backdrop for much of the analysis in this chapter. Several other studies of transracial adoptions have discussed cases like that of Jennifer Gold — troubled adolescent adoptees who have ambivalent and negative feelings toward their cultural origins, who appear to be marginally adapted to American culture and to their adoptive families (Kim 1977; Ladner 1977). How common are these difficulties among transculturally adopted adolescents? Are such problems more frequent among transculturally adopted adolescents than they are among adolescent adoptees who are racially similar to their adoptive parents? What accounts for the problems that some adolescent transracial adoptees, such as Jennifer Gold, experienced?

Data on the long-term adaptations of transracially adopted children remains fragmentary and inconclusive (Kim 1977; Kim, Hong, and Kim 1979; Simon and Altstein 1981). Do transracial adoptees eventually find themselves in a cultural no-man's-land, uncomfortable about their identification with a minority group, and never fully accepted as a members of the dominant white society? Many scholars argue that as transracial adoptees grow older, they are likely to experience increasing hostility and rejection by whites

(Ladner 1977; McRoy 1981; Simon and Altstein 1977). Adolescence is a difficult period in the best of circumstances. For the adoptees it would seem that the problems associated with this time of transition are likely to be compounded by having to come to grips with the anomaly of their adopted status. If we add to this the isolation associated with a minority status, we see the ingredients for producing a turbulent time for these young people and their families. Does the adolescent transracial adoptee encounter great difficulty in confronting these problems? Are the problems primarily those of adolescence? Of being adopted? Of racial difference? Such questions deserve our consideration.

We may also wonder what social factors are linked with adolescent adoptee stress, on the one hand, and with children's optimal adaptations, on the other. In some families adolescent adoptees seem to move through their lives with a minimum of friction and unhappiness. For other young people, like Jennifer Gold, trouble and problems seem to be enduring parts of their experience. The sources of Jennifer's difficulties — and of those of other transracially adopted adolescents — are by no means clear. Do they arise from the relatively late age at which some children are placed? Are they created by the trauma of separation and reattachment? Are they aggravated by the problems of a difficult life prior to placement? Do they follow from the uncertainties and instabilities of the adoptive parents — like Herb Gold's precarious employment? Do the insecurities and anxieties created by adoptive parents' infertility influence the adoptees' growth and development? Does the child's sense of racial pride contribute to his or her well-being? Are adjustment problems the outcome of a subtle, but persistent, conflict between dominant and minority cultures? These are the questions that will inform and direct the analysis that follows.

KOREAN CHILDREN: HOW THEY COMPARED
WITH OTHER GROUPS OF ADOPTEES

In the last two chapters we focused on Afro-Americans and Colombians — two of the major groups in our sample of transracial and transcultural adoptees — and evaluated their distinctive experiences. In this chapter we will review the common experiences of Korean adoptees, the largest group of transracial adoptees both in our sample and among the foreign-born adoptees now found in America. Our analysis in this chapter is based upon the 298 families in our 1975 sample who adopted children from Korea. Of these families, 161 replied to our follow-up questionnaire in 1981. Of special interest to us in this investigation were the 55 families that had an adopted Korean adolescent in 1981.

The adoption of Korean children by white Americans has been taking place for many years. Since the early 1950s the number of families adopting Korean children has increased substantially, to an average of approximately 2,500 yearly (Kim 1978). In the period since American agencies became established in Korea, over 50,000 children have been placed in the United States (Adams and Kim 1971; Kim 1978; U.S. Immigration and Naturalization Service 1972-78a). There have been numerous studies of the adaptations of Korean adoptees in the United States. Their results have shown that the overwhelming majority of these children adjust well to American society, with approximately three-fourths of the samples showing favorable adjustment and less than 10 percent indicating serious adjustment problems in their initial adaptations (Kim and Reid 1970; Keltie 1969; Gallay 1963; Welter 1965; Winick, Meyer, and Harris 1975; Nutt and Snyder 1973; Guilbault 1972).

Like the results of earlier studies, our data indicated that the greatest number of parents of Korean adopted children were fertile. Only 44 percent of the parents of Korean children said that infertility or subfertility was a consideration in their decision to adopt a Korean child. Sixty-six percent of the parents had other birth children in their families. The majority of these parents cited social and humanitarian reasons as most important in their decision to adopt. Most of them conformed to our conception of "preferential" adoptive parents.

Of all the groups of adoptive parents examined in this research — with the exception of the parents of Afro-American children — parents of Korean children showed the greatest willingness to adopt hard-to-place children. Sixty-one percent were favorably disposed to the adoption of an Afro-American child; 60 percent would have considered adopting a child eight years of age or older. Approximately a third would have considered adopting handicapped or retarded children. Clearly, this group of parents was especially receptive to providing homes for hard-to-place children.

In comparison with the transracial adoptive parents of Afro-Americans, the parents of Korean children encountered mostly favorable responses to their adoptions from the community and their extended families. (Table 5.2 shows the levels of support given for all the groups' children.) Between 60 and 75 percent of the parents, neighbors, and other relatives reacted approvingly to the adoptions of Korean children. This was a considerably more favorable response than the parents of Afro-American adoptees experienced, and somewhat less of a positive response than adoptive parents of white and Colombian children had.

In the main, adoptive parents of Korean children did not anticipate that their children would encounter particular difficulties because of their racial or cultural differences. In 1975 only 33 percent of these parents thought those differences might have some adverse effect on their child's dating relationships. Less than 10 percent thought they might interfere with their child's chances of getting a job or making friends. The results showed much the same pattern when children were six years older, at the time of our follow-up study. Given the generally supportive responses among kinfolk and other close associates, the absence of parental anxiety about their Korean adopted children's problems in dating, jobs, or friendships is readily understood.

A substantial minority of parents of Korean children actively encouraged their children to learn about and identify with their Korean background. Approximately two-fifths read things themselves or provided reading material to their children about Korean culture. An overwhelming majority of the parents — 87 percent — occasionally talked to their child about his or her Korean background. More than a third (37 percent) regularly went to museums or cultural events that dealt with their child's group. Considering the relative paucity of Koreans in America, it was surprising to note that as many as 17 percent of families lived in communities where Koreans were found in substantial numbers. Less than 10 percent lived in places where their children went to schools and had friends who included substantial numbers of Asians. Adoptive parents of Korean children did not offer the same encouragement for children to link themselves with their birth group as was noted for the adoptive parents of Afro-Americans. On the other hand, their commitment to cultivating their child's racial and ethnic affiliation was somewhat greater than was true among the parents of Colombians.

Given this generally facilitating climate, 48 percent of the adoptees identified themselves exclusively with their Korean racial heritage or with both their Asian birth group and their white families. Fifty-seven percent of all Korean adoptees expressed pride in their Asian background sometimes or often, and 64 percent expressed interest in their Korean heritage sometimes or often. The data suggested that even though some of the Korean children identified primarily with the ethnic background of their adoptive parents, they were likely to express pride and interest in their Asian heritage. Forty-one percent of all Korean adoptees were described as ever being ashamed of their ethnic background.

It is often suggested that transracially adopted children will be most likely to maintain their ethnic identity only when they live in areas where substantial numbers of their ethnic group are found. We discovered in our examination of transracially adopted Afro-American children that integrated residence and friendship patterns were positively associated with the development of a sense of pride and interest in their Afro-American heritage. Integrated communities and friendship networks are unlikely to have the same impact upon Korean adoptees, since their adoptive families are not concentrated in areas where Koreans or Korean-Americans are frequently found.

Yet, as our analysis in Chapter 4 indicated, when parents emphasize their adopted child's ethnic affiliation in a positive way, they are likely to inspire a sense of racial pride and interest in their transracially adopted children. Apparently the adoptive parents of Korean children do relatively well in imparting a sense of racial pride and identification. Although they largely live in segregated white America, between half and two-thirds of their Korean-born children showed frequent pride and interest in their ethnic heritage.

Parents of Korean children generally encouraged their adopted children to raise questions about their genealogical origins. Sixty-nine percent of these parents felt that they should share all the genealogical information they had with their child. Only 16 percent of the parents of Korean adoptees felt they should carefully limit the information about the birth family that they gave to their child. Given this generally encouraging atmosphere, children were often inclined to ask questions about their birth kin; 39 percent of the Korean adoptees asked such questions of their adoptive parents sometimes or often; and 15 percent had asked to see their adoption records.

Compared with Colombian children, Koreans showed greater curiosity about their birth families. While similar percentages of

Colombian adoptees were inclined to ask questions about birth parents, none of them asked to see their adoption records. None of the parents of Colombian children imagined that their child would ever search for his or her birth parents; by contrast, 14 percent of the parents of Korean felt their child would eventually pursue the search. When we consider the relatively greater numbers of fertile parents among the parents of Korean adopted children — and the greater ease with which fertile parents are likely to approach issues of genealogical questioning — such differences become more readily understandable. The interest in searching for birth relatives among Korean adoptees was comparable with that found among U.S.-born white adoptees, and somewhat less than that found for Afro-American adoptees.

DO RACIAL IDENTIFICATION PROBLEMS EXIST AMONG ADOLESCENT TRANSRACIAL ADOPTEES?

One of the issues that has been raised repeatedly in connection with transracially and transculturally adopted children is the question of their relationship to the culture and people of their birth. Critics of transracial adoption have frequently suggested that these children will not identify with their birth culture and will have little or no contact with the people among whom they were born. We have seen that this is not an accurate picture of the transracially adopted Afro-American children in our sample. Many transracially adopted Afro-American children identified with their Afro-American heritage as well as with their white parents; most were proud of and interested in Afro-American culture, and many lived in racially integrated communities. Parents of transracially adopted Afro-American children generally encouraged their children to develop and maintain ties to Afro-American culture. Only a few minimized their children's contacts and affiliation with black America.

The same patterns appeared to be true — to a somewhat lesser degree — in the responses of adoptive parents of Korean children and in their children's behavior. As we have indicated, these parents were decidedly less likely to live in integrated communities than were white adoptive parents of black children. While 17 percent of the parents of Korean adoptees lived in communities with a substantial Asian membership, 68 percent of the parents of

Afro-American adoptees lived in places where a significant proportion of the population was black.

Questions of the identification and the social relationships of transracially adopted Korean children have not been asked with the same frequency and intensity as those addressed to the situation of transracially adopted black children, but they are of increasing importance. Korean children and adolescents constitute the largest single group of transracially adopted children in the United States. They are coming into their adolescence and young adulthood at a time when the Korean population of the United States is rapidly increasing, when Asian-Americans as a group are becoming more assertive, and when the relationship of the United States to Asia is undergoing continuous change. It is not clear whether the majority of transracially adopted Koreans in the United States will choose to identify with their Asian background, whether they will identify themselves with the religious and ethnic communities of their adoptive families, or whether they will attempt to affirm both commitments.

Critics of transracial and transcultural adoptions have claimed that as the transracial adoptee grows older, he or she is likely to be subjected to increasing hostility and exclusionary treatment (Simon and Altstein 1977; Ladner 1977; McRoy 1981). This, in turn, is likely to cause the transracial adoptee to become culturally isolated and uncertain or ashamed about his or her identity. We were interested in investigating whether any factual basis could be established to support these claims.

Table 6.1 presents the data for our Korean respondents on their identifications, pride and interest in their Korean heritage, and their sense of shame and discomfort about their appearance. The data are broken down into two age groups: teenagers and younger children. Critics contend that there are likely to be mounting identification problems among older transracial adoptees. If there is validity to this claim, then it should be reflected in the contrast between the responses of younger and older adoptees.

These data seem to yield mixed support for the critics of transracial adoption. As the transracial adoptee grows older, there appears to be a greater affiliation with the dominant culture and a waning attachment to the birth group. Fewer of the older Korean adopted children identified primarily with other Koreans. The number of adolescent adoptees proud of or interested in their Korean heritage

TABLE 6.1
Race Pride, Interest, and Identification Among Transracially
Adopted Korean Adolescent and Younger Children
(percent)

	Younger Children (6-12)	Adolescents (13-21)
Child sometimes or often is proud of his/her racial group	67	40
Child sometimes or often shows interest in his/her racial group	69	50
Child identifies primarily with white society	48	63
Child never is ashamed of being Korean	56	66
Child never feels any discomfort about his/her appearance	36	40

declined. Yet, the data also showed that despite this withdrawal from their Korean origins, older adoptees did not feel increased shame or discomfort about their background.

Howard Sorenson, the adoptive parent of a 15-year-old Korean boy, commented upon his son's development:

> When Dan entered junior high, he began to lose a lot of his interest in Korean things. He didn't want to eat kim chee . . . or anything Korean, just American foods. . . like hot dogs and corn flakes. He was less interested in attending events at the Korean Community Church and more interested in his high school science club. When we adopted Dan, he was four, and he of course spoke Korean. Today, eleven years later, Dan still remembers a good deal of his Korean vocabulary, but he is generally reluctant to use it. I've also noticed some degree of anxiety and discomfort when we refer to his Korean background. To some extent I think this is the result of Dan's acceptance by his white high school friends. I'm not entirely happy about this, but Dan has to function in this country, among Americans, and not in Korea.

Howard Sorenson's comments suggest that the attempts of parents to encourage their children's sense of themselves as Korean are not reinforced by their children's experiences as adolescents. Beyond the early grades they are increasingly responsive to the definitions of their peers, who, while not hostile to their Korean background, do not see being Korean as important or interesting. Adolescent Korean adoptees are valued for their American qualities, not for their Korean backgrounds or attributes. This is apparently true even in those situations where other Korean or Asian children are present in the community or school. These other Asians are often assimilated individuals or families; in most instances they do not represent a distinct ethnic community.

Comparative analysis of the response of Korean, Colombian, and white adoptees showed that the Korean respondents were no more likely than the Colombians to feel ashamed of their national origins. Approximately 20 percent of both groups were inclined to feel ashamed of their affiliation. The reader will recall that in many instances Colombian children resembled whites closely enough to be considered "whites" by their parents, and most probably by the wider society.

Korean children — when compared with whites and Colombians — did show more discomfort about their appearance. Twenty-six percent of the Korean adoptees sometimes felt uncomfortable about how they looked, compared with 11 percent of the Colombians and 16 percent of the whites. The responses of the Korean children, however, did not appear to be age-linked. Older children and younger children alike seemed to be equally subject to this experience. Thus, given their greater difference from white American beauty standards, Koreans were likely to be judged and to evaluate themselves as less acceptable than were whites and Colombians.

We were also interested in whether Afro-American transracial adoptees — like their Korean counterparts — experienced declining racial pride, interest, and identification as they grew older. Table 6.2 presents the data on our Afro-American adoptees. The results suggested that black children were not as likely as the Koreans to distance themselves from the culture of their birth. The racial pride, interest, and identification expressed by younger Afro-American adoptees was similar to that found for teenagers. Older Afro-American adoptees were less likely to be to ashamed, but more likely to

TABLE 6.2
Race Pride, Interest, and Identification Among Transracially Adopted Afro-American Adolescent and Younger Children
(percent)

	Younger Children (6-12)	Adolescents (13-21)
Child sometimes or often is proud of his/her racial group	74	65
Child sometimes or often shows interest in his/her racial group	75	82
Child identifies primarily with white society	38	31
Child never is ashamed of his/her race group	58	73*
Child never feels any discomfort about his/her appearance	38	17*

*Chi square significant at the .05 level.

feel uncomfortable about their appearance. The explanation for this particular inconsistency was not apparent to us. It appeared to be another manifestation of the absence of a consistent association between the child's age and the measures of racial pride among Afro-American adoptees. Thus, the experience of growing older among Afro-Americans in whte homes did not appear to be linked to an attenuated ethnic identification, as it seemed to be for Korean adoptees.

These results suggested that, given the heightened involvement of Afro-American adoptees in the black community, older black children were encouraged to sustain their sense of racial pride and identification with the black community. We must also keep in mind that given the greater levels of antiblack attitudes in white society, blacks are given added encouragement to maintain high levels of pride and identification to counteract the low esteem in which they are held. We suspect that the integrated living and friendship patterns of adoptive families of Afro-American children contribute to the greater sense of racial identification found among their older adoptees.

THE ADJUSTMENTS OF ADOLESCENT KOREAN ADOPTEES

Comparisons with White Adolescent Adoptees

In reviewing adolescent adaptations in our 1981 follow-up study, we were struck by the lack of problems encountered in most homes. Table 6.3 shows the responses of Korean adoptees aged 13 and older, and compares their responses with those of white adoptees in the same age range.

TABLE 6.3
Adjustments of Korean and White Adoptees, Thirteen or Older, 1981
(percent)

	Korean Adoptees	*White Adoptees*
Child described as mostly or extremely well adjusted	74	62
Child described as being free of emotional adjustment problems	65	52
Child described as being free of growth or developmental problems	96	71
Child received professional help for problem behavior	9	33
Child's schoolwork above average	55	29
Child's interest in school described as above average	46	38
Child said to have some or frequent problems in getting along with peers	29	43
Child is sometimes or frequently uncomfortable about his/her appearance	28	19

The trends shown in Table 6.3 were consistent, indicating that the Korean adopted adolescents were well adapted in their American homes. Approximately three-fourths were described as well adjusted in their adoptive families. Considering the general tendency of older adoptees to have more frequent adjustment problems, this suggested that transracially adopted Korean adolescents were better adjusted than most adolescent adoptees. The apparently positive adaptation of the Koreans was confirmed when we compared them with their white American counterparts. Here we were surprised to find that the Korean adoptees were better adapted than white adolescents.

The trend was demonstrated in all of our adjustment indicators except one. Only in their discomfort about their appearance did the Koreans show more of a negative response than white adolescent adoptees. Korean children were more likely than the whites to be ashamed of their looks. Kim (1977) also has found discomfort about appearance to be one of the few areas where adopted Korean youth are likely to have problems. Despite this anxiety, Korean adoptees appeared to adapt especially well.

We suspected that these trends might have been influenced by variations in age between the two groups. We anticipated that the poorer adjustment of the white adolescent adoptees might be attributable to the fact that they were older than the Korean adoptees or were older at placement. Yet, when we compared both groups of children, there was no indication that this was the case.

Adolescent Korean adoptees tended to be older than their white counterparts. The mean age for the adolescent white adoptees in 1981 was 16.3; for the Koreans it was 17.4. While only a quarter of the Koreans were between 13 and 15, half of the adolescent whites belonged to that age group. Korean adoptees were also more likely to have been adopted at older ages. The average age at adoption for the Korean adolescents was 5.3 years; for the whites it was 3.2. Only 4 percent of the adolescent Koreans were adopted before they were a year old, compared with half among the white adolescent population. We must remember that all the evidence we have accumulated indicates that older children and those who are placed later are likely to have poorer adjustments.

Of course, these data remain incomplete; but the trends could have implications about the differences between preadoptive experiences of American and Korean children. The above patterns suggest that the quality of care available for children adopted from Korea may be better than that available to most homeless children in the United States. It may well reflect the deficiencies of the system of foster care in the United States. Being subjected to frequent changes in placement, as many American homeless children are, has damaging consequences. It is also possible that these differences could result from a tendency to make those children who have received the best preadoptive care in Korea available for foreign adoption. Both of these hypotheses raise interesting questions for further research.

Although a more definitive examination of these arguments was beyond the scope of the present research we felt that these questions were of sufficient interest and importance to merit some immediate study.

We attempted to pursue these questions further by discussing our findings and hypotheses with those familiar both with Korea and the inter-country adoptions of Korean children by American citizens. Our discussion did not support the hypotheses we advanced above. Material available in one of the few studies of the relinquishment of Korean children for inter-country adoption also suggested that prior to their adoption Korean children were exposed to extraordinary deprivation. Children who were of mixed racial background were also subjected to continual social ostracism (Whang 1976). We also discovered a certain amount of material suggesting that Korean social services as a whole are not well developed (Byma 1974). These subsequent findings tend to discredit some of our original hypotheses. However, pending a fuller examination of the services available to Korean children adopted abroad, we are reluctant to discount these possibilities altogether.

An alternative hypothesis was formulated by several persons familiar with Korea and the foreign adoptions of Korean children. They have observed that immigration to the United States is seen as a very desirable personal goal by many Koreans. Professor Dong Soo Kim of the School of Social Work of Norfolk State University suggested that, as a result of sharing such sentiments, Korean adoptees usually come to have very positive expectations of their American adoptive homes. He argued that in many cases these expectations become self-fulfilling prophecies. This viewpoint suggests that the high morale of Korean children toward their adoptions by American parents enables them to overcome problems created by their difficult preadoptive environments. This explanation is most interesting, but by no means fully demonstrated. The superior adjustment of older Korean adoptees may well have something important to tell us about how children survive and adapt. The subject deserves further thought and continued research.

The Social Context of Adjustment

We were interested in probing why some transracially adopted adolescents were having serious adjustment problems and others were not. Although comparatively few adolescent Korean adoptees were reported as having adjustment difficulties, there were those, like Jennifer Gold, whose adjustments were stressful. We wanted to understand what elements in their backgrounds and present environments influenced the problems these adolescents experienced.

Preadoptive and Developmental Influences

As we have pointed out elsewhere, the adjustment of adopted children depends very much on their preadoptive life histories — perhaps even on the health and emotional lives of their birth mothers prior to conception. Our adolescent Korean adoptees were no different from adoptees of other racial and ethnic backgrounds in this respect. The impact of later placement and the negative influence of the child's preadoptive history were obvious from our cross tabulation of children's maladjustments by age at placement. Among the teenage Korean children who were under two years of age when they were adopted, all had reportedly favorable adjustments; this contrasted with 70 percent who were said to be well adapted among those who were over two at the time of placement.

Age also influenced the adjustments of Korean adoptees. Increased age appeared to bring with it more numerous problems. Among the adoptees 16 years and older, 59 percent of the parents reported favorable adjustments for their children; for those under 15, 84 percent were reported as well adjusted. A multiple-regression analysis of children's maladjustments in both 1975 and 1981 suggested that these problems were developmental in nature and not, as some have suggested, the result of increased hostility encountered by the adoptees or their families as adolescence approached.

Family Influences

Our initial interest in family structure centered on the impact of the adoptive parents' infertility on the adjustment of Korean adolescents. Infertility, as we have noted, has been associated with a tendency to deny many of the differences between adoptive and nonadoptive parenthood. H. David Kirk (1964), David Anderson (1971), and others have argued that such denial results in increased stress and tension for both the adopting parents and the adoptee. Critics of transracial adoption have also argued that white families who adopt in response to their infertility are likely to deny the child's racial identification and, in so doing, create serious adjustment problems — difficulties that are seen as emerging with special intensity in adolescence. When we turned to our data, we found that adjustments were linked with parents' fertility; well-adjusted Korean adolescents tended to come from homes where parents were fertile. Eighty-two percent of the adolescent Korean children of fertile parents were described as being well adjusted, compared with 52 percent among the children of infertile parents.

The relationship between parents' infertility and their Korean children's poorer adoptive adjustments could be explained by the greater anxiety these parents have in accepting themselves as adoptive parents. In Chapter 3 our multiple-regression analysis indicated that with all other factors held constant, children's maladjustment scores were found to be higher among infertile adoptive parents. This pattern was demonstrated only in transracial adoptions. It would seem to be congruent with ideas advanced earlier. Infertile parents, it has been suggested, are made uneasy by the differences between their adopted children and the children who would have been born to them. These differences may remind them of their failure to fulfill the traditional expectations of parenthood.

Adolescence is a period of increased concern with personal identification and separation of the child's self from that of the parents. When the visible and socially significant difference of race is added to the stresses of this process of differentiation, it may lead to particular difficulties for parents who are in some measure anxious and ambivalent about their relationship to their children. Infertile adoptive parents, as we and other students of the family have argued, are more likely to be anxious and ambivalent. This anxiety is easily conveyed to adolescents and can compound their difficulties in adapting.

We suspected that there would be some variation in adjustments between parents who were actively affiliated with adoptive parent groups and those who were not. Yet, the data yielded no significant differences between active and inactive members of adoptive parent groups and between those who belonged to parent groups and those who did not. On the one hand, affiliates of adoptive parent groups are likely to find help and support in raising their adopted children through participation in such organizations. On the other hand, the fact that they join such organizations could indicate the presence of adjustment difficulties. On balance, these contradictory trends could conceivably cancel each other out.

Race and Responses to Race as Influences on Adjustment

Students of transracial adoption are generally agreed that contact with persons of his or her racial background is an important element in facilitating the adjustment of the transracially adopted child. We therefore hypothesized that adolescent Korean adoptees would be better adjusted in racially and ethnically diverse communities than elsewhere. Consequently we expected that residence in urban settings would facilitate the personal adaptation of the nonwhite adoptees in our sample. Our reasoning was further encouraged by the assumption that cities are more cosmopolitan, diverse, and, therefore, more tolerant places for ethnic and racial minorities. Suburban and, especially, rural places were regarded as the least likely places to be conducive to transracial adoptees' personal adaptation.

Our data did not confirm these expectations. The adolescent Korean adoptees who were reportedly well adjusted tended to live in rural communities. Over 90 percent of the older Korean adoptees living in rural communities were described as having problem-free adjustments, compared with 75 percent among urbanites, and 65 percent among those living in suburbs. The successful adjustment of Korean adolescents in rural communities is especially striking.

It is probable that our original hypothesis ignored the influence of the relative proportion of nonwhites in a community on the attitudes of the majority. As the proportion of nonwhites increases, so do the anxieties and prejudices of the white majority toward nonwhites. In rural areas of the Midwest, where most of our Korean adolescents living outside central cities and their suburbs were located, nonwhites are few and do not constitute a threat to the white majority. By contrast, American suburbs owe much of their existence as distinct communities to the desire of middle-class whites to insulate themselves from contact with working-class whites and nonwhites. Opposition to the integration of all-white suburban schools with nonwhites from the central cities is one of the many indications of this suburban insularity. In this context hostility toward nonwhite adolescents is likely to be significantly greater than in rural areas, which could have negative consequences on the adjustments of transracially adopted adolescents. Cities are also likely to have significant conflict between whites and nonwhites, but the immediate impact of this may well be moderated by the diversity of urban life. These contrasting directions in urban life could produce the intermediate adjustments of adolescent Korean adoptees living in central cities.

The influence of racial antagonism and hostility on adjustment is clear when the cross tabulation of these two variables is directly examined. When adoptive parents received supportive responses from their families, approximately half reported favorable adjustments among their transracially adopted Korean children. However, among parents whose families responded with ambivalence and disapproval, only one-third reported such satisfactory adjustments for their children. Parents whose neighbors responded positively to the adoption reported very favorable adjustments in 46 percent of the cases. Only 31 percent of the families whose neighbors responded negatively reported that their Korean children had similar adjustments.

Few of the parents of Korean adoptees experienced a steady stream of hostile comments directed toward their children. Half of these parents reported never having heard racial slurs directed at them or their children. Seventy-one percent of parents reporting hostile remarks said that it happened only once or twice. Less than 15 percent of our sample of families adopting Korean children indicated that they experienced hostility sometimes or often. Such experiences take their toll when they occur with some regularity. Of the families that reported experiencing verbal abuse sometimes or often, half reported frequent adjustment difficulties. Less than 30 percent of families hearing hostile remarks no more than once or twice reported similar difficulties. Thus, it is clear that continual racial hostility — when it occurs — abrades the smooth functioning of children's lives. Whether the frequency of such hostile responses is much greater for the transracial adoptee than they are for nonadopted black, Hispanic, or Asian children remains to be demonstrated.

Questions have been raised about the adjustment of nonwhites of mixed racial background in the United States. It has been argued that such individuals are particularly marginal, accepted by neither racial group, and consequently subject to serious adjustment difficulties. We attempted to investigate whether the children who were more visibly Asian in appearance would be more likely to be subjected to racial antagonism and exclusion, and more inclined to maladjustment. We divided our sample into two groups: those who were entirely of Asian appearance, and those whose appearances combined Asian and white features. Comparing and contrasting these groups yielded no significant differences. Both populations showed virtually similar percentages of adoptees who had heard negative comments about their looks, had felt ashamed about their racial background, and were said to be well adjusted. If it is possible to generalize from these findings to the numerous children from Southeast Asia of mixed parentage who are being considered for placement in the United States, then our data would seem to imply that their mixed-race background will not be a problem in their adjustments.

Transracially adopted children — indeed, the children of all racial minorities — are exposed not only to explicit hostility, but to more subtle assaults as well. Through its advertising, television programming, and visual arts, American culture projects a conception of the ideal human appearance that is limited to a particular racial and ethnic group. American ideas of beauty endorse the characteristics of white northern Europeans. In this context Korean children diverge from the cultural norm. It was, therefore, not surprising to find that Korean adoptees were more unhappy about their appearance than was true for white adoptees.

We found that 26 percent of the Korean adoptees of all ages reported some measure of unhappiness about their appearance, while only 16 percent of the white American-born adoptees and 11 percent of the Colombian adoptees — who are usually described by their parents as white — encountered such problems. Adolescent adoptees reported similar levels of displeasure with their physical characteristics. Nineteen percent of the American-born white adolescent adoptees reported that they felt unhappy about their looks, compared with 28 percent of the Korean adoptees in the same age range.

As the mother of one Korean adoptee commented to us:

> Jill was never easy with her appearance. It wasn't a constant concern, but it was there. She wanted blonde hair like Randy and Bob, eyes like Mom and Dad. I'm sure that growing up in a small town with a lot of Scandinavians didn't help. When we adopted Karen — from Vietnam — this seemed to ease things for Jill, and I think going to high school in ___, where there are a number of American Indian children and even one or two other Asian kids, didn't hurt. Jill has always had plenty of boy friends, but she's never been selected for the high school's Queen's Court [a local beauty and popularity contest]. I don't know that it's been a serious issue for her.

Afro-Americans, Asian-Americans, and others who do not share the idealized characteristics of northern and western Europe display their unhappiness in a number of ways — often resorting to elaborate grooming, hair styling, and even surgery to conform to cultural expectations for physical appearance. We were not surprised, therefore, to find that the Korean adolescents in our sample were often unhappy about their appearance and that this unhappiness led to poorer adjustment among these adoptees. Fifty-three percent of those Korean adoptees whose parents described them as unhappy about their appearance had moderate-to-serious adjustment problems. Less than 16 percent of those adolescents who had no uneasiness and discomfort about their features were reported as having such difficulties.

One of the critical influences presumably associated with children's adoptive adjustments is their sense of race pride and identification. However, in our chapter on Afro-American adoptees, we found no association between racial pride or identification and adoptive adjustments. We found no correlation between adoptive adjustments and any of the following variables: the child's racial pride, interest in racial heritage, shame about being black, and identification with Afro-Americans. This raised questions for us about whether racial pride and identification were in fact linked to adjustment. We suggested the possibility that racial pride and adjustment were separate and unrelated dimensions. In the case of Koreans, however, there appeared to be linkages between these variables.

Adoptees who showed more pride in their racial heritage were better adjusted than those who were less enthusiastic about their

Korean background. Among the adolescents who were reported as being sometimes or often proud of their racial heritage, 84 percent were reported as having favorable adjustments. Of those never showing pride in their Asian heritage, only 63 percent were reported as being well adjusted. Of children sometimes or often "interested in their racial heritage," 78 percent were reported as well adjusted. This compared with 68 percent among those who showed little interest in their racial heritage. Among the children who never indicated shame in their racial affiliation, 80 percent were reported as well adjusted, compared with 40 percent among children who sometimes or often were ashamed of being Asian. Among Korean children that identified primarily with white society, 71 percent were reported as being well adjusted, compared with 78 percent among the children who identified both with their Korean origins and with their adoptive parents. There seemed to be a consistent pattern indicating that adolescent Korean adoptees who were proud of their Asian background were better adapted in their adoptive families. The cross-tabulation data consistently showed more pronounced adjustment differences on each of these variables among the teenage Korean adoptees than among the younger Korean children.

Some questions remained about the sources of these linkages between adoptees' racial pride and their adjustments. Our evidence has shown that as our Korean adoptees grew older, they were likely to feel less pride in their racial heritage. Age has also been found to be associated with adoptive adjustment. The question then becomes one of establishing which factor — the child's age or sense of racial pride — was contributing more significantly to explaining adjustments. It is also possible that adjustments were independently influenced by both variables.

Factor analysis revealed two factors underlying all our pride, identification, and shame variables. Racial pride, interest, and identification formed one factor, and these three variables were combined into the simple additive scale "racial pride." Being ashamed of one's racial heritage and having discomfort about one's appearance formed another factor. This became the second variable, "shame," when these two items were combined into an additive scale. We then did a multiple-regression analysis among adolescent Koreans to try to unravel the sources of these adjustment variations. "Racial pride" and "shame" were entered as independent variables in a multiple regression of children's maladjustments along with children's ages, their ages at adoption, and the opposition parents experienced from families and communities.

The results indicated that each of these scales contributed significantly to explaining the variations in adjustment outcomes. "Shame" dominated, with a beta weight of .553. "Racial pride" also was significant, with a beta of .288. Age contributed significantly to adjustment variations, with a beta value of .273. Family opposition was another influential variable in the regression equation, with a beta value of .186. Together, all the variables contributed 45 percent of the variance. It is clear that racial pride and interest — or shame and uneasiness about one's appearance — were significant in explaining children's adaptations in their adoptive families. Among the Korean adolescents such factors had considerable importance. For Afro-Americans, however, these trends were not found.

The divergence between Afro-American and Korean adoptees prompted further analysis. Those adolescent Koreans who were ashamed of their backgrounds or who had little racial pride were poorly adjusted. This was not true for black adolescents. Koreans and blacks were likely to show more pride and interest in their racial backgrounds when their adoptive parents encouraged them to do so. The adoptive parents of Afro-Americans were more likely to positively emphasize their adopted child's racial background. Substantially more of these parents lived in integrated communities than was true for the parents of Korean adoptees. Considering the ready access to Afro-American communities in most parts of America, and the relatively scarcity of Korean communities, this pattern is easily understood. Living in proximity to other Asians was so infrequent that ethnic integration had virtually no impact on the racial pride and identification of Korean adoptees. By contrast, among the families adopting Afro-Americans there was a significant relationship between living in an integrated environment and children's racial pride and identification.

. What accounts for the very different patterns for the Afro-American adoptees and the Koreans? We suspect that it has much to do with the greater antipathy in America toward blacks. This hostility prompts most white families with black children to close ranks and encourage their children to develop high levels of racial pride and identification. The wide dispersion of Afro-Americans throughout American society also encourages these adoptees to maintain high levels of racial pride and identification. In contrast, the absence of contact with other Koreans weighs heavily on those adoptees whose families do not stress their child's national origins. In these families adolescents are likely to experience adjustment difficulties in the process of gaining acceptance by the majority, which places little positive value upon either Korean culture or Asian appearance.

These trends have important implications for the controversy surrounding transracial adoption. Critics of transracial adoption maintain that as the adoptees grow older, they are likely to become more isolated from and ashamed of their ethnic origins. These arguments appear to have some validity in the case of Korean adoptees. Given the nearly complete immersion of these children in white America, they are likely to find little support and encouragement for their Korean identities. Nevertheless, when their adoptive parents encourage a positive feeling for their children's Korean heritage, Korean adoptees are likely to experience better adjustments. Where parents ignore or minimize such identifications, children are more likely to have adjustment problems. Apparently this is particularly true among adolescents.

In the case of transracial Afro-American adoptions, the arguments of critics appear to have less validity. They appear to have underestimated the extent to which transracial adoptive families live in contact with the black community and to accord positive emphasis to their children's black heritage. A substantial majority of the transracial adoptive parents of black children live in integrated communities and strongly reinforce the development of race pride, interest, and identification among their children. Children usually develop much pride in their Afro-American heritage and, given their immersion in the black community, a sense of black pride and identification with being black is widespread. The development of a sense of racial pride and identification is so common among the Afro-American adoptees that it fails to distinguish reliably between those adoptees who are poorly and well adjusted.

SUMMARY AND IMPLICATIONS

This analysis of adolescent Korean adoptees has yielded some interesting and theoretically important results. It has demonstrated that a substantial majority of Korean children adapt well over the longer term in their adoptive American homes. In fact, our evidence shows that these children enjoy somewhat better adjustments than their inracially adopted white counterparts. Some analysts have claimed that as the transracial adoptees enter adolescence, they are likely to be subjected to increasing hostility from the dominant society. They also argue that, isolated from their racial and ethnic subculture, transracial adoptees are likely to face great difficulty during this stressful period. Our data simply do not support this view.

Yet, our findings did show that as many Korean adoptees grew older, there was a decline in their racial pride and identification. Those Korean adoptees who experienced a diminished sense of racial affiliation and pride had less favorable adoptive adjustments. These results offer some support for those who assert that there are inherent problems in transracial adoption. One must approach these data carefully, however. Even those Korean adoptees with lower levels of ethnic pride and identification were relatively well adjusted. Although their adjustments were not as favorable as those of Korean adoptees with higher levels of ethnic pride, there was no indication that they were poorly adapted.

Our data also indicated that as parents positively emphasize their transracially adopted child's racial identification, they encourage their child to be proud of his or her Korean heritage. In so doing, they reduce the possibility of adjustment difficulties. Such findings reinforce the conclusion of other analysts of transracial adoption whose data show that white parents can communicate a positive sense of racial identification to their nonwhite children. Those who have been dubious about transracial adoption have been particularly skeptical of the ability of transracially adopting parents to do this.

When white parents adopt black children and live within integrated communities, they are likely to enhance the racial interests and pride of their Afro-American adoptees. Given the small number of Koreans in the United States, it is difficult for the white adoptive parents of a Korean child to make their home and friendships within the Korean-American subculture. It remains exceedingly important for these parents to show their adopted Korean children that they are interested in their children's background, accord it respect and recognition, and think it desirable that their children share these sentiments. We would imagine that this would apply equally to the non-Asian adoptive parents of Vietnamese, Cambodian, and other Asian children.

With this kind of emphasis, children are likely to be proud of and interested in their Korean heritages — unashamed of their racial backgrounds — and better adapted in their adoptive families. For Colombian adoptees and probably for other children from Latin America — where the differences between these children and the dominant society are less obvious — we would expect that cultivating the child's sense of race pride and identification would be less important. These children are not likely to experience the same racial antagonism and exclusionary treatment as Asian and Afro-American children. As long as parents acknowledge and show respect for their adopted child's past, they will be likely to encourage their child's favorable adaptation, whether or not the child ultimately comes to identify himself or herself as white or as Hispanic-American.

7
Single-Parent Adoptions

Michael Benson, one of our respondents, typifies a new and expanding segment of society. He is a single adoptive parent. At age 39 he has been a father to 12-year-old Jimmy for three years.

Michael grew up in a large Irish Catholic family. He was one of six children; he remembers having close relationships and warm feelings for his family — especially his mother, brothers, and older sister — when he was younger. The relationship with his father, however, was distant and strained. Michael's father was an electrician who often worked in other cities. He had a history of problem drinking. It remains uncertain to this day whether his death from a fall off a scaffold on a construction job was connected with his alcohol abuse. Michael remembers the frequent fights between his mother and father. The memory of these conflicts is so deeply embedded in his psyche that Michael has vowed to make absolutely certain that he and his wife will be well suited for each other before making his own plunge into marriage. So far he hasn't found the right girl, although he continues to keep company with several women of whom he is fond.

Michael's interest in becoming a single adoptive parent arose rather unexpectedly. A psychologist, he learned about Jimmy at one of the schools in the district where he is employed. At that time, in 1971, Jimmy was an eight-year-old, mixed-race foster child whose behavior was extremely disruptive. He was diagnosed as a hyperactive child and was receiving medication to moderate his restless and excitable behavior. Although Jimmy was very antagonistic and wary at first, he and Michael eventually formed a close relationship. Jimmy began to trust Michael and confided in him; Michael found himself developing a deep interest in the boy and in his welfare. Michael began to conclude that Jimmy's problem behavior was closely linked with the instability in his family life. After learning from Jimmy's social worker that his chances of being adopted were especially remote, given the boy's age, mixed race, and history of emotional difficulties, Michael Benson began to think about whether he could become Jimmy's adoptive father.

At first the idea seemed ludicrous. How could he properly care for a child? Yet, the more he thought about it, the more sensible the idea seemed. Jimmy's prospects without him or somebody else were dim. At the rate he was going, Jimmy seemed to be a prime candidate for reform school and would most likely end up in such a place in the next few years, if not sooner. Also, Michael thought that the fact that Jimmy wasn't a baby made adoption considerably more attractive. After all, he could handle an older child a lot more easily than one who was still in diapers. In addition, his own work schedule was fairly flexible, which should make things a lot smoother. Most important, becoming an adoptive parent would give his life a focus and meaning. He was especially pleased with himself for having made the decision to adopt all by himself. When he mentioned his thoughts about adopting Jimmy to his family, he got a decidedly negative response; his oldest sister was the only family member to show encouragement. Everyone else in the family thought his plan was absolutely ridiculous, if not totally irresponsible. His friends generally indicated a similar skepticism about his intentions of becoming an adoptive parent. When he evaluated all the pros and cons he could think of, Michael felt sure that adopting Jimmy would make his life a great deal more worthwhile.

Once Michael committed himself to making the adoption, he had an extremely difficult time completing it, although Jimmy came to live with him about six months after his home study was completed. It was over two years before Jimmy officially became Michael's son. The agency that had custody of him seemed to make it extremely difficult and drawn out before all the papers were signed and presented to the state court. One case worker in particular was especially suspicious of his application, and as much as said to Michael that the reason he wanted to adopt the boy was to express his homosexual tendencies. Michael was outraged at these suspicions.

When the ordeal of the adoption application was over, Michael and Jimmy had a big celebration and went out to dinner in a fancy restaurant.

It hasn't been all fun for Michael and Jimmy as a family. When Jimmy first came to live with Michael, he kept wondering when he was going to be sent back to the agency; he didn't believe Michael when he said that he was going to adopt him. Michael felt that Jimmy really put him to the test to see whether he loved him. With the bed-wetting, stealing, and constantly changing array of other provocative acts, it was all he could do to keep his cool, to show Jimmy that he really was committed to him.

After a year Jimmy began to settle down a bit. First he didn't need the medication. Then his schoolwork improved. Michael still sometimes finds it hard to believe, and is especially proud that Jimmy is now an honor student. Jimmy has lots of friends, too. He's a good athlete, the star pitcher of his class softball team. Michael has been talking to Jimmy about adding another child to their family. Initially, Jimmy didn't want to have a brother; his memories of his foster brothers and sisters were not very positive. Michael tried to explain to him that the relationship he would have with his brother would be very different. Now Jimmy is beginning to get excited about the idea of having a brother. They are prepared to wait a long time for their application to be approved. If they have any luck, they think it may be two years before they'll have a new member in their family. In the meantime, they are looking for a larger apartment.

Betty St. James is another single adoptive parent who cooperated with our research. She is a 48-year-old white schoolteacher in Los Angeles. She has been a single adoptive parent since 1969, when she adopted four-year-old Colette. Betty adopted Linda, a Korean-born child of Asian and white ancestry, two years later.

Betty was married for a brief period when she was in her early twenties. During that time she became ill with colitis. After years of trying to control her condition with drugs, it finally became necessary for her to undergo an ileostomy. She is not sure just how her marriage may have contributed to her illness, or how the illness may have helped disrupt the closeness she had with her husband, but she is convinced that there was a relationship. Betty is not averse to marrying again, but before she does so, she is determined to be absolutely certain that there will be no illusions and deceptions between her and her mate. In the meantime she has taken her invalid, widowed mother in to live with her.

Betty's decision to become an adoptive parent was quite unpremeditated. She had read an article in a women's magazine about the experiences of Marjorie Margolis, a Philadelphia television news reporter and single adoptive mother of two girls. Her story prompted Betty to pull together a lot of feelings and thoughts that until then had been compartmentalized. Adoption seemed like a marvelous thing for her to do — she had always wanted children, and yet conventional family life had always eluded her. Her mother and relatives greatly encouraged her when they learned of her interest and her efforts to adopt a child. Her friends, however, seemed to think this was a mistake. Betty thought that they regarded her plan as one that would permanently inhibit her opportunities to remarry. Betty, however, didn't see it that way.

She had heard that single-parent adoptions had been done for some time in Los Angeles. Betty had few reservations about adopting almost any child except one that might have a serious or possibly fatal illness. Despite the fairly frequent incidence of single-parent adoptions in Los Angeles, it was nearly two years before she succeeded in becoming an adoptive mother.

Colette, Betty's first adopted child, has not been easy to deal with. At age four she seemed to have an unquenchable need to be loved. Betty felt that she was always doing bizarre things to get attention; she seemed to need almost continual physical stroking to be satisfied. It was very difficult at first, although with time Colette has settled down a great deal. Yet, she is still not on a par with children her age; she is a very slow learner and Betty often wonders whether she should be in a special program for the learning disabled. Betty's experiences with Linda have been far easier. Ever since she was adopted at age two, Linda has been a bright and inquisitive child, easily satisfied and healthy.

The two cases discussed above suggest some of the variety of experiences that led our respondents to become single adoptive parents and how they faced the challenges of single adoptive parenthood. These case studies seem to raise many questions about what prompts single adults to assume the burdens of adoptive parenthood. We may also wonder about how single individuals compare with couples as adoptive parents. Does the single person possess liabilities as an adoptive parent, compared with the greater resources and social supports available to adoptive couples? We may also wonder about the marginality and low esteem to which members of any new social movement are likely to be exposed – does this create a handicap with respect to single persons' abilities to function as effective adoptive parents? These questions, and others, have guided our research in this inquiry into single adoptive parents and their children.

Adoption by individuals represents a relatively unprecedented phenomenon in the field of American social services. In the past such a policy would have been considered "unthinkable" by most agency workers. Earlier viewpoints assumed that only couples possessed the necessary role models and resources that could offer children psychologically supportive experiences. Today, however, child care professionals are increasingly aware of the large number of children who are permanently estranged from their birth families. These professionals are intimately acquainted with the fates of children whose early lives consist of passage through a series of foster and institutional residences. Ultimately, these children are likely to be disproportionally overrepresented in reformatories, prisons, and mental institutions. Agency personnel have become increasingly receptive to new alternatives that could offer children permanency in a family context.

Child care professionals have also become aware of the changing nature of American family life: increasing divorce and the large numbers of children growing up without close association with both parents. As American family lifestyles have become varied and as single parenting has become more common, agency personnel have begun to consider placing children in one-parent homes, especially when institutionalization or long-term foster care would be the only likely alternative.

Perhaps the earliest relatively large-scale effort at single-parent placements was undertaken by the Los Angeles Department of Adoptions when 40 children were placed in single-parent homes during 1966 and 1967 (Branham 1970). More recently the Los Angeles Department of Adoptions reported that 826 children had been placed in single parent homes as of October 1, 1982 (personal communication, Mrs. Clara Holtzclaw, Los Angeles Dept. of Adoptions, October 12, 1982). Across the country the number of single-parent placements slowly and steadily continues to mount. In recent years the Los Angeles Department of Adoptions has been placing children in one-parent homes at a rate of approximately 60 per year. Single-parent adoptions have been made in a number of American cities, including Washington, D.C., Chicago, New York, Portland, Oregon, Minneapolis, Indianapolis, and Bridgeport, Connecticut (Kadushin 1970). Nationwide, approximately 3,000-5,000 single-parent adoptions have been effected.

Alfred Kadushin's research has been particularly influential in stimulating single-parent placements. Reviewing the research evidence on children reared in "fatherless" families in the areas of mental health, emotional adjustment, suicide, delinquency, and sexual identification, he found no compelling evidence that single-parent family life is inherently or necessarily pathogenic:

> Research seems to indicate that children are able to surmount the lack of a father and some of the real short-comings of a single parent home. . . . The material suggests a greater appreciation of the variety of different kinds of contexts in which children can be reared . . . without damage. (Kadushin 1970, p. 271)

Yet, the philosophy governing single-parent adoptions has viewed these placements as less desirable, and the prospective single adopter is perceived as an adoptive parent of last resort. In most situations single parents have been assigned older, minority, and handicapped children — the least preferred kinds of children, whose emotional, physical, and social needs are considerable, often exceeding those of most other children. Although consistent with the laws of supply and demand and the child welfare perspective, these placements appear paradoxical: those who are felt to possess the least resources to parent have been assigned the children who would seem to require the most demanding kinds of care.

Many of our questions about single-parent adoptions remain unanswered. How well do children adjust in single-parent homes? How well do their adjustments compare with those of children reared in two-parent adoptive homes? Moreover, what are the common social characteristics among single-parent adopters? How do these characteristics compare with those of adoptive couples? In selecting prospective single adoptive parents, agencies generally insist that applicants have close relationships with their extended families to aid with the many demanding tasks of child rearing. How essential are extended family involvements for facilitating children's adjustments?

Are there other sources of support that single parents utilize to meet the demands of child rearing?

REVIEWING PREVIOUS STUDIES

The limited research done to date indicates wholly positive results for the children adopted by single individuals. The earliest published study, based upon eight adoptive placements made by the Los Angeles Department of Adoptions, came to the following conclusion:

> Our experience with single-parent adoptive placements has, to date, been very promising. In no instance have we observed regression on the part of any of these children. There has been steady progress in the development of the child as a person in his adoptive home, and in several instances, the development has been truly dramatic. (Jordan and Little 1966, p. 538)

A late study, also conducted under the auspices of the Los Angeles Department of Adoptions, was based upon 36 single-parent placements (Branham 1970). All but one of these placements were with women. Blacks were overrepresented (almost 66 percent). Although the sample varied in its educational achievements, sample members tended to be more highly educated than most; half had completed at least some college. Most had close relationships with extended family members; 66 percent of the women had been married. Most sample members were employed, and incomes ranged from $3,000 to $13,000. Although this research was primarily descriptive, it was noted that "These thirty-six case records strongly suggest that the children involved have found true 'familiness.'"

Joan Shireman and Penny Johnson (1976) completed a study of 31 single-parent adoptions of black infants in the Chicago area between 1970 and 1972. Eighteen of these families were reinterviewed three years later. As in the Branham study, most single parents were women; most were black; most had been married. Although educational backgrounds, occupations, and incomes varied, comparable trends were noted in this sample. The Chicago group was relatively high in occupational status — half the sample were professionals with low-to-moderate incomes, the median income being $9,000. The group also appeared to be extended-family-oriented.

Although initial adjustments of the children tended to be somewhat negative, two months later their adjustments were reported to be problem-free by 81 percent of the parents. Trained interviewers substantially confirmed parental assessments. A follow-up study conducted three years later showed only two of the eighteen children in the reinterviewed families to have emotional adjustment problems.

Many questions, however, remain unanswered. Almost no information has been acquired on the smaller but growing body of male single adoptive parents.

Because these three studies have been completed with clients served by two agencies — the Los Angeles Department of Adoptions and the Chicago Child Care Society — it is unclear whether the social characteristics of these single parents accurately reflect the single-parent population, whether they represent selection criteria of the agencies, local features, or some combination of all three factors. A survey drawing single parents from a diversity of sources and localities would offer a better base to form a general picture of single adoptive parents.

Further, in discussing adjustments of adopted children in single-parent homes, studies should be designed that offer some kind of control population — for example, comparisons with children who were not placed in single-parent homes.

In this chapter we have attempted to address these matters in the collection of our own survey data. The 13 adoptive parent groups that cooperated with our research provided us with a sample of approximately 20 single-parent respondents. This group was augmented with a sample of respondents drawn from two adoptive parent organizations known to include large numbers of single adoptive parents. One of these organizations was a single-adoptive parent group with a national constituency; the other drew its ranks from the New York metropolitan area. Single parents in our sample obtained their children from a wide variety of agencies, from all parts of the country; some had made independent adoptions. Our final sample consisted of 58 single adoptive parents whose responses were compared with our remaining adoptive families, 679 couples. In 1981 we were able to contact 35 of our previous single-parent respondents and 337 adoptive couples.

FINDINGS

Of the 58 single adoptive parents in the sample, 15 were males and 43 were females. As a group they were much more likely to live in urban areas; couples, on the other hand, were much more likely to be suburbanites. Only 16 percent of the couples lived in urban areas, compared with 51 percent of single parents. Seventy percent of the couples lived in suburban areas, compared with 35 percent of single parents. These urban residence patterns of single adoptive parents probably reflect the residential patterns of single individuals, the higher levels of tolerance for unconventional lifestyles found in cities, and the wider availability of services such as clinics, day care centers, special schools, and medical facilities sought by single parents.

Single adoptive parents tended to be more highly educated than their adoptive couple counterparts. Seventy-five percent of the male and female single parents had completed some graduate study beyond the bachelor's degree level, compared with 47 percent of the married fathers and 33 percent of the married mothers. This relationship was statistically significant for the women, and approached significance for the men. Also, single parents generally held higher-status occupations; yet their incomes tended to trail behind those of couples. Only 22 percent of the single parents had annual incomes that exceeded $25,000, compared with 40 percent among the couples.

There are a number of reasons why the incomes of the single parents generally were below those of the couples. First, couples possess dual earning power. Second, women are overrepresented among the single parents, and it is widely known that women in nearly every occupational category earn less than men performing similar work. Also, women are more likely to pursue their occupations on a part-time basis. Virtually all the female single parents in the sample were employed; 87 percent were working full-time, 11 percent part-time, and only 2 percent are unemployed.

Other minority members are similarly subject to discrimination. Minority members were far more common among single parents of the sample. While only 2 percent of the married couples were nonwhite, 14 percent of the single parents were nonwhite.

Further, the single parents were concentrated primarily in two fields: education and social work. Typical occupations included social worker, professor of social work, coordinator of a school-based drug prevention program, elementary school teacher, special education teacher, university professor, teacher of Asian studies, and school psychologist. It is probable that those choosing careers in human services are more likely to be receptive to single-parent adoption. Moreover, occupational experiences with children and the needy tend to support and sustain motivations for single-parent adoption. Also, service professionals are more likely to know about children who available for adoption.

In terms of religious preferences no differences were noted between single parents and the married couples. Similarly, no differences were observed in the frequency of religious participation between the two groups. Single parents were somewhat more likely to describe their political viewpoints as liberal. Fifty-eight percent of the female single parents called themselves liberal, compared with 45 percent among the wives of the sample; this finding was significant at the .05 level. A similar trend prevailed among the men. Fifty-four percent of the male single parents were self-described liberals, versus 38 percent of the husbands; these differences approached, but did not achieve, statistical significance. The liberal perspectives of single parents may well reflect the occupational ideologies of educational and social service professionals.

While the literature would suggest that single parents are more likely to be closely affiliated with their extended families than married couples, the opposite trend was noted. Sixty-three percent of the adoptive couples saw their extended family members once a month or more often, compared with 55 percent among the single adoptive parents. Although the meaning of these findings is not certain, it is possible that the urban living patterns of the single parents may impose time and interest barriers against more frequent visiting with their usually suburban-based kin. Otherwise, in interaction with friends and organizational involvements, both groups showed similar patterns.

One other difference between the two groups was their relative ages. Although single fathers and husbands showed similarities in age, single mothers tended on the average to be older. Twenty-five percent were 45 or older, compared with only 11 percent of the wives. Fifty-six percent of the wives were less than 34 years of age, compared with only 38 percent of single mothers. These differences may reflect the greater period of time required to achieve sufficient resources, maturity, and desire to adopt a child as a single parent. And, in turn, this may correspond to agency requirements for prospective single adoptive parents.

Adoptive Experiences of Single Parents and Couples

Fifty-seven percent of the single adoptive parents were first-time adopters. Single parents tended to adopt children of the same sex; 80 percent of the fathers adopted boys and 75 percent of the mothers adopted girls.

As one might have expected, single parents tended to have more difficulties in completing their adoptions. Thirty-nine percent had made three or more previous attempts to adopt, compared with only 18 percent among the couples. Also, negative experiences with adoption professionals were more often reported by single parents. Eighteen percent found adoption agencies to be uncooperative, compared with only 6 percent among couples. Fifty-five percent found the Immigration and Naturalization Service to be uncooperative, compared with only 19 percent among couples. Recent changes in immigration laws should reduce frustrating experiences with the Immigration and Naturalization Service for single parents. There was a slight trend toward more single parents reporting uncooperative responses from regional social service departments, but it fell short of statistical significance. Among each of the specified caretakers — adoption agencies, the Immigration and Naturalization Service, social service departments — single male adopters tended to report more uncooperative responses. Also, the data revealed that courts were less likely to be helpful to single parents. While 59 percent of the couples found the courts helpful, only 36 percent of single parents described courts this way.

Alice Longley, a 37-year-old professor of social work and mother of 11-year-old Jennifer, offered some comments on the difficulties she and other single parents have in adopting:

> The problem I have found most disturbing, to the point of making me hesitant to attempt a second adoption, is the almost universal indifference of legal and social agencies to the single person who wishes to adopt. I have had to bear the most insulting insinuations that I am either sexually perverted or simply mad, or both, for wishing to adopt

a child. The law of this state permits single adoptions, but no "machinery," not even any petition forms, exists for doing so. The problems I encountered in trying to adopt Jennifer were enormously aggravating.

Single parents showed substantially greater willingness to adopt hard-to-place children, and these attitudes were reflected in the kinds of children they actually adopted. Seventy-nine percent would accept an older child, compared with 60 percent among adopting couples; 82 percent were willing to adopt a black child, compared with 56 percent among couples; 51 percent were willing to adopt a slightly retarded child, compared with 32 percent of couples; 40 percent were willing to adopt a handicapped child, compared with 35 percent among couples. Although substantially similar trends in attitude were noted for both single fathers and mothers, men showed a greater tendency to actually adopt hard-to-place children. Approximately 60 percent of the men adopted children six years of age or older, compared with 23 percent of the single mothers and 9 percent of the couples. Forty-seven percent had actually adopted blacks, compared with 30 percent among single mothers and 10 percent among couples. These patterns probably reflect the unwillingness of agencies to place children with male single parents.

As a group the single parents tended to adopt children who were older. Thirty-three percent adopted children six years or older, 22 percent adopted children between the ages of three and five, and 45 percent adopted children under three years of age. Couples, on the other hand, were much more likely to adopt infants; only 9 percent adopted children over six, and 74 percent adopted children under three years of age.

Several major areas where parents normally confront problems in raising children were investigated. Three areas were surveyed: physical health, emotional adjustment, and growth or development problems. Parents were asked to evaluate whether their children had problems in these areas often, sometimes, rarely, or never. Parents were also asked whether their adopted children had received any extensive medical care in the past year. The responses given by the single parents paralleled those given by adopting couples. No statistically significant differences were noted, except in one case where making adjustments was difficult.

Male and female single parents reported substantially similar responses in their appraisals of the problem areas. Single parents reported significantly more emotional adjustment problems than were true for couples. Forty-three percent reported problems sometimes or often, compared with 33 percent among the couples. Many earlier studies noted that adoptions of older children generally present more adjustment difficulties because the child's personality development is already well under way before he or she joins the adoptive family (Kadushin 1970). Therefore, we tried to control the age factor.

When age was controlled, we found that the relationship between single parenting and poorer emotional adjustment disappeared for younger children but persisted among children six years or older. Among a total of 79 adoptions of children six years or older, 77 percent of single parents reported emotional adjustment problems sometimes or often, compared with 52 percent among couples. This difference was statistically significant with chi square at the .02 level. It is our belief that these trends reflect existing placement realities. Single parents, as the agencies' adoptive placements of last resort, are more often obliged to accept children whose earlier experiences of deprivation, instability, and abuse have led to substantially more emotional adjustment problems. In addition, the professional experiences of these parents may lead them to recognize such problems more readily than other parents.

All the respondents were asked to offer a subjective evaluation of their child's overall adjustment. Approximately 68 percent reported excellent adjustment, 26 percent good, 4 percent fair, and 2 percent poor. Substantially similar responses were indicated by both single adoptive parents and couples; no apparent differences were noted between male and female single parents.

Children's adjustments are salient for their parent's sense of ego integrity and well-being. Therefore, we included two indirect measurements of adjustment. Parents were asked how long it took for the child to be considered "their own." Responses were divided into two groups; those taking place within a month or less, and those taking longer. Single parents took longer to consider their children as their own. While 36 percent of the single parents required more than a month to feel that the child was their own, only 26 percent of the couples required this much time. This difference fell a fraction short of the .05 level of significance.

Again we believed it advisable to control for the child's age at adoption. With age controlled, both groups required substantially similar time periods to fully accept their adopted children.

Examining gender differences among single parents on adjustment, it was found that males required more time to fully accept their adopted children than females. While 32 percent of female single parents took more than a month for the child to be regarded as their own, 53 percent of single fathers took this long. Yet, when the age of the child was adjusted for, these differences disappeared.

The other indirect measure of adjustment used was response to the following question: On the basis of your own experience, would you encourage others to adopt as you have adopted? Parents were offered the following response categories: yes; yes, with some reservation; no. Eighty-six percent of the adoptive couples responded with unreserved affirmation, compared with 72 percent among single mothers and 67 percent among single fathers. This difference was statistically significant. Yet, when we compared single adopting parents with couples adopting children of similar ages, the statistically significant association between these two variables dissolved. Apparently, when we adjusted for differences in the ages of the child at adoption, single parents and couples show substantially alike responses in recommending adoption to others. This factor would seem consistent with the interpretation that the older, more difficult nature of the children adopted by single parents is the source of much of the difference between the experiences of single parents and those of couples.

Agency workers frequently stress the importance of extended families in helping provide aid and support to the single adoptive parent with the many responsibilities of child rearing. In fact, most agencies engaged in single-parent placements insist that prospective applicants possess extended family resources before they will be approved. An attempt was made to test this assumption that extended family affiliations are associated with children's adjustments. Seventy percent of the single adoptive respondents who saw kin at least monthly reported well-adjusted children, compared with 63 percent among those seeing kin less often. This difference is too small to be meaningful. On investigating the two indirect measures of adjustment — the time it takes to regard the child as a member of the family and the willingness to recommend adoption to others — those who saw kin less often were no more likely to indicate adjustment difficulties than those seeing kin more frequently.

Yet, when the responses of extended families to the adoptions were investigated, it was found that positive reaction of parents correlated with better adjustments. Eighty percent of single parents whose parents responded positively to their adoptions had children judged to have excellent adjustments, compared with 40 percent among those whose parents responded with indifference, mixed reactions, or negatively. This difference was significant at the .02 level. Similar trends were noted with our indirect measures of adjustment.

Those whose parents responded positively tended to feel that their child became their own sooner. This association was statistically significant. They were also more likely to urge others to adopt; this association approached, but did not achieve, statistical significance. The patterns that were observed among the single parents were also noted among the adoptive couples. Thus, positive extended family support facilitates adoptive adjustments not just among single parents but among all adoptive parents.

Friends apparently play an analogous supportive role in the adoptive process. Seventy-two percent of single parents whose close friends responded positively felt their children were well adjusted, compared with only 46 percent among those whose close friends responded with indifference, mixed feelings, or negatively. This difference fell a fraction short of significance at the .05 level among the single parents, but was significant among the couples. Those whose close friends responded positively also were more likely to urge others to adopt; this difference was significant. The responses of close friends, however, is apparently unrelated to the time it takes for the child to become a member of the family.

Another area that was potentially important was society's response to the single adoptive parent. Does the community generally approve of or reject the single adoptive parent? We investigated what reactions adopting parents experienced from their parents, extended kin, close friends, and neighbors. Respondents were asked whether reactions had been positive, mixed, indifferent, or negative. On the whole, our single parents reported responses from their parents, other relatives, and neighbors that were substantially similar to those reported by the adoptive couples; no statistically significant differences were noted between the two groups. Positive responses ranged from a high of 74 percent among mothers' parents to a low of 64 percent among fathers' parents. Friends of single parents, however, were less likely to respond positively. While 89 percent of couples encountered positive responses from close friends, only 77 percent of the friends of single parents responded similarly. Male single parents were somewhat more likely to report their friends' disapproval, although this relationship fell short of statistical significance.

We have so far considered a number of variables that might influence the adjustment of children of single adoptive parents. We have found that the age of the child, the response of family members, friends, and neighbors, and single-parent status have some measurable impact on adopted children's adjustments. We do not know which of these variables is the most influential on adjustment outcomes. The adoption of an older child, for example, might conceivably be a more significant factor affecting variations in adjustments than whether parents oppose or support the adoption. Or perhaps single-parent status is more important in affecting adjustments than either the age of the child or the support or opposition of family and friends. In order to sort out the relationships among these variables and to estimate their relative importance, we included all of them in a multiple-regression analysis of children's adjustments. We also added the variable "age of the child at adoption" to this analysis because we have found it to be of extremely great importance in explaining adjustments in our previous work (Silverman and Feigelman 1981). We have found that the longer a child waits for adoptive placement, the poorer his or her adjustment is likely to be.

When we completed the analysis, we found that the response of family and friends and the age of the child influenced the adopted child's adjustment to about the same degree; the statistically significant beta weights ranged from values of .12 to .146. Also, whether a child was adopted by a single parent or a couple had no influence upon the child's adjustment; the beta weight here was .004, a statistically insignificant association. Another finding was that the child's age at adoption seemed to have a somewhat greater impact than any of the other variables (beta weight .181).

What this seems to show is that although being adopted by a single parent has no adverse adjustment impact on the child, waiting to be adopted does. The dangers and liabilities associated with letting a child remain without permanent placement, in the hope that he or she will eventually be placed with a couple, appear to be considerable. By contrast, the risks inherent in single-parent placement appear to be negligible or nonexistent. Such findings seem to have considerable significance for current placement practice. In far too many cases, single-parent placement is a policy alternative of last resort, occurring only when the prospects for couple placement seem especially remote. Such policies are not only costly in economic terms, in the additional dollars that must be spent for foster or institutional care, but, as our results show, in their extremely detrimental and damaging consequences for children's adjustments.

Single Parents and Their Children Six Years Later

We were particularly interested in following up our single-parent families to see how parents and children had adjusted six years later. A number of our respondents commented that problems that they had confronted at the initial stages of their adoptions either had been resolved or were much reduced in their intensity. Michael Benson commented:

> Many of the problems that Jimmy had resolved themselves in the first few years of our relationship. Stealing, lying, occasional bedwetting have all virtually disappeared. Jimmy is by no means always an easy young man to live with, but he doesn't have the serious disruptive problems he once had.

We wondered whether the Bensons' experiences were most typical. Of the 58 respondents in our 1975 research, we were able to resurvey 35 single-parent adoptive families in 1981. Regrettably, our subsequent survey did not yield sufficient numbers of male single-parent families to do separate analyses of this particular subgroup; only seven were resurveyed in 1981. Their responses, therefore, were grouped with the female single-parent respondents.

Six years later adoptive adjustments among the children raised by single parents indicated a pattern much like that of the children of adoptive couples. While there were some slight and consistent differences showing children raised by single parents to be experiencing more problems, in no case were these differences statistically significant. Twenty-three percent of single adoptive parents reported overall adjustment problems sometimes or often, compared with

16 percent among two-parent family respondents. Forty-three percent of single parents reported children as having emotional problems sometimes or often, compared with 38 percent of couples. Eleven percent of single parents reported growth problems with their children sometimes or often, compared with 12 percent among adoptive couples. Twenty-seven percent of single parents reported high scores on the Conners scale for their children, compared with 20 percent among adoptive couples. The Conners scale is a measure of children's hyperactivity (Conners 1969; 1973). Twenty percent of single parents had children who either were receiving or needed professional care for their problem behavior, compared with 12 percent reported by the families where there were two adoptive parents. All of these differences fell considerably short of statistical significance.

We also attempted to assess whether single parents acknowledged any greater role conflicts in assuming their parental obligations and in accepting adoption than was true for adoptive couples. We developed a scale consisting of seven items whereby role conflicts and regrets about adoption might be expressed. It included whether parents would agree or disagree with such statements as "Parenthood has been one of the most difficult times of my life"; "If I had to do it over again, I am not so sure I'd become an adoptive parent"; "You never know if you are doing the right thing for your child"; "My child takes up so much of my time and energy that I don't get a chance to pursue my career in the way I would like"; "Being an adoptive parent has brought me worries and anxieties that most parents don't have to deal with."

Our expectation was that single parents might have more role conflicts and regrets about having adopted than was true for couples. Yet, the data showed substantially similar degrees of agreement and disagreement on each item and on the cumulative score totals indicated by both single adoptive parents and couples. Apparently, being a single adoptive parent is no more likely to inspire role distress and conflict than being half of an adoptive couple.

We were also interested in assessing whether the social disapproval that was expressed to single adoptive parents by their social intimates persisted or diminished over time. The data suggested that responses of approval and disapproval did, for the most part, persist. The parents and other relatives of single parents showed substantially similar responses to those given by the kin of adoptive couples in

1975. These patterns held in 1981. In 1975 we also found that friends of single parents showed uniformly less approval of their adoptions than was true for adoptive couples; the same pattern held in 1981. Only 80 percent of single parents' friends responded positively to their adoptions six years later, compared with 90 percent among adoptive couples; this difference approached, but failed to achieve, statistical significance. We also noted that neighbors' responses were less approving in 1981 than they had been in 1975; while 75 percent of couples reported neighbors responding positively to their adoptions, only 60 percent of the single adoptive parents reported such responses. Single adoptive parents appear to encounter a lack of acceptance among their nonkin associates in the community.

SUMMARY

The data have documented trends that are probably well-known to many single adoptive parents: Single parents are much more likely to encounter resistance from the social agencies with which they must deal in completing their adoptions. They are more likely to be turned away and discouraged from adopting. Once they adopt, they are more likely to be subject to disapproval from their close friends than is true among other adopters. This uniformly discouraging response on the part of the community seems to be slightly more intense toward male single adoptive parents. Yet, these negative evaluations appear to be without foundation when one considers the outcomes of these adoptions. With few exceptions, both male and female single parents report experiences substantially similar to those of adoptive couples in raising their children.

The results obtained in this research offer positive support for the new and growing practice of single-parent adoption. With the exception of emotional adjustment problems, it was found that single adoptive parents report information on the variety and severity of problems encountered in raising their children that is substantially similar to the reports of adoptive couples. When controlling for the age of the children adopted, both direct and indirect assessments of children's overall adjustments show fundamentally corresponding patterns among single parents and adoptive couples. These findings confirm earlier studies on the success of the overwhelming majority of single-parent placements, and suggest that single parents are as viable a resource for adoptive placements as couples. In fact, given the present discrimination against single parents in the adoption process, the absence of spouse support, and their more limited economic resources, these findings suggest that single adoptive parents possess unusually high commitments to parenting.

Before being entirely confident that single parents offer benefits to waiting children that are similar to those found in two-parent homes, additional studies will be necessary. Future research should examine more objective indicators of adjustment, such as school records and psychological adjustment test scores, among comparable groups of children in single-parent and two-parent homes.

If future studies confirm the present results, then there would be a need for reconceptualization of a great many theories of child development. Many of these theories maintain that two-parent families are indispensable to successfully resolve Oedipus and Electra complexes, to offer role modeling opportunities, and to ensure the intergenerational transmission of cultural values and conforming behavior patterns. Most of the theories positing the inherent need for the two-parent family were conceived during the early and mid-twentieth century, at a time when sex roles were far more differentiated and segregated than is true today.

Toady, with married women participating in the labor force and pursuing careers in formerly male-dominated occupations in ever increasing numbers, with household and child-rearing tasks increasingly becoming shared by both men and women, with formal educational experiences of both sexes more nearly convergent, there is considerable mingling of sex roles. No longer are men the exclusive task specialists and women the providers of nurturance. With the increasing flexibility of contemporary sex roles, culturally appropriate role learning can be acquired from one parent as well as from two.

The findings outlined here also point to a need for reconsideration of the role of extended families in aiding and supporting the single adoptive parent. The mere availability of extended families, whether through living in the same community or frequent visits, has little to do with contributing to the success of single-parent adoptions. A core of positively responding intimates, composed of kin or close friends — rather than availability of kin per se — would seem to offer a good prognosis for adoption success.

8
The Adoption Search Controversy: Adoptive Parents' Attitudes and Adoptees' Inquiring Behavior

Adoption practices in America have always accorded a primary significance to serving the needs of adoptive parents, helping to preserve the intergenerational integrity of families that might have passed out of existence without the birth of heirs. The focus upon accommodating the needs of infertile adoptive parents has had a far-reaching impact on adoption laws. One of the many ways adoption laws have been directed toward meeting the needs of adoptive parents has been through the sealing of the adoption record and the original birth certificate of the adopted child. The practice of concealment is almost universal throughout the United States. Only four states do not have sealed record laws: Alabama, Arizona, Connecticut, and Kansas. Little is done in these states, however, to publicize the availability of records to adopted persons, and the general atmosphere, therefore, tends to encourage secrecy (Sorosky, Baran, and Pannor 1978).

In most adoptions the child is issued a new birth certificate upon his or her entry into the adoptive family. The new birth certificate was designed to relieve the adopted child of the stigma of the original birth record with its identity-spoiling information, often containing mention of an unknown father and illegitimate birth. Since the 1930s adopted children have been "reborn" in their adoptive families, complete with new identities in the form of new birth certificates, exactly as if they were born to their adoptive parents. The original birth certificates — with all their identity-damaging information — were sealed.

Such protective measures have been historically perceived as beneficial to all parties in the adoption triangle: adoptive parents, adoptees, and birth parents. The rights of adoptive parents were safeguarded and their family protected from the intrusions of news-hungry journalists and would-be blackmailers. Such practices have been seen as helpful in fostering the child's attachment to his or her new parents. These policies have also been regarded as consistent with the needs of the adopted child's birth parents, helpful in assuring them complete privacy and anonymity. It has been felt that such procedures reinforce the birth parents' intention to permanently relinquish parental ties and obligations. In such concealment practices, birth parents would be extremely reluctant to surrender children for adoption, given the great risks of subsequent damaging revelations. The practice of concealment has long been supported by adoption agencies. They have been fully cooperative in assuring all parties to the adoption complete concealment and total secrecy.

The practice of complete concealment has been subject to increasing questioning and attack. It has been recognized that while such practices serve the interests of many adoptive and birth parents, they may be inimical to the needs of adult adoptees. Many now claim that if adoptees are to emerge as psychologically healthy adults, they need to have more complete genealogical information about themselves. Without access to their adoption records and opportunities to search for their birth parents, many are likely to suffer genealogical confusion and bewilderment (Lifton 1979). Growing numbers of people are beginning to acknowledge that the concealment of adoption records diminishes the civil rights of the adult adoptee. The Child Welfare League of America recognizes the present state of conflict and flux with regard to the sealed records issue:

> Today's sealed record controversy cannot be dismissed as simply the expression of a few vocal dissidents; it must be viewed as a moot issue. In this debate open mindedness is essential and such open mindedness has to include consideration of the possibility that adult adoptees may be right in demanding the elimination of secrecy. Regardless of ultimate decisions, social agencies cannot evade the issues. They must confront them. Among the groups involved there will no doubt be struggle and differences, but these can be handled if there are respect and a beginning understanding each for the other. In these beginnings lie the evolution of future solutions. (Smith 1976, p. 74)

While adoption laws still favor earlier practices of concealment, increasing reexamination and change have begun to take shape. Adoption agencies have started to reevaluate their unqualified commitment to secrecy. In 1978 the Child Welfare League of America expressed itself on the issue:

> Services to natural parents should preserve confidentiality and keep knowledge of each other's identity from the natural and adoptive parents. Both should be advised, however, that the agency can no longer make firm assurances of confidentiality, in view of possible or future changes in the law or its interpretation. Parents may dispense with their right to privacy by authorizing disclosure of identifying information in writing, when the child attains legal majority. The statement may also include the parents' willingness to see the child. The agency has the responsibility to know present laws governing disclosure of information. (Child Welfare League of America 1978, p. 21)

The present period — with its relative surfeit of adoptive parents and its acute shortage of adoptable babies — has led adoption agencies to reconsider agency priorities, now placing greater emphasis upon serving the needs of the adoptee.

The current mood favoring the search has been stimulated by a number of factors. Adoptee rights groups such as Adoptees Liberty Movement Association (ALMA) and Orphan Voyage have become active advocates of adoptees' rights. These groups receive considerable national press, radio, and television coverage acquainting the public, adoption professionals, and legislators with their points of view. These activist organizations and their articulate spokespersons have helped to ignite the sparks of genealogical interest among thousands of adult adoptees. They have also brought the search issue to public attention.

We see the current search controversy as a outgrowth and an extension of the civil rights movement of the 1950s. The struggle of blacks for fuller equality became the impetus for the resurgence of American feminism. It also helped spawn the youth movement of the 1960s that resulted in the abolition of the draft, the termination of the war in Southeast Asia, and the extension of the right to vote to 18-year-olds. Such broadened civil rights concerns have been extended to children's liberties, making the child's rights movement a potent force. Children have legal protections increasingly similar to those available to adults. Advances have resulted in a widening array of new freedoms: opportunities for children to bring lawsuits in their own behalf, to be represented in court by their own counsel, to be subject to the same rules of evidence that are available to adults, and the right to be protected against assault and abuse. We see a direct connection between these more general social trends and the current adoptee rights movement. As society has developed conceptions of children's liberties, it has fostered a broadened perspective of the rights of the adopted person; specifically, it has encouraged the recognition of the rights of adopted children to fuller disclosure of information about themselves.

The concern with searching for birth parents also has links to growing interest in ethnic origins and pride. Since the mid-1960s we have seen various ethnic groups demonstrate a growing fascination with their collective identities, increasingly delving into their origins and family histories, as they attempt to achieve closer touch with their "roots." As these interests in genealogical matters have been gathering momentum in society generally, their presence has created an environment very conducive to encouraging "the search."

ADOPTIVE PARENTS: ENEMIES OF THE SEARCH?

Much of what has already been written on the search suggests that adoptive parents face this issue with deep dread and strong opposition. It is suggested that wherever possible, most adoptive parents would be likely to suppress any efforts of their adopted children to gain information about or to make any contact with their birth relatives. Previous writings on the search are replete with references to the antagonistic, uncooperative, and anxiety-riddled attitudes of adoptive parents.

For example, Triseliotis (1973) found that "There was a general reluctance among adoptive parents to reveal or share information about the child's original genealogy and also how he came to be adopted." Sorosky, Baran, and Pannor (1978) seemed to offer concurring evidence in their study:

> Adoptive parents have felt particularly threatened by the possibility of changes in the present policies (of unsealing adoption records). They fear that a liberalization of the sealed record law would lead to the loss of their adopted child to the birth parents. There is no evidence

to substantiate such fears. Many adoptive parents also view any interest by the child in his/her birth parents as an indication that they have failed as parents. (p. 62)

We find similar sentiments in the work of Betty Jean Lifton (1979):

The adoptive parents . . . are leading another kind of double life. Having spent years trying to conceive a baby of their own, they now pretend that adoption is the superior way of parenting: "Other people had to take what they got, but we were able to choose you." And while believing themselves to be doing everything for their child's well-being, they are actually withholding from them the very knowledge they need for their development into healthy adults. This double role of savior/ withholder eventually works against the adoptive parents, estranging them from the very children they want to hold close. . . . If we are to understand why it has been so hard for adoptive parents to accept their children's need to know, we must go back in time, back to those people making up the chosen-baby stories, and see the difficulty they had in admitting they were not the *real* or *blood* parents. . . . Much of the adoptive parents' anxiety centers around that phantom birth mother whom, until now, they have been able to dismiss *as if* dead. (pp. 8, 258)

These statements maintain a consistent theme: that adoptive parents are antagonistic to the search, and that their opposition arises from their fear of the loss of their child to his or her birth parents. While we, too, would suspect there are very few — if any — adoptive parents who wouldn't have a tinge of anxiety or fear at the prospect of their child having a reunion with his or her birth parents, we suspect that the opposition of adoptive parents to the search is being vastly overrated. In all fairness to Betty Jean Lifton's view, it must be acknowledged that she distinguishes between adoptive parents with biological children — whom she feels are likely to assist their adopted children in searching efforts — and adoptive parents without biological offspring. This latter group, Lifton feels, are likely to be opposed and uncooperative if their children attempt to inquire about and make contact with birth relatives.

There is one study that found overall approval among adoptive parents toward the searching efforts of their adopted children. The Children's Home Society of California's survey (1977) asked adoptive parents how they felt about the adoptees' search controversy.

Fifty-eight percent said they felt more or less or totally comfortable with the issue; only 36 percent responded negatively or quite uncomfortably. Respondents were also asked how they would react to the search of their own adult adopted children. Again similar trends were noted: 64 percent responded affirmatively and only 31 percent indicated that they would be quite uncomfortable or against it. Similar trends were revealed when respondents were asked how they would react if the birth parents of their adopted child contacted them, seeking reunion.

It should be acknowledged, however, that the Children's Home Society survey must be interpreted with some degree of caution. Nearly 30 percent of their respondents were not affiliated with this agency; they asked for copies of the survey when they heard it was being conducted. With such a high self-selection bias among the respondents, there is cause to wonder whether this population could be considered at all typical of adoptive parents.

Yet, our own research results concur with those obtained by the Children's Home Society of California. We found most parents to be positively disposed to the search. Sixty-one percent of our respondents agreed slightly or strongly with the idea of children learning about and making contact with their birth parents; only 22 percent indicated varying degrees of disapproval. Fifty percent showed varying degrees of disagreement with the statement that adoption records should remain sealed, while only 26 percent agreed with this idea. Fifty-seven percent showed varying degrees of agreement with the notion that adult adoptees should have unrestricted access to all the information contained in their adoption records, while only 27 percent showed disapproval. Adoptive parents were even ready, to a limited degree, to provide information access to younger adoptees. Forty-six percent agreed with the statement that minor adoptees should have some access to their adoption records, provided it was supervised by adoptive parents, social workers, and/or the courts, while 40 percent disagreed with this statement. Yet, on almost all of the policy-related questions we asked about the search, between half and three-fifths of adoptive parents favored more freedom for adoptees, and a quarter or so disagreed with these possible policy changes.

Where adoptive parents seemed to waiver in their enthusiasm for the search was in their willingness to extend similar rights of information and contact to birth parents. Only 19 percent would be willing to extend to birth parents the unrestricted right to contact their surrendered child when the child reached adulthood. Also, only 25 percent felt that birth parents should be entitled to updated information on their surrendered child's development. The responses of adoptive parents with one or more children over 18 years of age were much the same for these questions as those of all other respondents. These trends suggest that adoptive parents are receptive to increasing the rights of their adopted children, willing to grant them expanded freedom to gain genealogical information and to make contact with their birth parents if they should so desire it. Yet, they are not at all eager to extend similar liberties to birth parents; indeed, they are decidedly opposed to extending such benefits (see Table 8.1).

It may be claimed that our sample is not typical of American adoptive parents, with its high proportion of single adoptive parents, transracial adoptive families, and fertile parents. Yet, we still found

TABLE 8.1
Adoptive Parents' Attitudes Toward the Search

	Percent Agreeing	*Percent Disagreeing*
Approve of adoptees learning about their birth parents	61	22
Adoption records should remain sealed	26	50
Adult adoptees should have access to all information in their adoption record	57	27
Minor adoptees should have some (supervised) access to their adoption records	46	40
Birth parents should have the right to contact their surrendered child when child reaches adulthood	19	65
Birth parents should be entitled to updated information on their surrendered child's developments	25	57

relatively high expressions of approval among those subsegments of our sample who more nearly approximate the greatest numbers of American adoptive parents. Among infertile parents, 56 percent of our respondents agreed slightly or strongly with the idea of children learning about and making contact with their birth parents; only 26 percent of parents indicated varying degrees of disapproval. Forty-eight percent showed varying degrees of disagreement with the statement that adoption records should remain sealed, while 34 percent agreed with this idea. Forty-nine percent showed varying degrees of agreement with the notion that adult adoptees should have unrestricted access to all the information contained in their adoption records, while 32 percent showed disapproval. Although trends here show lower degrees of approval than are found in our sample as a whole, the results unmistakably show relatively higher approval of searching behavior (see Table 8.2).

Another fact that may be raised about our respondents is that they realistically face little actual likelihood that their adopted foreign-born child could or would search for his or her birth parents. We divided our respondents into two groups: those who had adopted American-born children and those with one or more foreign-born adoptees. Seventy of our 1981 respondents had only American-born adoptees, while 260 had adopted foreign-born children. The results showed that the parents of foreign-born adoptees exhibited slightly greater approval and acceptance of the search. Yet, it was also clear that a substantial reservoir of support for contact and communication between adopted children and birth parents existed among the adoptive parents of American-born children.

TABLE 8.2
Infertile Adoptive Parents' Attitudes Toward the Search

	Percent Agreeing	Percent Disagreeing
Approve of adoptees learning about their birth parents	56	26
Adoption records should remain sealed	34	48
Adult adoptees should have access to all information in their adoption record	49	32

When we looked at the levels of support for legislation easing the restrictions on searching, we found that 66 percent of the parents of foreign-born children supported such legislation, while 55 percent of parents with American-born adopted children felt similarly. Although levels of support for searching are reduced among parents of American-born children, a majority of them still support the easing of legal restrictions on the search. Between 45 and 60 percent approved of varying forms of expanded freedoms for adoptees to gain greater genealogical information, while only about 25 percent opposed such policies. It should also be noted that there is virtually no difference in the frequency with which these two groups of adoptive parents expected their oldest children to search. In both cases about one parent in six expects their eldest adoptee to search for his or her birth parents. Today's adoptive parents clearly are much more positively disposed to the search than earlier evidence would have led us to suspect.

FATHERS AND MOTHERS: DO THEY SHOW ANY DIFFERENCES IN APPROVING OF THE SEARCH?

One of the surprising facts we discovered upon first examining these data was the substantial differences between fathers and mothers in giving approval for the search. Mothers were far more positively disposed to searching than was true for fathers. While 67 percent of mothers favored adoptees' learning about and making contact with their birth parents, only 55 percent of fathers felt similarly. Adoptive fathers also favored maintaining sealed records to a greater extent than adoptive mothers did; of fathers, 31 percent expressed varying degrees of agreement with maintaining sealed records, compared with 23 percent of mothers. Also, 83 percent of mothers had offered their adopted children all the information they had about their origins, while only 68 percent of fathers behaved similarly. Among the large array of search policy-related attitude and behavior questions that were asked, there were a number of instances where no differences between the sexes were noted. Yet, we found no cases where mothers showed less approval for some aspect of searching than fathers did. For most of our questions mothers indicated slightly or substantially greater approval for the search than was true for their husbands (see Table 8.3).

TABLE 8.3
Approval of the Search Among Adoptive Mothers and Fathers

	Percent of adoptive mothers approving/ or doing so	*Percent of adoptive fathers approving/ or doing so*
Approve of adoptees learning about their birth parents	67	55
Adoption records should remain sealed	23	31
Offered their adopted children all the information they had about their origins	83	68

What accounts for the greater receptivity of females to the search? It should be noted that earlier studies have found that females are disproportionally overrepresented among the ranks of those seeking reunions with their natural parents (Sorosky, Baran, and Pannor 1978; Reynolds and Chiappise 1975). Our own results showed females to be slightly more likely to ask for information about their birth parents and siblings than was true of males. We think that the greater interest and approval that women display toward the search stems from the position they occupy in American families.

Much family research suggests that women appear to occupy a pivotal position in the maintenance of kinship ties. Studies done in England and in the United States among the working classes show women to be at the center of the kinship circle. The wife's mother frequently finds housing for the newly married couple in her own neighborhood, she helps prepare the wife for her domestic and child care roles, and the married couple frequently benefits from the baby-sitting and other services that are usually furnished by the wife's relatives. In this setting of living in close proximity and depending upon each other for favors, social life usually revolves around inter-acting with the wife's relatives. There is no parallel associational network between the husband and his kinfolk (Young and Wilmott 1964). Women also play a dominant role in planning social activities.

They make the telephone calls and convene the family for holidays and family celebrations (Komarovsky 1967).

Studies of the American middle classes do not confirm similar patterns of matrifocal residence that have been shown for the working classes. However, they show a greater emphasis on the kin connection with the wife's family than with the husband's (Sweetser 1968; Booth 1972). Bert Adams (1968) has noted that females know more kin, on the average, than their husbands; they recognize family relationships as a more important part of their lives; they generally tend to be affectionately closer to kin; and they are in more frequent contact with siblings and secondary kin than their husbands. Given such greater involvement in the kin network and greater salience of family membership for women, it is no wonder that they are much more sympathetic to the search issue than men.

Jeffrey Rosenfeld (1974) has noted that the status of American women is much more dependent on their family ties than is the case for American men. Rosenfeld observes that women are more often involved in organizations, such as the Daughters of the American Revolution, that are dedicated to preserving family status distinctions. Women's organizations, such as the DAR, have several times the membership of comparable organizations for men. Given this emphasis among women, it is not unexpected that they should be both more likely to approve of attempts to maintain continuity and possibly more inclined to initiate search efforts.

SOCIAL CHARACTERISTICS OF PARENTS APPROVING OF THE SEARCH

We wanted to identify which adoptive parents would be most supportive of their adopted children's reunion-seeking behavior. Betty Jean Lifton (1979) suggests that adoptive parents with birth offspring are more likely to be sympathetic to the search than their counterparts without birth children. As we mentioned in Chapter 3, preferential adopters were significantly more supportive of the search than was true for infertile parents. Sixty-eight percent of preferential parents showed varying degrees of approval of the trend to help adoptees learn about their birth parents and make contact with them, compared with 56 percent among infertile adoptive parents.

We also anticipated that more support for searching would be found among those who are more likely to embrace newer social movements in general: the more highly educated, politically liberal, and secularly oriented members of society. Correlatively, we expected the least support among the less educated, politically conservative, conventionally religious and traditionally inclined elements in society. We also hypothesized that members of adoptive parent groups would be more receptive to the search than non-members. We expected that their attempts to conduct frank and open discussions of serious adoption issues would help to promote more empathetic behavior and more understanding and appreciation of the wants and needs of adopted children.

For the most part, the data seemed to be consistent with our expectations. Among mothers who were college graduates or more highly educated, 74 percent showed varying degrees of approval for the search, compared with 54 percent among mothers who completed high school. Approval of the search was also related to the wife's political preference. Seventy-five percent of liberal wives were positively disposed to the search, compared with 62 percent among wives having conservative political orientations. The tendency to approve of reunion-seeking behavior was significantly related to religious participation. Among those mothers who never participated in religious services, 77 percent approved of the search, in contrast with 64 percent among the wives who went to religious services weekly or more often. We also found statistically significant differences between those affiliated with one of the three major faiths and those who didn't profess any religious membership; 81 percent of those who weren't affiliated with any faith approved of the search, compared with 65 percent of adherents of the three dominant American religions.

Mothers who belonged to adoptive parents groups were more likely to approve of children learning about and making contact with their biological parents. Seventy-six percent of mothers in parent groups favored the search, compared with 47 percent who weren't affiliated with such organizations. Most of the predicted trends that were found in the data for mothers were matched by parallel trends for fathers. In the case of fathers, however, the associations appeared to be less consistent and strong.

There was also a trend that showed women who approved of mothers having careers to be more favorably oriented to their child's

TABLE 8.4
Social and Political Characteristics of Parents and Approval
of the Search

	Percent of mothers approving of the search
Among those with four or more years of college	74
Among high school graduates	54
Political liberals	75
Political conservatives	62
Never participating in religious services	77
Participating once a week or more	64
No religious affiliation	81
Religiously affiliated	65
Parent group affiliates	66
Nonmembers of parent groups	47

efforts to contact birth parents. Fifty-nine percent of women who approved of mothers having careers outside the home favored the search, compared with 45 percent of mothers who disapproved of mothers working. Thus, in summary, we observed that mothers who are more highly educated, fertile, politically liberal, religiously inactive, and accepting of women in the work force tend to be far more receptive to their children's reunion-seeking behavior (see Table 8.4).

PARENTS' SEARCH ATTITUDES AND
ADOPTEES' INQUIRING BEHAVIOR

One of the important questions we wanted to explore in this chapter was the relationship between the support and approving response of parents regarding the search and children's reunion-seeking. The point seemed fundamental — and perhaps obvious — but we anticipated that parents with approving attitudes, who offer greater encouragement, aid, and information to their children, would have children who would be more likely to ask questions about their origins and be more likely to engage in the search.

Literature on the search has made some mention of the positive and supportive role of adoptive parents in leading adoptees to the search. It has also been noted by some analysts, such as Triseliotis (1973), that adoptees are more likely to pursue the search when they have had strained relationships with their adoptive parents and when they've found out about their adoptive status relatively late in life — during adolescence. In this instance parents' apparent negative responses and withholding of genealogical information tend to inspire an adaptive, if not counteractive, response on the part of their children. Sorosky, Baran, and Pannor (1978) maintain that the more open and honest the communication is between parents and child about the adoption, the greater the likelihood that the child will be well adjusted psychologically, whether or not he or she ultimately decides to search for his or her birth parents: "The more open the communication about all adoption-related matters, the less likely the adolescent will have to resort to excessive fantasizing or acting out in an attempt to fill in . . . identity lacunae" (p. 113). Betty Jean Lifton (1979) also suggests a connection between parents' attitudes and children's behavior:

> The whole subject of telling [the child about being adopted and offer-ing genealogical information] should be faced squarely. . . . No matter what the age, the child will sense the parents' discomfort or ease with the topic. If they are tight and secretive, he will be too; if they are open and accepting, so will he [be]. If they act as if it is a disaster area, he will regard it as one; if they act as if it is a natural condition, which they can accept or deal with, he will feel more at home in his own skin, and in the family. (p. 202)

Parents' attitudes about the search — whether overt or covert — tend to influence their adopted children to openly discuss their origins and pursue reunion-seeking efforts. The attitudes they express spur the child to proceed as parents offer approval and encourage-ment. Correlatively, the child may be inclined to desist as he or she perceives that parents may be threatened by or disapprove of these questions. When parents provide a more hostile environment to the search, the child may learn to suppress these interests so as not to incur the parents' wrath, and perhaps lose the parents' love. Having already lost one set of parents, the child who receives discourage-ment may unconsciously decide that finding out about his or her origins is not really all that important. Some may learn, too, to keep these questions secret and go underground in their quest to learn more about themselves. Earlier research suggests that only a minority of adoptees go underground in their pursuit of the search. In the largest number of cases — two-thirds of the sample of those who had successfully made reunions with their birth relatives — adoptees had shared this information with their adoptive parents. The number of cases where adoptees did not tell parents about their searches included cases where adoptive parents were no longer living (Sorosky, Baran, and Pannor 1978).

Looking at our data, we found consistent support for our hypotheses. When parents approve of the search, adopted children are more likely to ask for information about birth parents and natural siblings; 55 percent reported children asking such questions sometimes or often when mothers approved of the search, compared with 29 percent when mothers disapproved. Seventeen percent had children who asked to see their adoption records when mothers approved of the search, compared with 11 percent when mothers disapproved. These differences approached, but failed to achieve, statistical significance. Twenty-four percent of mothers approving of the search thought their adopted children probably would or definitely would seek their birth parents, compared with 7 percent among disapproving mothers. Twelve out of the thirteen children who successfully completed reunions with their birth parents came from homes where parents approved of searching (see Table 8.5).

One of our respondents, who expressed particularly favorable sentiments toward the search — a parent of a 16-year-old adopted

TABLE 8.5
Parents' Attitudes and Childrens' Searching Behavior

	Approving Parents	Disapproving Parents
Adoptee has asked for information about birth parents	55	29
Child asked to see their adoption record	17	11
Child probably or definitely would search	24	7

son, born in Korea and adopted close to his third birthday — commented:

> In the last year or so Johnny has begun to talk about his family in Korea. We know he has at least one younger sister. John has always been aware that he is Korean, but until now he hasn't connected it with people whom he might be related to. He wants to write to his younger sister. We think it is a good idea, but we don't know how to arrange it. We're trying to find out. The funny thing about all this is that we have Korean friends whose teenage kids can't stand the idea of going back to Korea for a summer vacation to visit their families.

As a group our adoptive parents were most encouraging in responding to the questions of their adopted children; 83 percent of mothers indicated that they offered children all the information that they had when children asked about their birth parents; the remaining 17 percent carefully limited the information the child was given, or deferred or discouraged the questioning.

WHEN ADOPTED CHILDREN ARE TOLD THEY ARE ADOPTED AND REUNION-SEEKING BEHAVIOR

In the past, professional opinions were deeply divided about how important it is for adoptees to have full information about themselves. Some experts maintained that the less the adopted child knew about their origins, the better. They argued that in the absence of such information, adoptees were better able to adjust to their adoptive families and to acquire socially conforming behavior patterns (Kohlsaat and Johnson 1954). Many other experts have contested this claim, maintaining that family secrets diminish the energies that would otherwise be available for mutually satisfying family interactions (Sands and Rothenberg 1976). They claim that the adopted child's psychological health is best facilitated by full disclosure. Complete and truthful information about one's background also spares the adoptee the prospect of being traumatized in later life by inadvertent revelations of the adoption by kin or close friends of the family.

As the experts were unable to reach a consensus, so were most adoptive parents. Some parents shared all the information they had about the adoption with their children; others told children very little; some completely concealed the child's adoption. Now experts generally agree that open disclosure is the soundest way to facilitate the best psychological health of the child. Indeed, few adoptive parents today conceal the fact of adoption from their adopted children. In our 1981 survey — which included families that had at least one child six years of age or older — we found none that hadn't told their children they were adopted.

Another current controversial matter concerns when it is most appropriate to tell children they are adopted: early in life or when they are older. Advocates of telling children early in life include psychiatrist Robert Knight (1941), who maintains that telling children early relieves parents of the continuous dread that the child may hear of it from a third party: "The child who learns early would be very likely to think very little of it and forget about it" (p. 65).

Others, such as Herbert Weider, advocate telling children later, maintaining that the adoptee does not have the ego strength to master the information until he or she is over six. He believes that children who are told early carry a burden of knowing, may be highly inclined to fantasize, and may ultimately experience learning difficulties and underachievement in school (Weider 1977). Others, such as Robert Jay Lifton, place more emphasis on parents' attitudes about telling than on the chronological age at which the child is told he or she was adopted. Most important of all, Lifton suggests, is that parents have a relaxed attitude about conveying genealogical information to the child:

> Telling does not have to be flaunted or pressed upon the child. In fact, parents should take the pressure off the issue of when, so as not to falsify by not telling, or find themselves confessing to a toddler out of guilt or ostensibly expert opinion. By being more relaxed about telling, the parent will be able to tell in the most natural way possible according to the child's curiosity and need. (cited in Betty Jean Lifton 1979, p. 193)

There is also speculation that the timing of when children are told they are adopted is related to the tendency to pursue the search. In Triseliotis' study (1973) — based on 70 adults who engaged in varying degrees of reunion-seeking efforts in Scotland — it was found that those who had actually searched for their birth kin tended to find out they were adopted relatively late in life, during adolescence. By contrast, those who merely wanted information about their birth relatives tended to learn about their adopted status much earlier. Sorosky, Baran, and Pannor's research (1975), based upon 50 cases, found that their sample of searchers tended to learn they were adopted relatively late in life. The median age at which the group learned they were adopted was seven. We would suspect, therefore, that those showing deeper levels of interest in reunions would be among those learning that they were adopted at later ages.

Among our responding families, 60 percent had told their children they were adopted before three years of age, 16 percent between ages three and five, and 5 percent after six years of age; the remaining 19 percent knew they were adopted before being placed their adoptive parents' home. We investigated the timing of when children were told they were adopted, cross-tabulating it with all the items in our adjustment inventory. The results showed no consistent pattern. When children were told they were adopted — whether early or late in life — was in no way associated with the quality of their adjustments.

We also cross-tabulated this variable with all the items on reunion-seeking behavior — the frequency with which children asked for information about birth parents and biological siblings, the requests of children to see their adoption records, the parental expectation that their children would seek their birth relatives, and the likelihood that children successfully searched for and found their birth parents. Again, the results showed no consistent or statistically significant pattern. We could not say with any assurance that those finding out that they were adopted earlier or later in life were any more or less likely to be among those asking questions about origins or engaging in the search.

Given these findings, the data appear to come closest to supporting Lifton's contention that when children are told they are adopted matters less than the manner in which it is done. The findings also cast doubt on the significance of when children are told they are adopted and its impact on searching behavior. Earlier studies of these questions did not include control populations of adoptees who did not pursue searching efforts. The absence of controls may be a critical factor. Conceivably, also, patterns of searching behavior that may have held for earlier generations of adoptees may not remain true for later ones — searching has become so much more widely discussed and accepted.

RAISING GENEALOGICAL QUESTIONS AND REUNION-SEEKING BEHAVIOR AMONG OUR RESPONDENTS

Most of the available studies on the search have been based on relatively small samples; few have included control groups of non-searching adoptees. It is difficult to judge just how frequent searching behavior is among adoptees in general, and in particular among adopted adults. In one of the few studies of this kind available, Jean Paton (1954) reported that half of her sample of 40 adult adoptees had made some attempt to search for their birth parents. In the Children's Home Society of California survey — the only large sample survey — based upon 309 respondents, it was found that among adult adoptees 14 percent had successfully found their birth parents; another 18 percent had looked for birth relatives, but were unsuccessful in establishing contact with them. Given the various limitations of earlier studies, we wondered whether these figures were typical for adoptees in general. We investigated this question among our 1981 sample of 373 adoptive families, 129 of whom had at least one child aged 18 or older at the time of the study. We were also interested in assessing how frequent searching was among younger adoptees.

Among all our respondents we found that the inclination to ask for information about birth parents and siblings was rather widespread. Only 31 percent of parents reported that children never asked for such information; 25 percent said they had asked for such information once or twice; 38 percent of respondents had children who reportedly asked for such information sometimes; and 6 percent had children who sought such information often. Among families with older children the responses were substantially alike.

Actual searching seemed to be uncommon. We thought that if a child asked to see his or her birth record, that would be a good behavioral indicator of searching for birth relatives. Among all respondents 85 percent of parents said that children never asked to see their adoption records. The remaining 15 percent had done so, with varying degrees of frequency. Among families with one or more children 18 or older, 20 percent had children who asked to see their adoption records. Only 4 percent of families reported that an adopted child had successfully made contact with his or her birth parents. Among those with one or more 18-year-olds, 6 percent reported children who made contact with birth parents.

The results showed that our adoptees were slightly more likely to have reunion experiences with siblings, with 8 percent having successfully contacted a sibling. We also asked parents to speculate on the likelihood that their children would search for birth parents in the future. Only 18 percent felt their children probably or definitely would search for birth parents; 37 percent were uncertain; and 44 percent felt their children probably or definitely would not search for birth parents. Among those parents with older children, substantially similar figures were given.

These figures seem to suggest that while genealogical curiosity appears to be widespread among adoptees, relatively few actually pursue the search. There seems to be a notable discrepancy between the data obtained by Jean Paton and the trends indicated by our respondents. We see at least two factors that may account for these differences in results. First, most of our responding families had younger adopted children; even the ones with adults tended to have younger adult family members than would be found in the adult population at large. Second, among our respondents there was a high proportion of foreign-born adopted children. Foreign adoptions pose distinctive problems for those seeking to make reunions, in dealing with the varied political, linguistic, cultural, and economic obstacles that must be overcome. Such differences may explain why the search was so rare among our sample members.

Yet, when we subdivided our sample into families with foreign-born adopted children and those with American-born adoptees, we found that the responses toward searching were much the same in both groups. Whatever trends could be found, showed that families with foreign-born children possessed greater interest in searching than was noted in adoptive families with American-born adoptees. The number of families with children who had actually made contact with parents or siblings among both groups was too small to make reliable comparisons.

If anything, whatever trends we did observe seemed to indicate that searching and genealogical questioning were greater when there were foreign-born adopted children in the family. Forty-five percent of families with foreign-born adoptees reported children asking for information about birth parents sometimes or often, compared with 36 percent among the parents of American-born adoptees. Although this difference appears fairly considerable, it fell a fraction short of statistical significance at the .05 level. In 15 percent of families with foreign-born children, the children had asked to see their adoption records, compared with only 8 percent among the adoptive families with American-born children. Among both sets of families almost equal percentages expected that children would eventually seek their birth parents, with approximately one-sixth anticipating that reunions would eventually be made. Our data do not confirm earlier researchers' findings of widespread searching among adoptees. Much uncertainty still remains in gauging the incidence of genealogical questioning and reunion-seeking in the adult adoptee population at large.

DIFFERENCES BETWEEN SEARCHERS AND NONSEARCHERS

Why do some adoptees want to search for their birth parents and others do not? What social and personal factors are associated with the inclination to seek their birth kindred? Is the interest in searching associated with some psychological maladaptation, or is it linked to optimal psychological adjustment? Analysts seem to differ in their assessment of the psychological significance of the search and what it reflects about the psychological well-being of adoptees. Some analysts, such as John Triseliotis (1973), maintain that the search is linked to psychological maladjustment. He contends that there are two important dimensions to the realm of searching behavior: asking questions about genealogical origins and actually pursuing the search. In his research on searchers he found that adoptees who merely sought information about themselves, but were disinterested in seeking reunions, tended to have better self-images and more positive relationships with their adoptive parents. Those who actually sought reunions tended to have problems in these areas.

By contrast, Betty Jean Lifton (1979) tends to see the psychological adjustment aspects of the search in completely positive terms. She sees the search as purging the individual of his or her unresolved fantasies and self-doubts associated with being adopted: "Not knowing [about one's natural origins], then, would appear to be incompatible with a secure self-image" (Lifton, 1979, p. 50).

Others, such as Sorosky, Baran, and Pannor (1978), suggest that adoptees who search are likely to represent a broad array of psychological types. Some adoptees' searches are based upon neurotic needs and poor nurturing; others, who are basically curious and questioning individuals — with psychologically sound foundations from their adoptive family experiences — are also inclined to initiate the search and seek reunion. Given such a wide variety of viewpoints, we were reluctant to predict whether searchers came from the ranks of the psychologically maladapted or well-adjusted.

Following up our viewpoint that searchers would tend to come from homes where parents approved of and encouraged the search, we anticipated that they would tend to come from homes where parents were fertile, more highly educated, liberal, and detached from conservative religious and political institutions. We also anticipated that parents' membership in adoptive parents' groups would be associated with the inclination to search.

We used the interest in seeing one's adoption record as a behavioral indicator of searching. Considering the generally younger age level of our respondents, we felt that the request to examine one's adoption record represented a particularly meaningful indication of searching. It may be recalled that 15 percent of all responding families — and 20 percent of those with children 18 and older — had children who expressed such interests. The question we posed was what distinguishing features this group of families had, compared with all other adoptive families.

Statistically significant or nearly significant differences were found for most our hypotheses. Searchers tended to come from homes where the following characteristics prevailed: parents were fertile, mothers and fathers were highly educated and politically liberal, husbands and wives never participated in religious activities, and neither parent was affiliated with one of the three major religious faiths. However, there was no statistically significant association between the tendency to have a searching child and the parents' adoptive parent group affiliation. Similar statistically significant or nearly significant trends held for families who had one or more 18-year-olds.

We also noted a number of other interesting trends of statistically significant or nearly significant magnitude. The tendency to have a searching child was more common when women approved of combining motherhood and career, when they were employed themselves, when husbands and wives shared child care tasks, in larger families, and in single-parent households. These associations, upon first examination, seem puzzling. Yet, as we have noted elsewhere in this volume, all these variables are associated with the tendency to adopt older children. When we examined these hypotheses in relation to families with older children, in all instances the relationships dissolved. There was only one instance where the relationship remained: a single-parent family. For the moment let us pass over this finding; we will deal with it shortly. However, with the exception of single-parent households, all the above associations seem to be by-products of the older ages of the children in these families.

In order to examine the relationship between adjustment and searching, we compared children who had asked for information about their adoption record and those who had not. Comparisons were made among families whose oldest adopted child was the principal focus of our questionnaires. It was only on this child that we had collected adjustment information. There were 242 such families in our sample.

When it came to comparing the adjustments of children who were searching and those who were not, we found an unmistakable trend. The families of searchers reported significantly more adjustment problems with their children than was true for nonsearchers' families. Searchers' parents reported more children who were somewhat or poorly adjusted, compared with those whose children weren't looking. The figures were 25 percent and 17 percent, a difference that fell short of statistical significance.

In a great many other places we found evidence of poorer emotional and social adjustments in the families where children were engaged in reunion-seeking behavior. While only 13 percent of nonsearchers' parents reported their children as doing poorly in school, 22 percent of searchers' parents gave similar reports for their children. The parents of searchers reported their children had less interest in school and lower motivation to learn; only 32 percent of searchers' parents reported their children as highly motivated, compared with 59 percent among nonsearchers. Parents of searchers also reported that fewer of their children were getting along well with their siblings. Thirty percent of searchers were reportedly getting along well with siblings, compared with 43 percent among nonsearchers (see Table 8.6).

TABLE 8.6
Childrens' Adjustments and Their Involvements in Searching

	Among Children Asking To See Their Adoption Records	Among Children Not Asking to See Records
Percent of children reported as having some or many adjustment problems	25	17
Percent reported to be doing poorly in school	22	13
Percent reported to be highly motivated to learn	32	59
Percent reported to be getting along well with siblings	30	43
Percent receiving professional treatment for problem behavior	18	8
Percent reported to have emotional adjustment problems sometimes or often	46	35
Percent of children reportedly uncomfortable about their appearance	35	21

Parents of searchers were more likely to report that their children needed professional treatment for problem behavior. While only 8 percent of nonsearchers' parents indicated the need for professional help, 18 percent of searchers' parents indicated such a need. Parents of searchers were also more likely to report emotional problems among their children than was true for nonsearchers; 46 percent of searchers' parents reported such problems sometimes or often among the children, compared with 35 percent among nonsearchers' parents. We also noted that the parents of searchers were more likely to indicate their children displayed discomfort about their appearance:

35 percent of searchers were reported to have such feelings occasionally or often, compared with 21 percent among nonsearchers.

The trends show a very consistent pattern, with parents of children who were interested in seeing their adoption records among those most likely to describe their children as having adjustment problems. When we examined these relationships in families who had at least one 18-year-old adopted child, the patterns did not remain statistically significant in every instance, but they did persist.

We suspected that the affinity between searching and maladjustment could be a product of age. As we have established elsewhere in our analysis, older children tend to have poorer emotional and social adjustments than their younger adoptive counterparts. Older children, also, are more likely to have been adopted at later ages, another factor we have found linked with poorer adjustments. In order to effectively control for all these variables, we put each of them into a multiple-regression equation with adjustment as the dependent variable. We created an additive scale of the tendency to search, summing the responses of families who reported children who were believed to be inclined to search, who were asking questions about birth parents, who were asking to see their adoption records, and who had contacted birth parents. Using factor analysis, we found that these variables formed a single factor. The results of this analysis showed that the search index and age exerted independent influences on adjustment outcomes; the beta weight for the search index was .159, a statistically significant result, when age was present in the equation. Thus, the link between searching and maladjustment seems to be clearly indicated.

Earlier studies of searching behavior found that those who search for birth kindred overwhelmingly tend to be females (Sorosky, Baran, and Pannor 1978; Reynolds and Chiappise 1975). We found some slight evidence supporting this trend, with girls asking more often for information about birth kin than boys; 42 percent of girls asked such questions often, compared with 27 percent among boys. Yet, we found that girls were no more overrepresented than boys among those who wanted to see their adoption records, or among those who had successfully found their birth parents.

Previous research found that those who engage in the search are more likely to be only children (Sorosky, Baran, and Pannor 1978). Sorosky, Baran, and Pannor found that 60 percent of their respondents were raised as only children, an obvious overrepresentation.

Yet, among our respondents we did not find any evidence of more search-related behavior — higher frequencies of asking questions about birth kin, asking to see adoption records, or finding birth parents — among only children, compared with children in larger families. We also found that searching was more common among older adoptees; approximately one-third more of those between 21 and 26 had asked to see their adoption records than those between 16 and 20.

We also tried to investigate whether there were any other important linkable differences between families who had a child who was reunited with birth parents and those who did not. The few cases we had of successful reunion-seeking — 16 in all — make this analysis extremely tentative and suggestive. For some variables, missing responses were in such high proportions that the analysis had to be abandoned. Trends indicated that successful reunion-seeking was somewhat more common when mothers were more educated and liberal, when families belonged to adoptive parent groups, and when children were described as more poorly adjusted. Successful searchers also were adopted at later ages, and came from large adoption families or from single-parent households.

We imagine that in a great number of cases of successful reunion-seeking behavior, children were adopted relatively late in childhood. They may have been in and out of the foster care system. The intermittent contact they may have had with their birth parents established a sufficiently enduring bond for them to seek their parents as adults. We suspect that in many instances of older-child, single-parent adoptions, from the very beginning it may have been understood by all parties that the child would have contact and continuing association with his or her birth kin.

Many Domhoff, one of our single adoptive parents, told us that her 17-year-old daughter Karen had occasional contact with her birth mother:

> Karen had a number of homes when she was younger. She lived with her mother's sister on and off for a few years, then she was placed in a series of foster homes. From time to time Karen lived with her birth mother, but she could never manage to keep her family together. It was pretty clear, even before the adoption was final, that Karen would continue to see her birth mother and her aunt. Actually Karen is a good deal closer to her aunt than her birth mother. I've never had any

problem with this. I'm glad that she has a sense of continuity that other adopted children might miss. I do think Karen has a lot of unresolved anger toward her birth mother — it's going to take her a while to sort it all out.

SEARCHING ACROSS RACIAL AND CULTURAL BOUNDARIES

No study has yet probed the interest of transracial and transcultural adoptees in contacting their birth kin. Our data, however, makes it possible to address this question. Contact between transracial adoptees and their birth kin raises the issue of racial as well as family boundaries. The transracial adoptee who attempts to contact his or her birth parents is affirming a racial identification as well as a family tie. Inquiries about birth kin on the part of transracial adoptees, even if they go no further than requests for information, could prove threatening to adoptive parents.

Parents of transracial adoptees who are ambivalent or uneasy about their child's nonwhite background could easily find queries about their children's birth kin uncomfortable. Fathers and mothers who are ambivalent about their child's racial background may discourage their children from raising these questions. Such persuasion could be on quite a subtle level. The child or adolescent can easily sense the parents' attitudes and never raise the question. If the adoptee has learned from his or her family and friends that racial status is either undesirable or unimportant he or she is less likely to raise questions about birth kin.

We believe that the interest of transracial adoptees in their birth kin will be a product of the attitudes toward their racial or cultural background held by their family, friends, and neighbors. It is our expectation that those adoptive parents who are most supportive of their children's interest in their racial background will also be those most likely to encourage their children's contact with their birth kin. In Chapter 4 we found that the white parents of black adoptees strongly supported their children's attachment to the black community and their interest in contacting their birth kin. Parents of black transracial adoptees were more supportive of their children's inclination to search for their birth kin than were the white parents of white adoptees. Our data on families adopting Colombian and Korean children in Chapters 5 and 6 revealed that they were less supportive of their children's attachments to their ethnic communities than are the parents of black transracial adoptees. Extrapolating from this data we believe that the parents of Colombian and Korean adoptees are likely to be less supportive of their children's interests in their birth kin and that their children will express less inclination to contact their birth parents.

Our findings support most of these expectations. Data from Table 8.7 reveals that 26 percent of all black transracial adoptees in our sample asked to see their adoption and birth records while only 15 percent of the Korean adoptees and none of the Colombian children have asked for similar information. Thirty-nine percent of the parents of black transracial adoptees expected them to search for their birth parents. In contrast, only fourteen percent of the adoptive parents of Korean children and none of the parents of Colombian adoptees thought their children would search for birth kin. It is possible that the expectation that Korean adoptees will actually search for their birth kin is reduced by the difficulties of conducting such an inquiry in another culture. Such problems would also arise in the case of the Colombian children. The parents of white adoptees expected their children to search for birth kin in 21 percent of the cases. This probably reflects the greater age of the white adoptees.

TABLE 8.7
Adoptee's Interest in Adoption Records, Birth Kin, and Contacting Birth Parents by Ethnicity

	Whites	Colombians	Koreans	Afro-Americans
Child sometimes or often asks for information about birth relatives	48	43	39	63
Child asked to see adoption record	10	0	15	26
Child probably or definitely will search for birth parents	21	0	14	39

TABLE 8.8
Attitudes of Adoptive Parents Toward the Interest of Their Adopted Children in Their Birth Kin by the Adoptees' Ethnicity

	Whites	Colombians	Koreans	Afro-Americans
Fathers oppose sealed adoption records	28	53	51	75
Fathers believe adult adoptees should be able to contact birth parents	48	47	59	82
Parents limited the information they gave to the child about their background	27	7	16	8

Parental attitudes described in Table 8.8 closely corresponded to their children's behavior. Eighty-two percent of the white fathers of black adopted children believe that adult adoptees should be able to contact their birth parents, while only 59 percent of the fathers of Korean adoptees and 47 percent of the fathers of adopted Colombian children support such access. The parents of black transracial adoptees also opposed existing laws sealing adoption records with more vigor than the parents of adopted Korean or Colombian children. All transracially adopting families were more likely to support legal changes than were the parents of white inracially adopted children. Seventy-five percent of the fathers of black adoptees favored unsealing adoption records as did 51 percent of the Korean adoptees' fathers and 53 percent of the fathers of Colombian adopted children, but only 28 percent of the white adoptee's fathers did so.

When we turn to the behavior of adoptive parents we see that for the most part their actions conform to their attitudes, but we do see some anomalies. The parents of black adoptees made few attempts to restrict the inquiries of their adopted children, certainly less often than the parents of Korean or white adopted children. Only 8 percent of the white adoptive fathers of black children limited the amount of information on birth kin that they gave to their children, while 16 percent of the fathers of Korean adoptees limited such information. Colombian parents, however, placed few restrictions on their adopted children, limiting inquiries in only 7 percent of the cases.

Much of the disinclination to limit information about birth kin displayed by the parents of Colombian children probably results from their youth at the time of the study. Most were less than ten years old at the time of the follow-up. It is possible that the resistance of parents of Colombian adoptees to providing such information will grow as their children mature and have real opportunities to inquire about their past and pursue the search.

It seems clear that the interest of transracially adopted children in searching for their birth kin is a product of the larger pattern of race relations. Afro-American children, whose race is an inescapable part of their social status and whose adoptive parents are largely sympathetic to Afro-Americans and their culture, express great interest not only in searching for their birth parents but in the black community and its culture. Koreans are much more easily assimilated into the culture and community of white America, and, hence, the issue of contact with one's birth kin is less crucial. Colombians, who are often physically homogeneous with white Americans, are even more easily assimilated than Koreans. As a result Colombian adoptees are less likely to be concerned with their birth culture or kin.

The patterns of interest in birth kin that we have described above may well change. Shifting national and international tensions may bring about alterations in the relative status of ethnic groups in the United States. These changes will, in turn, create new meanings for the racial and ethnic heritage of transracial adoptees.

SUMMARY AND SIGNIFICANCE: IMPLICATIONS FOR SOCIAL WORK PRACTICE

Our findings add to the small, but rapidly expanding, literature on the search of adoptees for their birth relatives. For one thing, the data indicate that most adoptive parents seem to be far more receptive to the idea of reunion-seeking by their children than earlier studies would have led us to suspect. Apparently the increasing public discussions of this issue have led to greater understanding and support among adoptive parents for the rights of adoptees to full disclosure of information about themselves. Earlier studies on the search have found that all members of the adoption triangle — adoptive parents, adoptees, and birth parents — share a common frustration and disappointment in not receiving adequate information about the adoption and the other parties involved in it (Sorosky, Baran, and Pannor 1978; Children's Home Society of California 1977).

If disinterest and disapproval among adoptive parents formed a basis in the past for creating and maintaining present-day concealment practices, then changing sentiments among all parties would seem to point to a need to revise such policies. Our data — along with the results of practically every other study done on the search — call for the abandonment of current concealment practices; they suggest a reorganization of adoption policies so that agencies would routinely collect sufficient medical and social background information from all parties in the adoption triangle. Such information could be periodically updated, and made available in a nonidentifying manner to adult adoptees and birth and adoptive parents. Such policy and practical changes, our own and other studies show, would be received favorably by the overwhelming majority of all parties to adoptions.

Although our data indicate that adoptive parents are far more receptive to unsealing adoption records than has generally been recognized, many placement organizations take a more conservative stance. In 1976 Mary Ann Jones of the Child Welfare League of America, describing the response of a majority of member agencies to a questionnaire study of policy in this area concluded that:

Although most agencies report that they believe "the search" to be part of a natural quest for identity, and nearly all agencies urge the post-adoptive services be made more responsive to returning adult adoptees, *still* they do not believe that the laws should be changed to permit the adult adoptee access to the information in court or agency records on request, either now or in the future. Their objections to opening current records center on the obligation they feel to protect the anonymity of their former clients, the biological parents. But their objections go beyond the protection of prior commitments: most of the agencies believe that they should *continue* to guarantee anonymity to both the biological and adoptive parents. Although they may decide to conduct searches or disclose identifying information in the future, they want that decision to be made on a case-by-case basis rather than dictated by a general policy. (Jones 1976, p. 30).

While increasing numbers of social workers today have become more receptive to the search, many social workers and their agencies continue to favor sealed records. Such practices are felt to be consistent with general policies of client confidentiality. They also enhance the power and authority of the social service professional. Whatever position that agencies and workers adopt, doubtless, they will encounter opposition in some quarters. A minority of more conservative adoptive parents remain steadfastly opposed to any changes in laws or agency policies affecting the unsealing of adoption records. Yet, as our findings suggest, they will be more likely to satisfy most adoptive parents by facilitating access to adoption records.

Apparently overlooked in earlier search studies, another result that our investigation demonstrates is the formative role that adoptive parents play in encouraging adoptees' genealogical questioning and reunion-seeking behavior. As parents approve of such activities, they more often tend to inspire and elicit such actions among their adopted children. We would imagine that as mutual respect and support flow between parents and children, parents are likely to offer much substantial support and guidance in their children's reunion-seeking efforts. Parental disapproval, on the other hand, may lead adoptees to abandon such questioning or to pursue the search surreptitiously. We would imagine that in such instances, parents disapproval would be likely to widen the gulf of differences and to increase conflict between parents and children. We have also found that adoptive parent groups play a useful role in encouraging parents to develop accepting attitudes of searching behavior.

These data have also shown that genealogical questioning is extremely widespread among adoptees, yet actual searching and contact with birth relatives remain relatively rare. Such findings seem to be somewhat at variance with the results of earlier studies. Whether our results are due to ignorance on the part of our adoptive parent respondents in not fully knowing their children's actual searching efforts, or to the particular composition of our sample with its higher proportions of younger and foreign-born adoptees, or whether these patterns would typify adoptee searching behavior more generally, awaits future research.

We have also found that mothers seem to be substantially more approving and supportive of their adopted children's genealogical questioning and reunion-seeking than fathers. We have explained this trend as a by-product of the pivotal role women hold in American kinship relations. The clinical implications of these trends, for the time being, remain uncertain. Given a situation in which a great difference of opinion on the search existed between mothers and fathers, there could be very unhealthy psychological effects on adoptees. Under these conditions, if a child showed interests in searching, he or she would gain the approval and support of one parent, and the intense displeasure of the other. Abstaining from genealogical questioning would evoke similar consequences. It would be a "Catch-22" situation, very likely to cause the adoptee much anguish and turmoil. Such conditions could conceivably be linked with the association we found between reunion-seeking efforts and poorer psychological adjustments.

Other analysts have speculated, and in some cases have presented data suggesting, that the timing of when children are told they are adopted has an influence on their emotional adjustments and on the likelihood that they will search for their birth relatives. Our data show that virtually all adoptive parents today tell their children they are adopted; the greatest majority (60 percent) tell their children before they are three years old. In contrast with other studies, our data indicated that whether children were told early or late mattered little in explaining variations in their psychological well-being and their likelihood to engage in reunion-seeking behavior. Perhaps the way in which children are told they are adopted is more important than the particular chronological moment at which this information is offered.

We also found an association between children's reunion-seeking behavior and a variety of emotional and social adjustment problems. Children who engaged in more searching efforts were felt by their adoptive parents to be more poorly adjusted psychologically than their counterparts who had not pursued the search. The implications of these trends remain unclear. Several possible interpretations for these patterns present themselves.

It is altogether conceivable that while parents may approve of the search in the abstract and in general — even be inclined to offer some assistance to searching efforts — they may be quite distraught and fearful with the particular prospect of their child's actually engaging in reunion-seeking behavior. They may connect these feelings in such a way that they see their child's behavior as a source of disappointment and irritation.

It is also possible that the poorer adjustments among adoptees who search result from problems in the adoptive parent-child relationship.

Adoptive parents frequently deny the differences between adoption and birth parenthood; this denial can result in problems for both parent and child. In this situation the child's interest in pursuing the search could easily reflect the tensions generated by denial. This pattern remains to be empirically established.

Another equally plausible alternative is that the children who are searching for their birth parents do, indeed, present more difficult behavior patterns. Considering the age of our respondents' children — the greatest number were preteens and teenagers — it is entirely possible that these children are in the midst of adolescent turmoil. No longer revering their adoptive parents in the way they did when they were younger, they may experience a sense of loss and become contemptuous toward them. This sense of loss may be compounded with a sense of grief and self-pity for having lost their birth parents and with wondering who they are. Feelings of inadequacy compound when they consider that they were relinquished as infants. Such concerns may inspire much fantasizing and acting-out behavior, with children becoming troublesome in their actions. It is quite possible that, under these circumstances, the search may be a very disruptive event within the adoptive family.

We might speculate that among older, more mature adoptees the search may be associated with good psychological health, or at least with the absence of maladaptive psychological aspects. Other analysts suggest that the search may be linked with good psychological health among adoptees and a strengthening of the adoptive parent-child bond (Lifton 1979; Sorosky, Baran, and Pannor 1978). Our evidence, from the vantage point of the adoptive parent, finds little confirmation of this pattern. More research will be necessary to specify the conditions under which psychological adjustments are facilitated or frustrated by adoptees' reunion-seeking behavior.

We might also mention that these results point to the identification of at least one other type of search in addition to the most common quest of finding birth parents by children who were relinquished as infants. We have identified a group of adoptees who may have had intermittent contact with birth parents during their early childhood years; they may have been in and out of foster homes and eventually were placed for adoption in later childhood. Such children often seek their birth parents as adults. They are also more likely to be adopted by single parents. We suspect that their experiences in searching and their reunions are likely to be very different from those of adoptees who have been separated from birth parents since infancy. More information needs to be collected on this distinctive subgroup of adoptees.

9
Adoption Overview

Our book has focused upon changing trends in adoptive relationships in American society. We have emphasized the linkages between changes in American family patterns and their impact on current adoption practices. Several emergent trends have been particularly important in reshaping adoption practices. Newer family patterns have given greater emphasis to sharing work and child care roles. With the rising tide of divorce, single-parent households are far more acceptable. Our society now affords greater recognition to reconstituted, communal, and other nontraditional family patterns. Prevailing conceptions of masculinity and femininity are no longer as closely identified with procreation, as they once were. All of these changes have favored adoption and have given encouragement to thousands of fertile couples and single adults to form families by adoption.

Recent medical advances have aided some prospective parents who would have been likely to adopt. Nevertheless, owing to changes in the patterns of family living, the extent of infertility remains relatively undiminished. Increasing cohabitation, economic pressures, and the expanding importance of work for women have led couples to marry later. Unwed mothers are now more inclined to retain custody of their children. Such tendencies have added to the numbers of infertile couples and have made it more difficult for them to find infants to adopt. Given the prevailing shortage of infants available for adoption in the United States, it could even be claimed that the difficulties associated with infertility have intensified for infertile couples.

For the general public adoption remains associated with infertility. Considerable numbers of Americans continue to believe that the only people interested in seeking adoption are those who cannot conceive children. It is certainly true that in terms of nonrelative adoptions, the majority of today's adoptive parents are adopting in response to infertility. Yet, the public has not begun to acknowledge that sizable numbers — and expanding proportions — of today's adoptive parents consist of fertile couples and single adults.

It is against the backdrop of these trends that we were prompted to do our study. We wanted to investigate how these newer types of "preferential" adoptive parents responded to adoption. We wondered how their more social and humanitarian motivations would affect their adjustments and the adaptations of their children. We wanted to know whether their motivations were adequate to meet the challenges of adoptive parenthood.

Our results indicated that preferential adoptive parents — whether they were fertile couples or single adults — were no less able to respond to the nurturing needs of their adoptive children than was true of traditional infertile parents. When all other important differences were adjusted for, we found their children to be at least as well adapted as the children adopted by infertile couples. Although these parents were likely to encounter more opposition from their extended families and communities than traditional adoptive parents, this lack of support had relatively little adverse impact upon their own and their children's adaptations. These parents did not come to adoption with the sense of anxiety and role handicap that is common among many infertile parents. They also had a rich backlog of parenting experiences from raising their birth children that apparently proved helpful to them. We found no evidence to indicate that such families were deficient in meeting the needs of waiting children.

Our results showed that these preferential parents were more inclined to adopt all types of hard-to-place children, whether the children were stigmatized by age, race or ethnic affiliation, mental or physical disabilities. Fertile couples and single adults felt freer to initiate efforts to construct families and parent-child relationships outside the limits imposed by traditional conceptions of family formation.

These changes have have broad implications for the recruitment of adoptive parents. Child welfare practitioners frequently assume that the number of prospective adoptive parents willing to provide homes for special-needs children is especially limited. Our evidence suggests that the number of such receptive families is growing, and may be more widespread than commonly thought. Our evidence also suggests that some groups traditionally excluded from consideration for adoptive parenthood — fertile couples, families with working wives, single parents, and less affluent families — may be among those particularly receptive to providing homes for hard-to-place children.

Case workers and administrators frequently believe that prevailing adoption practices fully acknowledge the changing American family and the newer groups of potential adoptive parents. Many expect that previous barriers to placement no longer apply, anticipating that the enlightened views they share about adoption are widely employed in current adoption practices. Yet, the comments of a significant minority of our respondents would seem to indicate otherwise. Ted Callahan, the 37-year-old adoptive parent of a nine-year-old boy, Jim, made the following comments on his attempts to adopt a second child:

> After Jim had been in our home for three years, we wanted to adopt a second child. We didn't think we'd have a problem because Marie and I were willing to adopt an older child or a child with emotional problems. We were surprised when a worker from an agency we applied to told us that the fact we already had children in our home reduced our chances for another placement. I actually think the agency was put off by our interest. It was almost as if there was something not quite right about people who were interested in kids with emotional problems. I could hardly believe their response because they had persuaded us to adopt Jim four years earlier. They had told us before he was placed with us that Jim had a lot of emotional problems.

In the same vein Jane Croce, a 39-year-old teacher of learning-disabled children and a prospective single adoptive parent, said:

> I've been trying to adopt a child for the last three years, and I'm beginning to think I'll never do it. I know that a lot of others in the Greater _____ Area Single Parents Association have had the same experience, but it doesn't make it easier to deal with. It makes me very angry because I know that there are a lot of older kids who need to be placed — I work with some of them in the school system. I try hard not to

get very angry with the people at ＿＿ Children's Services. I'm afraid if I lose my temper, I'll ruin any chance I have of adopting a child with them.

Our many discussions with single adoptive parents and their questionnaire responses consistently indicated a pattern of struggling unremittingly — for years in many cases — before eventually getting children placed with them. While fertile couples reported less difficulty in their dealings with placement agencies, the comments of these parents frequently suggested that it was often necessary for them to act as adversaries in order to get children. Apparently, earlier attitudes giving priority to relatively young, economically secure, infertile, and childless couples as the most desirable adoptive parents still apply in some quarters. This seems to be a particular problem in Asian and Latin American countries, where the desire of single or fertile parents to adopt is often treated with considerable suspicion. If the placement needs of waiting children are to be fully met, such stereotypes will have to be relinquished.

It is widely assumed that single parents should be a placement choice of last resort. Both laymen and social service professionals often feel that single adults are less able to parent successfully, if for no other reason than the fact that they lack a spouse with whom the burdens of child care can be shared. The findings of our study reveal that it is the children who are hardest to place — those with the greatest potential for difficulties in adapting to their adoptive homes — who are offered to single parents. Despite the greater range of problems these parents encountered, our evidence suggested that single parents were as effective as couples in raising their adopted children. Another assumption that has limited single-parent placements is the belief that such adoptions can work only where there is an extensive and supportive network of kin. Our data suggested that this is not so. For many single parents a network of friends, neighbors, and co-workers may be equally effective in reducing the burdens of parenting.

Our research has compared the experiences of infertile and fertile adoptive parents. Although both groups are faced with many of the same realities in their experience of adoptive parenthood, the meaning of the adoptive relationship may be profoundly different at many points. We found the theories of H. David Kirk to be particularly helpful in interpreting these differences. Kirk argues that infertile couples are often likely to feel very anxious about becoming adoptive parents, perceiving a deficiency within themselves in their failure to bear offspring. In response to their great uneasiness about adoption, many infertile parents are likely to deny the differences between biological and adoptive parenthood.

Consistent with this line of analysis, our findings indicated that these anxieties and role handicaps were reflected in the adoption preferences of infertile parents; they tended to adopt infants racially and ethnically like themselves, much like the children they might have given birth to, had they been able to conceive. Infertile parents, we also found, were less inclined to favor open adoptions, and were less amenable to offering information and support to their adoptees who raised questions about their genealogical origins. Fertile parents, not burdened by the need to deny or come to terms with infertility, do not experience the feelings of infertile adoptive parents that their child is both a reminder of failure and a symbol of fulfillment.

The interaction between parental infertility and the adaptation of the adoptee is complex one. The adopted children of infertile parents appeared to encounter more adjustment problems when they were first placed in their adoptive homes. These problems were by no means severe enough to threaten the adoptive relationship; they were not overwhelming in most cases. It is quite clear, however, that these children faced greater difficulties than those placed in the homes of fertile parents. In many cases, particularly those in which parents and adopted children were of the same racial background, the problems were transitory; they diminished in the first few years after placement.

Among transracially adopted children, however, the difficulties created by infertility were more likely to persist. We found this to be true for adolescent Korean transracial adoptees. These children were less likely to be well adjusted when they were living in homes where parents were infertile than when they were adopted by fertile parents. Such findings may not be all that surprising theoretically, when we consider that these transracially adopted children are visibly different from the children their adoptive parents might have conceived had they been fertile. It is precisely this difference that apparently creates a strain in adoptive relationships, continually reminding parents — and their socially significant others — of their failure to conceive.

At the same time it should be reiterated that we are talking about rather small, although consistent, differences between the children adopted by fertile and infertile couples. Although the children of infertile adoptive parents did encounter more problems in some instances, their overall adaptations were generally positive. The implication here, we think, is not that infertile placements — transracial or intraracial — are excessively difficult, but that some reasonable attention must be paid to the problems and difficulties that infertility creates for parents and adopted children.

Infertility often implies adjustment difficulties for the adoptive parents. It is likely to remain an important issue for adoptive parents, adoptees, and social service professionals in the coming years. Present trends toward later marriages will inevitably add to the numbers of infertile couples seeking to adopt children. Many of those adopted — given the small numbers of American-born infants available — will be foreign-born and nonwhite. Problems generated by infertility are likely to be more pronounced where racial and cultural differences separate parent and child. Professional treatment and peer support are likely to be of considerable benefit in alleviating the stress encountered by many infertile adoptive parents.

Current trends in family patterns — with the greater involvement of fertile couples in adoptions — offer possibilities for reducing some of the stigma now linked with adoption and infertility. Negative feelings toward adoption could diminish with a wider understanding that for many, adoption represents a positive choice, not simply a response to failure. A greater appreciation of the intrinsic rewards of adoption could bring about declining prejudice and stigma. Such changed attitudes could have an important impact on reducing the role difficulties felt by infertile adopting parents.

One of the most controversial topics associated with adoptions is transracial and transcultural adoption. Interestingly, when these placements first began in large numbers, at the close of World War II, they provoked little debate. At that time they were seen as a humanitarian response to aid the war-ravaged countries of Europe and Asia. Although foreign adoptions from Europe sharply diminished with successful war relief and economic development efforts, they continued to expand from Asia. There, with chronic economic underdevelopment, lingering warfare (particularly in Korea and Vietnam), and the continuing presence of American soldiers, conditions favored the persistence and expansion of transracial adoptions. Transracial adoptions were also stimulated by the diffusion and development of American social services in Asia, especially in Korea.

As the transracial adoptions of Korean children increased, this stimulated efforts to place American-born minorities in white homes. Since the late 1950s there have been rising numbers of transracial placements of homeless Native American and Afro-American children. The important role played by military and political conflict abroad in initiating the process of transracial placements in the United States has been matched by equally dramatic changes in American race relations that have made such placements more acceptable.

Racism has long been an important undercurrent in American life. Over much of the twentieth century American immigration laws greatly discouraged the entry of non-Western European peoples. Prior to World War II a xenophobic mentality pervaded the country, leading many to be concerned about the dangers of American families harboring "inferior racial stocks." This climate not only effectively discouraged transracial placements, but also served as very strong deterrent to intraracial placements. Adopting parents wanted to be sure that the child they were about to take into their families was not a carrier of "defective genes" for amoral or criminal tendencies. Such anxieties led to prolonged waiting periods before infants were put into homes, so that undesirable genetic traits could be detected. In this context transracial placements on any regular basis were not possible.

During the last several decades antiminority attitudes appear to have moderated somewhat. Immigration laws have been relaxed, permitting considerably more non-Western Europeans to become American citizens. The inclusion of nonwhites in the programs of the New Deal and the antiracist stance of the U.S. government in response to the blatantly racist policies of the German enemy helped to discredit the racism in many areas of American life. In more recent years increasing civil rights protests, expanding educational opportunities, and greater interracial interaction have diminished racism in the United States. The more liberal climate since the 1960s has been essential for encouraging rising transracial adoptions.

At first the adoptions of Asian children by white American parents represented a significant departure from earlier practices. Yet, these adoptions did not have the same impact as the adoptions of black children by white parents. The first black/white transracial placements of this sort were made in the late 1950s and early 1960s, in response to the increasing numbers of homeless black children for whom agencies were unable to find black placements. At first they comprised an isolated few cases; most were done in the United States, although some placements were made in Canada.

Initially these transracial placements were generally applauded or ignored by social service professionals and the black community. Social workers displayed some anxiety about their workability, but little doubt about their need or desirability. As the emphasis of the civil rights movement shifted from the dismantling of Jim Crow laws in the American South to the mobilization of black communities everywhere in the country, a change in attitude became apparent. An increase in opposition to transracial placements developed within the black community.

As the number of transracial adoptions underwent its most dramatic expansion, during the late 1960s, steadily mounting criticism was voiced. In 1972 the opposition to transracial adoptions peaked when the National Association of Black Social Workers expressed "vehement opposition" to the practice. As a result of the criticism of transracial adoption, there has been a noticeable decline in the adoption of black children by white parents. There are now virtually no whites adopting Native American children in the United States. Yet, the adoption of Asians by whites has remained almost constant, with some slight downward trend; and there has been a moderate increase in Latin American children adopted by white parents.

Among the objections leveled against transracial adoption by its critics is the view that it results in cultural genocide. Its detractors contend that transracial adoption takes children away from their homelands and strips them of their connection to their community and culture. They assert that the practice is psychologically crippling to the children involved, leaving them in a cultural no-man's-land, never fully accepted in the majority culture and maladapted for effective participation within the culture of their birth. Its opponents charge that the transracial adoptee is likely to experience a deep sense of personal isolation, identity confusion, and poor self-esteem. They also maintain that transracially adopted children will be unable to cope effectively with the hostility and rejection of white society as they grow up in white families.

None of the empirical studies done to date on transracial adoption have tried to seriously examine the sociopolitical objections of critics. However, much attention has been focused on their psychological arguments. Data accumulated so far have presented little evidence in support of their contentions. Many studies have been done on the initial adaptations of transracially adopted children. The consistent finding of all these studies is that approximately three-fourths of transracially adopted children adapt well in their new homes, and less than a quarter have moderate-to-serious maladjustment problems. The studies of racial awareness, identification, and self-esteem of transracially adopted children have not indicated any evidence of problems among these children. Critics have countered that the racism of white society against transracial adoptees is not likely to become virulent until these children approach or reach adolescence. They contend that most of these studies say very little about how the children will adapt as they grow older.

Evidence on longer-term adaptations remains limited, but it is beginning to accumulate. One study of Korean adolescent adoptees found that the overwhelming majority of these children had little Korean identity but — according to a widely accepted psychological self-concept inventory — had developed a healthy self-concept relative to other adolescents (Kim 1977). Another study conducted in Great Britain of 36 black, Asian, and mixed-race children adopted by white parents came up with virtually similar findings (Gill and Jackson 1983). Still another study — half of whose sample consisted of adolescent adoptees — found no significant differences in self-esteem scores between a sample of black transracial adoptees and a control group of black inracially adopted children (McRoy, Zurcher, Lauderdale, and Anderson 1981). This last-mentioned study was the first of its kind to include a control population of inracially adopted minority children. Our own survey evidence concurs with these findings.

We found little support for the arguments of those who contend that the placement of black children in white homes will produce damaging psychological consequences for these children. The claim that the black transracial adoptee will inevitably lack a sense of racial pride and identification as a result of being raised in a white family does not seem to be confirmed by our data. We also found that over the six-year period of our study, the social and psychological adjustments of black transracial adoptees were comparable with those of inracially adopted white adoptees. Our evidence suggested that the deterioration of the health and well-being of black children resulting from delays in permanent placement was more serious than any problem resulting from transracial adoption.

Our evidence also challenges the frequently made assumption of the need to live in an integrated community in order to provide adequately for the psychological health of the black transracial adoptee. We found that the transracial adopting families who had integrated living patterns were more likely to foster black identifications among their children, yet their children were no more likely to be well adjusted than those who lived in more racially segregated surroundings.

We also found that where transracial adoptive parents take concrete steps to encourage the identification of their children with the black community, they are likely to be successful at creating a sense of racial pride in their children. These efforts are more effective in fostering racial pride than immersion in the black community alone. Adoptive parents' commitment to familiarizing their black children with Afro-American culture was a more important determinant than their pattern of integrated living for fostering a sense of racial pride and interest among their children.

Thus, our data on transracially adopted Afro-Americans provided little support for most of the contentions of those critical of transracial adoption. Black transracial adoptees showed no more evidence of maladjustment than similar white inracial adoptees. Most transracial adoptive families lived in integrated communities; white parents were often committed to familiarizing their black adoptees with Afro-American culture. As a result the majority of these children were proud of and interested in their black heritage. According to their parents, most identified with the black community. None displayed strong negative feelings for their Afro-American heritage or appearance. Ironically, our data indicated that those who were proud of their black heritage — and closely identified with the black community — were no more likely to be well adapted in their adoptive homes than those who were not proud.

On the whole our evidence on transracially adopted Korean adolescents showed that they were especially well adjusted in their adoptive homes. Six years after our original survey, these adoptees were found to be slightly better adapted in their adoptive homes than comparable groups of white inracial adoptees. Despite the fact that the adolescent Korean adoptees were older when we did our survey and when they were first adopted — factors usually linked with poorer adjustments — these children showed better adaptations than their inracially adopted controls.

Nevertheless, analysis of the experiences of adolescent Korean adoptees offered some support for those critical of transracial adoption. Most of these children lived in white communities. As Korean adoptees entered adolescence, there was a tendency for some to lose their sense of racial pride and to become more ashamed of their Korean origins. These children were also more likely to have adjustment problems than their counterparts who remained proud of being Korean. Yet, as adoptive parents strove to cultivate positive feelings for their adopted children's ethnic identities, they were usually able to avoid such adjustment difficulties with their Korean children. The data suggested that the greatest numbers of adoptive parents of Korean children offered sufficient positive emphasis to their children's backgrounds so that they did not confront these problems.

Our findings illuminate some of the longer-term social psychological consequences of transracial adoption. Given the prevalence of antiblack sentiments in America, transracial adoptive families with Afro-American adoptees are likely to draw together to insulate themselves against racist viewpoints and actions. White adoptive parents tend to offer their Afro-American adoptees positive perspectives on their racial heritage. They also tend to live in integrated communities. These actions engender racial pride and identification with the black community, although they have little impact on the adjustments of black adoptees. As these transracially adopting parents provide their children with constancy, love, and emotional support, they seem able to raise children who are well adjusted.

White adoptive parents of Korean-born children are not subject to the same degree of bigotry that experienced by the adoptive parents of Afro-Americans. Given the more limited possibilities for living in Korean-American communities, adoptive parents of Korean children are likely to live in white communities. Yet, adoptive parents generally are interested in their children's backgrounds, they usually accord respect and positive recognition to them, and think it desirable that their children share these sentiments. Most often they succeed in raising children who think well of their Korean birth and have good feelings about themselves. Despite their lack of close affiliation with other Koreans, these children give every indication of adapting well. Although a sizable minority of these adoptees do not identify with their Korean background, most seem to be getting along well not only in their adoptive families but also in their schools and communities.

For Latin American transracial adoptees, the one group that seems to be expanding, the pattern appears to be much like that found for Koreans. These children — Colombians and other Hispanic adoptees from South and Central America — seem to be exposed to the least prejudice and bigotry of all the major groups of transracial adoptees. In many instances children's appearances are not essentially different from those of white Americans. Considering the general physical similarities of the children, and the frequent problems of infertility among their adoptive parents, parents are inclined to accord little importance to their children's ethnic backgrounds. Parents also are not especially likely to live in integrated Hispanic communities. Although parents do not emphasize their children's backgrounds, most do not seem to disavow them; they apparently acknowledge their children's past and give their origins positive treatment. Although these children seemed least likely of all to possess strong ethnic or racial identifications, they appeared to have established high levels of self-esteem and were likely to be favorably adapted in their families, schools, and communities.

All of these findings on transracial adoption and those of other researchers are beginning to raise serious questions about the appropriateness of abandoning transracial adoptions. Our evidence indicates that whatever problems may be generated by transracial adoption, the benefits to the child outweigh the costs. There is no evidence that any of the serious problems of adjustment or racial self-esteem suggested by the critics of transracial adoption are present in any meaningful proportion of nonwhite children who have been adopted by white parents. There is, of course, evidence from our own study and others that the developmental and emotional damage sustained by black children without permanent placement is considerable. Despite the very meaningful advances that have been made in the placement of minority children in minority families, large numbers of black and Hispanic children remain in foster and institutional care. For these nonwhite children, transracial adoption may be the only realistic possibility for their permanent placement.

Our findings support the position that transracial adoption remains a viable option for the placement of homeless nonwhite children. If policy makers and social workers fail to consider it as a possibility, then they are likely to condemn those children who cannot be placed in minority homes to serious and lasting emotional and developmental damage.

We should note that not all of the objections raised by black social workers and others in the black community focused on the question of the adoptees' adjustment and racial identity. One very salient criticism had to with the inability of white-dominated social service agencies to find homes for black children in the black community. As the careful research done by Dawn Day (1979) demonstrates, these charges were substantially correct. The subsequent efforts made to place black children in black homes also illustrate the inadequacy of previous efforts. Our research in no way disputes either the argument that more should be done to place black children in black homes or that past efforts to do so were less than satisfactory.

Currently expanded efforts to place black children in black homes still leave large numbers of them in foster and institutional care. If transracial placement is ruled out for these children, a significant proportion of them will not grow up in permanent homes and families.

Transracial adoption raises in a very pointed fashion a number of questions about contact between adopted children and their birth parents. This is another of the most disputed issues that adoptees and their birth and adoptive parents face today. It has created considerable conflict not only among social service professionals but also within families. Our research provides some information on a number of assumptions made in the debate over whether adoptees should be permitted to have contact with or knowledge about their birth parents.

Our findings reveal that adoptive parents seem to be more receptive to the idea of contact between their children and their birth parents than earlier studies would have led us to suspect. Even infertile parents — who are less favorable to such contact — demonstrated considerable support for legislation and policies that would extend the rights of adoptees to contact or learn about their birth parents. Apparently the increasing public discussion of this issue has led to a widening understanding and support among adoptive parents for the rights of adoptees. Earlier studies found that all parties to the adoption triangle — adoptive parents, adoptees, and birth parents — share a common frustration and disappointment in not receiving adequate information about the adoption and the other parties involved (Sorosky, Baran, and Pannor 1978; Children's Home Society of California 1977).

If disinterest and disapproval among adoptive parents formed a basis in the past for creating and maintaining present-day concealment practices, then changing sentiments among all parties would seem to point to a need to revise such policies. Our data, along with most other research, calls for the abandonment of current concealment practices; it suggests a reorganization of adoption policies under which agencies would routinely collect sufficient medical and social background information from all parties in the adoption triangle. Such information could be periodically updated, and made available in a nonidentifying manner to adult adoptees and birth and adoptive parents. Such policy and practical changes, our own and other studies show, would be received favorably by the majority of all parties to the adoption.

Apparently overlooked in earlier studies, our investigation also points to the formative role that adoptive parents play in encouraging adoptees' interest in their preplacement lives. When parents are open to questions about their children's backgrounds, they tend to develop the children's active interests. We would imagine that as mutual respect and support flow between parents and children, parents are likely to offer much substantial support and guidance in their children's reunion-seeking efforts. Parental disapproval, on the other hand, may lead adoptees to abandon such questioning or to pursue the search covertly. In such instances parental disapproval would increase the tension between parents and their adopted children. We have also found that adoptive parent groups play a useful role in encouraging parents to develop accepting attitudes toward searching behavior.

Our data have also shown that genealogical questioning is extremely widespread among adoptees, yet actual searching and contact with birth relatives remain relatively rare. Such findings seem to be somewhat at variance with the results of earlier studies. Those earlier studies, however, tended to be based upon samples of adoptees who were in the process of searching for their birth parents. Our sample is more broadly based, and this may well explain the differences in the findings. A more definitive answer to the incidence of interest in and attempts to locate birth parents awaits future research.

We have also found that mothers seem to be substantially more supportive of their adopted children's interest in their birth parents than fathers. We have explained this as a product of the pivotal role women play in American family structure. The clinical implications of these trends, for the time being, remain uncertain. Given a situation in which a great difference of opinion on the search existed between mother and father, very unhealthy psychological results could be produced for the adoptee.

We also found among our adoptive families an association between the children's reunion-seeking behavior and a variety of emotional and social adjustment problems. Parents whose children engaged in more searching efforts were felt to be more poorly adjusted psychologically than their counterparts who had not pursued the search. The implications of these trends remain unclear. Several possible interpretations for these patterns present themselves.

It is altogether conceivable that while parents may approve of the search in the abstract and in general — even be inclined to offer some assistance in searching efforts — they may be quite distraught and fearful with the particular prospect of their child actually attempting to engage in reunion-seeking behavior. They may link these feelings in such a way that they see their child's behavior as a source of disappointment and irritation.

It is also possible that the poorer adjustments among adoptees who search result from problems in the adoptive parent-child relationship. Adoptive parents frequently deny the differences between adoption and biological parenthood; this denial can result in problems for both parent and child. In this situation the child's interest in pursuing the search could easily reflect the tensions generated by denial. Yet, this pattern remains to be empirically established. Further research will be necessary to fully specify the conditions under which psychological adjustments are facilitated or frustrated by adoptees' reunion-seeking behavior.

References

Adams, Bert. 1968. *Kinship in an Urban Setting*. Chicago: Markham Publishing Co.

Adams, John, and Hy Bok Kim. 1971. "A Fresh Look at Intercountry Adoptions." *Children* 18 (Nov./Dec.): 214-21.

Anderson, David C. 1971. *Children of Special Value*. New York: St. Martin's Press.

Bernard, Jessie. 1981. "Facing the Future." *Society/Transaction* 18, no. 2 (Jan./Feb.): 53-59.

Blood, Robert O., and Alan Wolfe. 1956. *Husbands and Wives*. New York: The Free Press.

Bonham, Gordon Scott. 1977. "Who Adopts: The Relationship of Adoption and Social Demographic Characteristics of Women." *Journal of Marriage and the Family* 39 (2) (May): 295-306.

Booth, Alan. 1972. "Sex and Social Participation." *American Sociological Review* 37 (Apr.): 183-93.

Bowlby, John. 1952. *Maternal Care and Mental Health*. Geneva: World Health Organization.

Braden, Josephine. 1970. "Adoption in a Changing World." *Social Casework* 5 (Oct.): 486.

Branham, Ethel. 1970. "One Parent Adoptions." *Children* 17 (May/June): 103-07.

Byma, Sydney. 1974. "Overseas Adoptions Threaten Development of Local Services," *Canadian Welfare* 50 (May-June): 7-11.

Chambers, Donald. 1970. "Willingness to Adopt Atypical Children." *Child Welfare* 49, no. 5 (May): 275-79.

Chestang, Leon. 1972. "The Dilemma of Biracial Adoption." *Social Work* 17 (May): 100-15.

Children's Home Society of California. 1977. "The Changing Face of Adoption." Los Angeles: Children's Home Society, pamphlet.

Child Welfare League of America. 1959. *Standards for Adoptive Practice*. New York: Child Welfare League of America.

_____. 1978. *Standards for Adoption Service, Revised Edition*. New York: Child Welfare League of America.

Conners, C. K. 1969. "A Teacher Rating Scale for Use in Drug Studies with Children." *American Journal of Psychiatry* 126 (Dec.): 152-56.

_____. 1973. "Rating Scales in Drug Studies with Children." *Psychopharmacology Bulletin*, special issue, "Pharmacotherapy of Children," pp. 24-84.

Commission on Population Growth and the American Future. 1972. *Population and the American Future*. Washington, D.C.: U.S. Government Printing Office.

Cummings, Judith. 1983. "Homosexual Views Adoption Approval as Victory." *New York Times* (Monday, Jan. 10): B-5.

Davis, Mary. 1961. "Adoptive Placement of American Indian Children with Non-Indian Families." *Child Welfare* 40 (June): 12-15.

Day, Dawn. 1979. *The Adoption of Black Children: Counteracting Institutional Discrimination*. Lexington, Mass.: Lexington Books.

DeLeon, Judy, and Judy Westerberg. 1980. "Who Adopts Retarded Children?" Westfield, N.J.: Spaulding for Children. Unpublished paper.

DiVirgilio, Letitia. 1956. "Adjustment of Foreign Born Children in Their Adoptive Homes." *Child Welfare* 35 (Nov.): 15-21.

Dukel, Abraham. 1955. "Jewish Attitudes to Child Adoption." In Michael Shapiro, ed., *Study of Adoption Practice, II*. New York: Child Welfare League of America.

Dyer, Everett D. 1963. "Parenthood as Crisis: A Restudy." *Marriage and Family Living* 25 (May): 196-201.

Falk, Lawrence. 1970. "A Comparative Study of Transracial and Inracial Adoptions." *Child Welfare* 49 (Feb.): 82-88.

Fanshel, David. 1972. *Far from the Reservation*. Metuchen, N.J.: Scarecrow Press.

_____. 1978. "Children Discharged from Foster Care in New York City: Where to – When – at What Age?" *Child Welfare* 57, no. 3 (Sept./Oct.): 467-83.

_____. 1979. "Preschoolers Entering Foster Care in New York City: The Need to Stress Plans for Permanency." *Child Welfare* 58, no. 2 (Feb.): 67-87.

Farber, Bernard. 1964. *Family Organization and Interaction*. San Francisco: Chandler Publishing Co.

_____. 1972. *Family and Kinship in Modern Society*. Glenview, Ill.: Scott Foresman.

Feigelman, William, and Arnold R. Silverman. 1977. "Single Parent Adoptions." *Social Casework* 58, no. 7 (July): 418-25.

_____. 1979. "Preferential Adoption: A New Mode of Family Formation." *Social Casework* 60 (May): 296-305.

Fraiberg, Selma. 1977. *Every Child's Birthright: In Defense of Mothering*. New York: Basic Books.

Freud, Anna, and Dorothy Burlingham. 1973. *Infants Without Families: Report on the Hampstead Nurseries: The Writings of Anna Freud*. 3. New York: International Universities Press, 182-83.

Fricke, Harriet. 1965. "Interracial Adoption: The Little Revolution." *Social Work* 10 (July): 92-97.

Gallay, Grace. 1963. "Interracial Adoptions." *Canadian Welfare* 39, (Nov./Dec.): 248-50.

Gallup, George. 1979. "The Gallup Poll: Public Opinion, 1978." Wilmington, Delaware: Scholarly Resources: 217-22.

Gill, Owen, and Barbara Jackson. 1983. *Adoption and Race: Black, Asian and Mixed Race Children in White Families*. New York: St. Martin's Press.

Glick, Paul, and Arthur Norton. 1977. "Marrying, Divorcing and Living Together in the United States Today." *Population Bulletin* 32, no. 5 (Oct.): 2-39.

Goldstein, Joseph, Anna Freud, and Albert Solnit. 1973. *Beyond the Best Interests of the Child*. New York: The Free Press.

Goldstein, Sidney, and Calvin Goldscheider. 1968. *Jewish Americans*. Englewood Cliffs, N.J.: Prentice-Hall.

Grow, Lucille, and Deborah Shapiro. 1974. *Black Children – White Parents*. New York: Child Welfare League of America.

Gruber, Allen. 1973. "Foster Home Care in Massachusetts: A Study of Foster Children, Their Biological and Foster Parents." Boston: Governor's Commission on Adoption and Foster Care.

Guilbault, Claude, and Jean Guilbault. 1972. "A Descriptive Study of the Adjustment of Korean Children Adopted by Families in Minnesota." Master's thesis, University of Wisconsin.

Haring, Barbara. 1976. "Adoption Statistics Annual Data 1975." New York: Child Welfare League of America.

Herzog, Elizabeth, Cecilia Sudia, and Jane Harwood. 1971. "Some Opinions on Finding Families for Black Children." *Children* 18 (July/Aug.): 143-48.

Hobbs, Daniel F. 1965. "Parenthood as Crisis: A Third Study." *Journal of Marriage and the Family* 27 (Aug.): 367-72.

Howard, Alicia, David Royse, and John Skerl. 1977. "Transracial Adoption: The Black Community Perspective." *Social Work* 22 (May): 184-89.

Jones, Mary Ann. 1976. "The Sealed Adoption Record Controversy Report of a Survey of Agency Policy, Practice and Opinions." New York, N.Y.: Child Welfare League of America, pamphlet, 1-30.

Jordan, Velma, and William Little. 1966. "Early Comments on Single Parent Adoptive Homes." *Child Welfare* 45 (Nov.): 536-38.

Kadushin, Alfred. 1962. "A Study of Parents of Hard-to-Place Children." *Social Casework* 43, no. 5 (May): 227-33.

_____. 1970a. *Adopting Older Children*. New York: Columbia University Press.

_____. 1970b. "Single Parent Adoptions: An Overview and Some Relevant Research." *Social Service Review* 44 (Sept.): 263-74.

_____. 1977. "Child Welfare: Adoption and Foster Care." In *Encyclopedia of Social Work, I,* pp. 114-25. Washington, D.C.: National Association of Social Workers.

Kahn, Alfred. 1979. *Social Policy and Social Services.* New York: Random House.

Kanter, Rosabeth M. 1974. "Communes in Cities." *Working Papers for a New Society* II (Summer): 36-44.

Kardiner, Abram, and Lionel Ovesey. 1951. *The Mark of Oppression.* New York: W. W. Norton.

Karon, Bernard. 1958. *The Negro Personality.* New York: Springer.

Keller, Suzanne. 1971. "Does the Family Have a Future?" *Journal of Comparative Family Studies* 2 (Spring): 1-14.

Keltie, Patricia. 1969. "The Adjustment of Korean Children Adopted by Couples in the Chicago Area." Master's thesis, Jane Addams School of Social Work, University of Illinois.

Kihss, Peter. 1981. "Study Criticizes Emergency Foster-Care Programs." *New York Times,* January 18, p. 36.

Kim, Dong Soo. 1977. "How They Fare in American Homes: A Follow-up Study of Adopted Korean Children in U.S. Homes." *Children Today* 6 (Mar./Apr.): 2-6, 36.

_____. 1978. "Issues in Transracial and Transcultural Adoption." *Social Casework* 59 (Oct.): 477-86.

Kim, Hi Taik, and Elaine Reid. 1970. "After a Long Journey." Master's thesis, University of Minnesota.

Kim, S. P., S. Hong, and B. S. Kim. 1979. "Adoption of Korean Children by New York Area Couples, a Preliminary Study." *Child Welfare* 58, no. 7 (July/Aug.): 419-27.

Kirk, H. David. 1964. *Shared Fate.* New York: The Free Press.

Kleiman, Dena. 1979. "Anguished Search to Cure Infertility." *New York Times Magazine,* Dec. 16, pp. 38, 60-69, 149-151.

Knight, Robert. 1941. "Some Problems Involved in Selecting and Rearing Adopted Children." *The Menninger Clinic Bulletin* 5 (Jan.) :65-74.

Kohlsaat, Barbara, and A. Johnson. 1954. "Some Suggestions for Practice in Infant Adoptions." *Social Casework* 35 (Mar.): 93.

Komarovsky, Mirra. 1967. *Blue Collar Marriage*. New York: Vintage.

Ladner, Joyce. 1977. *Mixed Families: Adopting Across Racial Boundaries*. Garden City, N.Y.: Doubleday.

Lasch, Christopher. 1976. "The Family as a Haven in a Heartless World." *Salmagundi* (Fall): 42-55.

Lawder, Elizabeth, et al. 1969. *A Follow up Study of Adoptions: Post Placement Functioning of Adoption Families*. New York: Child Welfare League of America.

Lee, Gary. 1981. "Marriage and Aging." *Society/Transaction* 18, no. 2 (Jan./Feb.): 68-71.

LeMasters, E. E. 1957. "Parenthood as Crisis." *Marriage and Family Living* 19 (Nov.): 352-55.

Leslie, Gerald. 1982. *The Family in Social Context*. 5th ed. New York: Oxford University Press.

Lifton, Betty Jean. 1979. *Lost and Found: The Adoption Experience*. New York: Dial Press.

Lipset, Seymour M. 1960. *Political Man*. Garden City, N.Y.: Doubleday.

López de Rodriguez, Cecilia, and José Olinto Rueda. 1979. "La transición demográfica en Colombia y sus consecuencias sociales y económicas." *Revista de planeación y desarrollo* 11, no. 1 (Jan./Apr.):

Lott, Bernice. 1973. "Who Wants the Children?: Some Relationships Among Attitudes Toward Children, Parents, and the Liberation of Women." *American Psychologist* 28 (July): 573-82.

Margolin, C. R. 1978. "Salvation vs. Liberation: The Movement for Child Rights in a Historical Context." *Social Problems* 25, no. 4 (Apr.): 441-52.

Massachusetts Adoption Resource Exchange. *Annual Report*. 1969-72. Cited in Thomas Nutt. "Issues in Supply and Demand in Adoption." in *Proceedings of the Fourth North American Conference on Adoptable Children*. Washington: D.C.: Council on Advocacy for Children, 1974.

McRoy, Ruth. 1981. "A Comparative Study of the Self-Concept of Transracially and Inracially Adopted Black Children." Ph.D. dissertation, School of Social Work, University of Texas at Austin.

McRoy, Ruth, L. Zurcher, M. Lauderdale, and R. Anderson. 1982. "Self-Esteem and Racial Identity in Transracial and Inracial Adoptees." *Social Work* 27, no. 6 (Nov.): 522-26.

McTaggert, Lynn. 1980. *The Baby Brokers*. New York: Dial Press.

Meezan, William, Sanford Katz, and Eva Russo 1978. *Adoptions Without Agencies: A Study of Independent Adoptions*. New York: Child Welfare League of America.

National Center for Health Statistics. 1974. "Summary Report: Final Natality Statistics, 1971.'" *Monthly Vital Statistics Report* (DHEW Pub. no. (HRA) 75-1120) 23, no. 3 (May): 1-8.

National Commission on Children in Need of Parents, 1979. 1982. "Who Knows, Who Cares?: The Forgotten Children in Foster Care," cited in the *Proceedings of the Eighth North American Conference on Adoptable Children*, New York: N.Y.: Council on Advocacy For Children (August) mimeo.

Neal, Leora. 1979. "No Child Should be Denied His Heritage." Letter to *New York Times*, Aug. 28, Op. Ed. page.

Nelson-Erichsen, Jean, and Heino Erichsen. 1981. *Gamines: How to Adopt from Latin America*. Minneapolis: Dillon Press.

Editorial Staff. 1978. "Saving the Family." *Newsweek*, May 15, pp. 63-74.

Nutt, Thomas A., and John Snyder. 1973. "Transracial Adoption." Cambridge, Mass.: Department of Sociology, Massachusetts Institute of Technology. Unpublished monograph.

Opportunity. 1969-76. "Survey of Adoption of Black Children." Portland Ore.: Boys and Girls Aid Society of Oregon.

Paton, Jean. 1954. *The Adopted Break Silence*. Acton, Calif.: Life History Study Center.

Pfohl, Steven. 1977. "The 'Discovery' of Child Abuse." *Social Problems* 24, no. 3 (Feb.): 310-23.

Provence, Sally, and Rose Lipton. 1962. *Infants in Institutions*. New York: International Universities Press.

Rathbun, Constance, Letitia DiVirgilio, and Samuel Waldfogel. 1958. "The Restitutive Process in Children Following Radical Separation from Family and Culture." *American Journal of Orthopsychiatry* 28 (Apr.): 408-15.

Rathbun, Constance, et al. 1965. "Later Adjustment of Children Following Radical Separation from Family and Culture." *American Journal of Orthopsychiatry* 35 (Apr.):

Resnick, Rosa, and Gloria Munoz de Rodriguez. 1982. "Intercountry Adoptions Between the United States and Colombia: Final Report." New York: International Social Services.

Reynolds, William, and D. Chiappise. 1975. "The Search by Adopted Persons for Their Natural Parents: A Research Project Comparing Those Who Search and Those Who Do Not." Paper presented at the meetings of the American Psychology-Law Society, Chicago.

Rosenberg, Morris, and Roberta Simmons. 1971. *Black and White Self Esteem: The Urban School Child*. Washington, D.C.: American Sociological Association.

Rosenfeld, Jeffrey. 1974. "Inheritance: A Sex-Related System of Exchange." In Rose L. Coser, ed., *The Family: Its Structures and Functions*. New York: St. Martin's Press.

St. John, N. 1975. *School Desegregation: Outcomes for Children*. New York: John Wiley.

Sands, R. M., and E. Rothenberg. 1976. "Adoption in 1976: Unresolved Problems, Unrealized Goals, New Perspectives." Paper presented at the annual meetings of the American Association of Psychiatric Services for Children, San Francisco.

Scarr, Sandra, and Richard A. Weinberg. 1976. "IQ Test Performance of Black Children Adopted by White Families." *American Psychologist* 31 (Oct.): 726-39.

Selznick, Gertrude, and Stephan Steinberg. 1969. *The Tenacity of Prejudice*. Westport, Conn.: Greenwood Press.

Shireman, Joan, and Penny Johnson. 1976. "Single Persons as Adoptive Parents." *Social Service Review* 50 (Mar.): 103-16.

Silverman, Arnold R. 1980. "The Assimilation and Adjustment of Transracially Adopted Children in the United States." Ph.D. dissertation, University of Wisconsin-Madison.

Silverman, Arnold R., and William Feigelman. 1981. "The Adjustment of Black Children Adopted by White Families." *Social Casework* 62, no. 9 (Nov.): 529-36.

Simon, Rita J., and Howard Altstein. 1977. *Transracial Adoption*. New York: John Wiley.

_____. 1981. *Transracial Adoption: A Follow-up*. Lexington, Mass.: Lexington Books.

Smith, R. 1976. "The Sealed Adoption Record Controversy and Social Agency Response." *Child Welfare* 55 (Feb.): 73-74.

Sorosky, Arthur, Annette Baran, and Reuben Pannor. 1975. "Identity Conflicts in Adoptees." *American Journal of Orthopsychiatry* 45: 18-27.

_____. 1978. *The Adoption Triangle*. Garden City, N.Y.: Doubleday/Anchor.

Spitz, Rene. 1945. "Hospitalism." In *The Psychoanalytic Study of the Child*, I, pp. 53-74. New York: International Universities Press.

Stack, Carol. 1975. *All Our Kin: Survival in the Black Community*. New York: Harper and Row.

Stark, Rodney, and Charles Glock. 1968. *American Piety: The Nature of Religious Commitment*. Berkeley and Los Angeles: University of California Press.

Sweetser, Dorian. 1972. "Intergenerational Ties in Finnish Urban Families." *American Sociological Review* 33 (Apr.): 236-46.

Triseliotis, John. 1973. *In Search of Origins: The Experiences of Adopted People*. London: Routledge and Kegan Paul.

U.S. Department of Health and Human Services. 1981. *Children's Bureau Initiatives for the Adoption of Minority Children*. Publication DHHS no. OHDS 81-30300. Washington, D.C.: U.S. Dept. of Health and Human Services.

U.S. Immigration and Naturalization Service. 1983. "Immigrant Orphans Admitted to the United States Year Ended 1980." Washington, D.C.: U.S. Immigration and Naturalization Service.

Wieder, Herbert. 1977. "On Being Told of Adoption." *The Psychoanalytic Quarterly* 46, no. 1, 1-22.

Welter, Marianne. 1965. *Adopted Older Foreign and American Children*. New York: International Social Service.

Westoff, Leslie Aldridge. 1976. "Kids with Kids." *New York Times Magazine*, Feb. 22, pp. 14-15, 63-65.

Whang, Minsum Sung. 1976. "An Exploratory Descriptive Study of Inter-Country Adoption of Korean Children Children With Known Parents." Unpublished Master's Thesis, University of Hawaii.

Winick, Myron, K. Meyer, and R. Harris. 1975. "Malnutrition and Environmental Enrichment by Early Adoption." *Science* 190 (Dec. 19): 1173.

Young, Michael, and Peter Wilmott. 1964. *Family and Kinship in East London*. Baltimore: Pelican Books.

Zastrow, Charles. 1977. *Outcome of Black Children/White Parent Adoptions*. San Francisco: R and E Research Associates.

Index

About the Authors

WILLIAM FEIGELMAN is professor of sociology at Nassau Community College, Garden City, New York. He has written extensively in the area of sociology, and is the author of two sociology undergraduate text/anthologies used in many American colleges. His first book, *Sociology Full Circle: Contemporary Readings on Society*, was originally published in 1972 by Praeger Publishers, and is currently being revised for a fourth edition. His articles and reviews have appeared in *Urban Life and Culture*, *Contemporary Society*, *Social Casework*, *Group*, and *Journal of Social Welfare*.

Professor Feigelman was born in Brooklyn, New York. His undergraduate education was completed at the City College of New York. His graduate study of sociology was undertaken at Washington University, St. Louis. He has received awards for his academic work from the National Institutes of Health and the Research Foundation of the State University of New York. Professor Feigelman is married and the father of two children, one of whom was adopted from Bogotá, Colombia. His personal experience as a transcultural adoptive parent helped ignite the interests that gave rise to this study.

ARNOLD R. SILVERMAN is professor of sociology at Nassau Community College, Garden City, New York. Before joining the faculty at Nassau, he had been on the faculties of Fordham and Rutgers universities. Professor Silverman has written widely on issues of race and the family. He is the author of numerous articles and reviews appearing in *American Sociological Review*, *Journal of Health and Human Behavior*, *Contemporary Sociology*, *Social Casework*, *Group*, and *Journal of Social Welfare*. His collaborative work with Stanley Lieberson, "Precipitants and Underlying Conditions of Race Riots," has been reprinted in numerous textbooks and anthologies.

Professor Silverman was born in Philadelphia. He received his A.B. degree from Temple University in Philadelphia and his Ph.D. in sociology from the University of Wisconsin at Madison. He has received many grants and fellowships, including awards from the National Institute of Mental Health, the National Endowment for the Humanities, the Research Foundation of the State University of New York, and the Andrew W. Mellon Foundation. Dr. Silverman is married and the father of two children.